Sell Your Business Your Way

SELL YOUR BUSINESS YOUR WAY

GETTING OUT, GETTING RICH, AND GETTING ON WITH YOUR LIFE

Rick Rickertsen
with Robert Gunther

AMACOM
AMERICAN MANAGEMENT ASSOCIATION
NEW YORK • ATLANTA • BRUSSELS • CHICAGO • MEXICO CITY • SAN FRANCISCO
SHANGHAI • TOKYO • TORONTO • WASHINGTON, D.C.

Special discounts on bulk quantities of AMACOM books
are available to corporations, professional associations, and other
organizations. For details, contact Special Sales Department,
AMACOM, a division of American Management Association,
1601 Broadway, New York, NY 10019.
Tel.: 212-903-8316.   Fax: 212-903-8083.
Web Site: www.amacombooks.org

This publication is designed to provide accurate and authoritative
information in regard to the subject matter covered. It is sold with the
understanding that the publisher is not engaged in rendering legal,
accounting, or other professional service. If legal advice or other expert
assistance is required, the services of a competent professional person
should be sought.

Library of Congress Cataloging-in-Publication Data

Rickertsen, Rick.
      Sell your business your way : getting out, getting rich, and getting on with your
life / Rick Rickertsen with Robert Gunther.
         p.   cm.
      Includes bibliographical references and index.
      ISBN-13: 978-0-8144-0896-4
      ISBN-10: 0-8144-0896-6
      1. Sale of business enterprises.   I. Gunther, Robert E., 1960–   II. Title.
   HD1393.25.R53   2006
   658.1'64—dc22
                                                                    2006008839

Printing number

10   9   8   7   6   5   4   3   2   1

778 1580

As always, for Iris and Ocke

CONTENTS

DURING THE LEVERAGED BUYOUT CRAZE of the 1980s, a number of corporations—the car rental company Avis comes to mind—made several trips between the public and private sector. It was as if Wall Street had gotten into the business of selling round-trip tickets to the stock market. Each time a company changed hands, the corporate managers and their investment bankers invoked some higher principle. When Avis went private, it was to harness the greater efficiency and enthusiasm of managers who were also owners; when Avis went public again, it was because the company could not grow as it deserved to without greater access to capital. On and on it went, in a kind of endless spin cycle. The main consequence of a lot of this activity was to enrich investment bankers who were, in effect, churning entire companies. In some cases, the investment bankers were simply colluding with corporate managers; but in many cases, they were preying on the insecurities and ignorance of those managers. In either case, a lot of people at the mercy of Wall Street would have been better off if the two processes at the heart of high finance—taking a company public and taking a company private—had been de-mystified.

Now they have been—and by a former investment banker, Rick Rickertsen. A few years ago, Rick wrote an interesting book called *Buyout*, which advised corporate managers how to take their public companies private without undergoing a body cavity search by Wall Street. That book was a paean to the owner-manager. Only when he became an owner could the manager reap the fruits of his labor, cease to be a wage slave, and join capitalism's most exalted ranks of those who could safely ignore the advice of Wall Street investment bankers. Now Rick has written another interesting book, *Sell Your Business Your Way*, and it instructs people how to do pretty much the opposite thing. But the symmetry is not perfect. Rick has no intention of turning you, the business owner, back into a wage slave. His ambition for his readers has, if anything, grown. In *Buyout*, he showed you how you, too, can fly first class. In *Sell Your Business Your Way*, he shows you how to stop flying commercial and get into your own private jet. In *Buyout*, he sought to put you beyond the greedy grasp of Wall Street investment bankers. Here he helps put you in the position to actually purchase a few Wall Street investment bankers, and do whatever you want with them.

I love Rick's impulse to make high finance simple and accessible. "Wall Street loves people to think what they do is a mystical Black Box totally incomprehensible to the normal man," he says. "It enables them to keep their fees up. But this is wrong, of course." Anyone who has built a business should be grateful to his democratizing instincts. He could have charged you millions for the privilege of hiring him to your company. Instead, he is asking only the price of a hardcover book.

—Michael Lewis

IT WAS YOUR SWEAT AND BLOOD that built the business. Maybe you started from scratch with an idea and a few bucks, or came in later to grow or manage the enterprise. Your ingenuity landed your first big clients. When the dark times came, it was your passion that carried it through. You made the tough decisions. This business is your "baby." It has your DNA all over it. It has more of you in it than anything you have ever done in your life.

But now you are thinking about selling your business. You may want to do something different, or hit the links to enjoy a well deserved retirement. Perhaps you want to start your next business, or just can't stand the sight of another airport lounge. Maybe you want to spend more time with your (other) children or grandchildren. But there is only one way to reach these dreams: You have to make an exit from your business.

Over the years, you've fired close associates, taken bold risks in entering new markets, and sat in front of bankers with hat in hand. But nothing has prepared you for this. Entrepreneurs who are phenomenally successful in building their businesses are often just as phenomenally unsuccessful in selling them. They are too involved. Their oversized egos, which were so crucial on the way up, won't let them see the business through the eyes of a buyer. Their companies are too tangled up in their families. You've put together many deals in the past, but none of them were this significant and this personal. You've put your heart into your business. How can you *not* be emotional when you are facing the biggest deal of your life?

If you think you don't need to consider a sale, think again. You may think you'll pass the baton effortlessly to your children. You've seen the smiling photos of father and son Ralph and Brian Roberts at Comcast. These are the exceptions. While the 2003 American Family Business Survey found that nearly 88 percent of business owners expected to keep their firms in the family, other research shows that only about a third of businesses make it to the second generation. By the fourth generation, only about 3 percent of companies are still in family hands. All the rest of these businesses—two-thirds in the first generation—were sold or closed. Do you think you can beat those odds? A sale is certainly preferable.

You can't put this off. This is something you need to think about now. The most successful sales require *years* of preparation. I've always been surprised at how ill-prepared many business owners are for the sale of their lives. They have not done the groundwork. They have not articulated their goals. They cannot see the world through the eyes of buyers. They don't know how to mitigate risks to maximize the price of their business. Like all parents, they think that their baby is more beautiful than any other. As a result, many owners are getting less than their businesses are worth or failing to meet their nonfinancial goals.

You can do better. This book will show you how. It offers an insider's view of the buying and selling process. I share my own insights from nearly twenty years in the deal business. I have worked on hundreds of transactions and closed more than fifty. I've been a buyer and a seller, and I've worked with buyers and sellers. I've done some tremendous deals and led some real stinkers. On the following pages, I'll also share the knowledge of entrepreneurs who have sold their businesses. One of these owners watched the biggest deal of his lifetime slip through his fingers and the other aced a deal that turned his small company into millions in cash at the top of the market. We'll examine how a pair of seasoned business owners brought in a new partner and walked into the succession plan from hell. We also offer the knowledge of a stellar group of subject-area experts from leading firms such as The Global Consulting Partnership, Goldman Sachs, PricewaterhouseCoopers, and Hogan & Hartson on issues from family dynamics and succession to estate and tax planning.

In this book we reveal all. By the end of this book, the highlights of everything important that I know from decades of experience about selling a business, as well as the knowledge of experts, you will know—the inside secrets, the things that buyers certainly don't want you to know, and the things that advisers with different vantage points might not be able to tell you. This will save you money and help you get more value from the sale of your business—however you define value.

THE GOAL OF THIS BOOK IS SIMPLE

Why reveal this information? While I enjoy seeing investments pay off, my biggest passion has always been working with people who own and run companies to help them succeed. My first book, *Buyout*, was written to inspire managers to take control of their destinies and live the American Business Dream. This book is written to empower entrepreneurs to get maximum value when they make the most important decision of their business lives: to sell their companies.

In my extensive work with owner-operated and family-held companies, nothing is more exciting than having lunch with an entrepreneur who has built his company into a success. A friend of mine tells how he recently walked into the corporate offices of a major food company and saw an intriguing diorama hanging on the wall. The scene was a South Philadelphia butcher shop with a brothel in the rooms upstairs. The world may see this company for what it is today, a hugely successful, multimillion-dollar enterprise. But in the owner's eyes, the business is still that little butcher shop with a buxom woman leaning out of the upstairs window. It may be a mature business, but for the entrepreneur, it will always be his baby. Their eyes fire up as they tell the war stories of their successes and failures. Their pride in their companies is mesmerizing. I have found business owners to be such a wonderful, complex, and talented group of people. Their passion is infectious.

Entrepreneurs built the backbone of the American economy. They create the most jobs and help to build strong families. They take enormous risks and make unbelievable and untold personal sacrifices to build these businesses. They jump on airplanes on Sundays, miss their families, and sign bank notes that may put their houses at risk, all in the name of building their enterprises. When they make their biggest decision, to sell the company, they have every right to believe that their "baby" is the most beautiful in the world. The goal of this book is simple: to help one entrepreneur sell his or her company for 10 percent more than may have been received otherwise. If it helps two entrepreneurs, so much the better. If it is a thousand, even better still.

This book is for the entrepreneur. Thank you for building your company. Few understand what you went through to make it all go. It is my pleasure to offer you insights on how to run the last mile of this race successfully—to make a graceful and profitable exit. Then, enjoy your success. You deserve it!

Rick Rickertsen

ACKNOWLEDGMENTS

AS ANY READER KNOWS, just lifting most books requires effort. Reading a book, much more. But constructing and actually writing one of those babies, well, that is a bear. It's lonely, hard work that requires real passion and dedication. My highest kudos to anyone who has ever completed a book, and even more thanks to all of you wonderful people who still enjoy a good book over a shimmering blog or cathode ray tube.

This book would never have been completed without the incredible work and effort of my coauthor, Robert Gunther. He is smart, hardworking, and tremendously business-savvy. Thank you, Robert.

Thanks to my agent, Al Zuckerman, of Writers House for his great work in taking this idea out to the world. And sincere thanks to Jacquie Flynn, Niels Buessem, and the tremendous folks at AMACOM for their support and confidence. I hope this book is a big winner for them.

This book would not have half its quality content were it not for the terrific entrepreneurs who were willing to tell us their stories. My heartfelt thanks to Barbara Meade and Carla Cohen, the lovely founders of a D.C. landmark: Politics & Prose Bookstore. May it go on forever. And thank you so much to Leo Mullen of the NavigationArts, the greatest seller around; to Joe Wesley of Tradesman International, a tremendous entrepreneur; and to the creative and tenacious "Bill Chambers" (you know who you are!) for telling us these great and compelling stories.

Our domain experts made this an infinitely better book, and I cannot thank you enough. To Mark Brenner and David Pellegrini of The Global Consulting Partnership, thank you for all of your time, input, and great care. More long lunches! And a huge thank-you to our great friends at Goldman Sachs, Scott Belveal, Steve Torbeck, and Cristina Hug for helping all entrepreneurs figure out how to make more dough! Also, for their tremendous advice on how to prepare for a sale, our major thanks to Michael Kennedy of Price-waterhouseCoopers and Molly James of Hogan & Hartson. And our thanks to Bill Morrissett of Edgeview Partners for helping us understand the investment banking role and engagement.

Huge thanks to the finest writer I know, Michael Lewis, for his tremendous support, creativity, and inspiration. No one turns a sentence like ML.

Many friends were very helpful. First, my business partner George McCabe, and our trusty killer at Pine Creek, Scott Bryant, had invaluable input. And without Jennifer Walaitis, nothing would ever get done! I much appreciate as well the support of Bill Walton and John Fruehwirth of Allied Capital. Also, my lifelong thanks to Big Bob Calton, Billy Campbell, Chris Nassetta, Kelvin Davis, David Solomon, and John Waldron for their spiritual input, which is generally proffered most eloquently in the desert of Nevada. My thanks also to Herb and Herbert Allen, David Bonderman, Howard Millstein, John Hart, and Fred Malek for their ongoing support.

Last, and never least, thanks to the finest parents a guy could have. Mom is kicking cancer's butt, and Dad is just too good to be true.

Sell Your Business Your Way

A MOMENT OF TRUTH

Looking in the Mirror

SELLING YOUR BUSINESS is a moment of truth. It defines the value of your life's work. The deal reflects your goals and values. It will affect your relationship with your family and your employees. The outcome will determine your future opportunities. Everything you've worked so long and hard for comes to a crescendo in this one critical deal.

The sale process also brings with it many moments of truth along the way—times when you have to make tough decisions or when things fall apart or come together. Selling a business is not a simple process. It involves deep soul searching and enormous complexity. It involves many players and many moving parts. There is a lot that can go wrong, and there is no better feeling than when it all comes together. As in building the business, there is a fair measure of skill involved, as well as a healthy dose of luck. But I also believe that with thorough preparation and forethought, you can create your own luck. That is one of the goals of this book.

Every sale is different, but all of them take unexpected twists and turns. In the following vignettes, we introduce several entrepreneurs as they faced their own moments of truth in the deal process. They share their triumphs and failures, demonstrating the rich textures of the deal process and some of the core lessons about putting together a successful deal. We will return to their stories throughout the book to illustrate key issues and aspects of the deal process, but for now, we consider these business owners at the point where deals are made or destroyed—their own moments of truth.

THREE CASES

Throughout the book, we'll revisit the three cases discussed in this chapter and look at how the owners addressed different steps of the sale process:

Homeland Designs: Bill Chambers had a $40 million deal lined up with a strategic buyer, but it unwound before he could close the deal.

Iconix: Leo Mullen moved his business from print design to online, brought in professional managers, and sold the business successfully for $26 million.

Politics & Prose: The partners of this independent bookstore brought in a new partner who was expected to buy the business for $1.2 million. But the resulting organizational turmoil ditched the deal.

HOMELAND DESIGNS: WHAT DOES NOT KILL YOU MAKES YOU STRONGER

"Forty million bucks," thought Bill Chambers[1] to himself as he took a long, deadly serious look in the mirror. "What the hell had gone wrong?" The face staring back at him in the fall of 2002 was 59 years old but looked more like 42. Good genes, hard work, and a smart lifestyle. Still, he felt he had gotten a lot older in the past year. He splashed a bit of water on his face. Nine months ago, he believed he had realized the dream of his business life. That was the day he signed a letter of intent to sell his company, his baby, Homeland Designs, for $40 million. Forty million dollars. He had liked the sound of that.

He had acquired the business years earlier, when he had completed his own buyout from the company's founder in 1985 for over $1 million. Chambers had grown the business for 22 years. They had been through so much together. There had been three brutal industry downturns where he had nearly lost it all. There was an unsuccessful plan for an international deal that brought family members into the core and spun them back out again. Chambers had launched new product lines and broken new ground in direct marketing. Now the company had grown from $12 million in sales and paltry profits to more than $60 million in sales and $10 million in cash flow! And he had done it all before his sixtieth birthday. It was every entrepreneur's dream. Now he just needed to pull off the final act.

Nine months ago, he had the biggest deal of his life all queued up and ready to go. A competitor was ready, willing, and able to take the reins. The buyer had committed to pay him 40 million bucks. And that was just the cash at closing. There were another five to fifteen million scoots around the corner in the form of an earnout. Not too shabby, he thought, for a guy from Westchester who pretty much started out with nothing. Not too bad at all. With other equity holders in the firm, he considered his piece of the wire instructions: $20 million. After paying Uncle Sam, he would still have 15 large in the bank. Interest alone would pay him 600 grand a year on that nut. He had the letter of agreement in his hand. He was planning a Caribbean and European trip with his gorgeous wife. He was visualizing the boat he always wanted to command.

And then the dream dissolved.

Chambers stared into the eyes in the mirror. What the hell had gone wrong? Nine months after signing that lovely agreement, all was dashed. The 40 million bucks. The vacation. The retirement party. The graceful exit into the sunset. Gone.

Heaven could wait. He was in hell.

Not only was his $40 million deal deader than Napoleon, but there was much worse news. He had taken his eye off the business to work on the deal, and now the company desperately needed his attention. Dealmaking had been a massive distraction. Instead of focusing on his customers, he was off meeting in mahogany conference rooms with legal eagles and Turnbull & Associates–clad investment bankers. While Chambers was dealmaking and dreaming about how he would spend his part of the 40 million, sales were falling and profits were down. And, with the worst possible timing, his biggest customer had filed for Chapter 11. He had thought that the new owner could worry about ramping up the business again. Now *he* was the new owner.

To add insult to injury, like the father of the bride when the groom changed his mind on the way to the altar, Chambers still had to pay the wedding expenses. He was the proud owner of $750,000 in broken deal expense, $300,000 of which was owed to his law firm.

Now he had to go back to senior managers and let them know the deal was dead. If there was anxiety and confusion when the deal was pending, this would be shock and awe! He knew they would be wondering: What would happen next? How would the company pull out of its dive? Would Chambers try for another sale? Did they have a future with the company? Did anyone?

Chambers shook his head, and water dripped onto the marble double sink of his bathroom. What had gone wrong? As always, he took the hit himself. I screwed this up, he thought. Too greedy at crunch time. Weak deadlines that made the process drag on and nearly took the business down with it. So many mistakes.

He splashed a bit more water on his face, and a wide smile stretched across his face. He had been here before, he thought. He had come back from the grave. He had kept the business alive against the odds. And he learned from the experience every time. This was just another lesson. He'd bring this company back and put together an even better deal. Now, he knew a lot more about what can go right and what can go wrong. Growing his business had been the best education in his life. And this deal was no exception. He smiled again into the mirror. One of his favorite expressions popped into his head as his smile spread: "What doesn't kill you makes you stronger."

After all, he wasn't in it for the money. Being mega-rich had never been his primary goal. He and his wife had never "lived large," and they had plenty of money to meet their needs by any standard. His family was what mattered, as did doing the right thing. He would redouble his efforts to build the business. He would fight through this downturn as he had done through others in the past. He still had faith in his business, and in himself.

But coming so close to the Promised Land had made him more sure than ever that he wanted to make it out the other side. The face looking back from the mirror was not as young as it used to be. He'd be 60 soon, and Armand Hammer he was not. He didn't want to run the business forever. He wanted a better life and to make the graceful exit he'd dreamed about within a few years. Once he had the business on a solid footing again, he'd go back to the table, stronger and much more knowledgeable.

He had earned his MBA in deal-making during this fiasco. It was a dress rehearsal—a very expensive dress rehearsal, admittedly. This time he would get it all right, starting with hiring a professional manager to help operate the business so he could focus on growth opportunities. He had learned legions. Now he had work to do to prepare for the next deal. Losing the $40 million was a shock, but he wasn't dead. In fact, he was stronger than ever.

ICONIX: NEVER UNDERESTIMATE A VIKING

To hear Leo Mullen tell it, he just was very lucky. He had studied philosophy as an undergrad at Penn State and then went on to a fellowship in graphic design and filmmaking. His father, a lawyer with a practice in a small town in the middle of Pennsylvania, had hoped against hope that one of his five children would take over the law practice. When Mullen was home, the old man, who couldn't hide his disappointment in his philosopher son, would pretend to look through the want ads of the newspaper and pointedly note how few advertisements there were for philosophy majors. His father's favorite comment was, "You'd have a better chance of getting a job as a Viking."

Mullen came to Washington, D.C., in 1973 to see an old girlfriend in Georgetown for a couple of days. He never left. The visit led to a job at an advertising agency, where his future wife, Helene Patterson, hired him for a design position. A few years later, when he was asked to sign a noncompete agreement at the design firm where he was working, he decided on the way to the water cooler that he couldn't do it. So he just quit. He had a baby on the way, a Volvo station wagon, and three kayaks—but no job. Three months later, his wife also quit, and they set up a small graphic design firm in 1978, called Invisions. Their early clients included a crushed stone manufacturer and the company that made Wite-Out correction fluid. He worked hard but it was a good life, coming in early to work, going running, and then taking a nap in the afternoon.

One afternoon, as Mullen was napping, the phone rang. It was Marriott Corporation. Invisions had been recommended by a client to do Marriott's annual report. Marriott was twenty times larger than any of their current clients. Mullen knew that if he closed them, he'd be off to the races. After they landed that account, other major companies followed quickly. They had to scramble to hire people. Specializing in annual reports had become a lucrative business.

But one day in early 1992, a client showed Mullen the EDGAR electronic database. They were looking for a document, and the client said, "Let's go online and look at it." Mullen had never been online before, but in that instant he understood that his world was fundamentally changing. Companies were only required to make their annual reports available, not to put them into print. It was the same feeling that he had when they were working on the Wite-Out account and he bought his first personal computer. After seeing the EDGAR database, Mullen went back to the office and said to Patterson, "We're toast." He was as scared as he had ever been in his life. He could see his family standing destitute in Union Station with tin cups.

Faced with the extinction of the print business, Mullen began pouring capital into building an online business. He retained earnings from the company's $4 million in revenue and slashed bonuses to a third of what they would have been. This was tough on morale because a lot of people had worked hard that year. They had achieved record revenue and record earnings. Patterson, who was co-founder and CFO of the firm, was one of his critics. Was this a fool's errand? They had a successful business. Why should they change it for some crazy new technology?

But Mullen persevered. He had a hunch that the Internet would change the world in fundamental ways. While he was wrong about the exact changes, his instincts took him in the right direction. In 1993, he launched a new subsidiary, dubbed Iconix, led by two senior people from Invisions. The business was slow to take off at first, but when the dot-com frenzy kicked into high gear, they went up with it. "I overestimated the speed that the Internet was coming, but underestimated its impact," Mullen said. They created the first websites for Marriott, US Airways, and other clients.

Iconix was so wildly successful that it became the tail that wagged the dog. The strength of Iconix in online strategy and engineering services actually became a feeder for clients into the print business as companies began to integrate their channels. By 1999, Mullen engineered a reverse merger between the two companies. The subsidiary had swallowed its parent. It also meant that Mullen was finally dispensable to the business.

He was ready to leave. Although he was only 45 years old, he was fond of quoting Indiana Jones: "It's not the years, it's the miles." He had put in a lot of miles. Iconix had opened offices in Paris and on the West Coast, so Mullen found himself crisscrossing the globe. He'd fly home on Fridays to see his daughters' ballet recitals or soccer games, only to be back in Europe on Monday morning. In 1998, he walked into Helene's office and said, "I'm 45 years old and I've been at a dead run ever since you hired me. How many years ago was that? How do we exit this?"

In all, it took seven years to get to the point of making a deal. Mullen and Patterson had built Iconix and made themselves dispensable by bringing in professional management (as we'll examine in Chapter 3). Now they were ready to deal. They received a flurry of offers but turned them down on the basis of instinct or values. "I didn't want to do anything with someone I didn't trust," Mullen said. "Dogs are the best judges of trust I've met. You have to get in touch with the voice inside of you, and you never go wrong."

Iconix ultimately sold to a group of investors as part of a roll-up of five different businesses in four locations. Mullen and Patterson walked away with $26.5 million—more than two times 12 months' forward revenue. They generously gave away 20 percent to their employees, recognition of their help in building the business and the importance to the business of keeping talent. While the owners of the other firms into the roll-up took lots of paper in the new firm (dubbed Iconixx, with an extra "x"), Mullen trusted his instincts (and the advice of his wife) to take most of his payment in cash.

At first, it didn't look like a wise move to take all that cash. After the deal was put together, he took a family vacation to Ireland for a couple of weeks in August 1999. He was pacing the floor with seller's remorse, thinking that he should have taken stock. The market was continuing to roar ahead, and the company was now valued at 12 times forward 12 months of earnings. But soon the bottom fell out, and these paper profits dissolved into cyberspace. Taking cash turned out to be a stroke of genius. How many of the other owners had given a second thought to the structure of the payout?

While wildly successful financially, the process was not without its pain for Mullen. He saw his organization shaken and stirred under new leadership, and he ultimately resigned. After retiring, he found himself setting up whiteboards in the living room until he started his next business. But he had achieved a remarkable transformation. He had started with a $5 million graphic design business that was so dependent on him that it might have produced $2 million in a sale. He attached Iconix to it and turned it into a business that sold for a 2x multiple of the entire business, print and digital. He walked away with $26 million. Not bad for a Viking.

POLITICS & PROSE: A TALE OF SUSPENSE AND HORROR

Barbara Meade and Carla Cohen had been so busy building Politics & Prose into one of the nation's most successful independent bookstores that they hadn't stopped to think about what would happen next. Since founding the store as its only employees in 1984, they had made it an icon in the Washington area. President Bill Clinton stopped by to browse the stacks. A string of leading authors had launched books there. In 1999, they were named Bookseller of the Year by *Publisher's Weekly*. A day-in-the-life profile on the bookstore in the *Washington Post* in December 2000 included the following brief discussion about what would happen after the partners retired:

> Conversation curves wistfully toward the future and what will happen to Politics & Prose when Cohen and Meade— both 64 years old—retire. They are looking for someone to take over the high-maintenance operation in the next few years.
>
> Aaron, Cohen's son, would be a logical successor. . . . Meade recites advice from her lawyer. "Do your children a favor and don't saddle them with the family farm."[2]

It was just a brief passage in a 3,220-word story. The partners didn't give it a second thought. Little did they know where those remarks would lead.

When the article appeared, the phone started ringing. Cohen and Meade received five calls from suitors who wanted to look at buying the business. "The first time around, it happened accidentally," recalled Meade in a small office stacked with books in the back of their store on Connecticut Avenue. "We didn't think about it."

Most of the potential investors or buyers took a quick look and didn't think they'd get the returns they were looking for. (The owners give away most of their profits to employees at the end of each year.) But one of the calls came from a longtime customer who had just sold his T-shirt business and was interested in exploring taking over the bookstore. He had an appraisal done on the business, which had $6 million in sales and 6 percent net profits, before profit sharing with employees. The deal called for the new partner to join the staff of the store for a few trial months, then purchase a one-third interest for $400,000, and finally have the option to take full control in five years.

It all happened quickly. Meade and Cohen were so busy running the business that they never even discussed the proposal carefully, even with one another, let alone with outside advisers. They never took it to their advisory board. And, worst of all, they never discussed it with their employees. This turned out to be a big mistake. Employees at the store were given great autonomy, and the owners treated the business as a family business, even though they are not related. This formula had produced low turnover and high morale.

While Meade and Cohen differed in their interests and personalities, they had always agreed on one thing: Their primary goals for the business were never about the money. Their exit strategy was no different. As Meade wrote in a booklet celebrating their fifteenth anniversary in 1999, "I think that in a male partnership, there is a tremendous emphasis put on money; making it, keeping it, and divvying it up. I can't remember a single quarrel that Carla and I have had over money. From our female perspective, the money is less important than the quality of relationships we have with each other, with our customers, and with the staff." These relationships were about to be put to the test.

If the partners had wanted to maximize the price, selling to a large chain such as Barnes & Noble would have probably produced top dollar. But for a store that saw itself as the last bastion in independence in a homogenized world, it was unthinkable. "It would betray what we believe in and stand for," Cohen said flatly. The owners had chosen a transition plan that they thought would keep Politics & Prose intact, sustaining their commitment to the community and employees. While it would limit their responsibilities and give them time for other things (like reading), they expected that the new partnership would allow them to continue to work at the store. They would ride off gracefully into the sunset.

When the new potential partner came into the store for the trial period in the spring of 2001, his lack of openness with employees created immediate suspicion about this mysterious newcomer. They had no idea what he was doing there. When he began acting more like an owner, suspicion turned to resentment. He had a particularly prickly relationship with the store's general manager. When after a few months the new partner bought into his first third of the business, Meade and Cohen realized they needed to make an announcement to employees. They gathered the staff in an empty office building, and welcomed their new partner. "We thought they were going to be happy," said Meade. "Across the board, everyone's jaw dropped, and the general manager looked like a bolt of lightning had hit him."

At first, Meade and Cohen attributed the problems to difficulties between the general manager and the new partner. After six months of work with an organizational psychologist, they ended up replacing the general manager with the partner. But the staff still felt he was too bottom line–oriented and in their face, not at all in line with the more decentralized management style that Meade and Cohen had practiced. A paternal kiss to an employee on her birthday set a match to this powder keg. The employee quit. The staff was in an uproar. Meade flew back from vacation in Colorado. The organizational psychologist first met with the entire staff and then with the three partners. The best course seemed to be for the new partner to leave.

But without a bailout clause, it took months of mediation and negotiation to work out an agreement. It included returning his investment as well as making "alimony" payments for four years. Months later, and roughly $300,000 poorer, Meade and Cohen had their business back.

"We did everything wrong," Meade recalled. "We didn't have our own lawyer. There was no bailout clause to unwind the agreement."

Fortunately, the business continued to do well despite the internal turmoil, posting 6 percent growth in revenues in 2004. The staff was more galvanized than ever in support of the store. The owners identified a new general manager from their current staff. In that sense, they were successful in surviving this ordeal. It was an expensive lesson, but Meade and Cohen had learned a lot. As they both moved toward their seventieth birthdays, they were still firmly at the helm.

While they had made many mistakes in growing the business,

this one was one of the largest and most expensive. "We grew the business, little by little," Meade said. "We learned as we went along and made small mistakes. This was different." They had rushed into a deal without carefully thinking about the implications. Although they had an advisory board, they never took the matter to the board.

What happens next? When we met with them in mid-2005, they were thinking about an ESOP or seeking out another buyer. They had involved their advisory board this time, hired a consultant to help think through the possibilities, and had a policy of absolute transparency with employees.

All of the plans they envisioned called for the founding partners to continue to be involved in the store. As they discussed their plans, an employee ducked into the office of the two partners to discuss ordering extra copies of a new book. Shoppers browsed through the aisles of books outside the door. The store was alive, and Meade and Cohen were at its heart. While they continued to explore the possibilities, they were in no hurry this time. As Cohen said, "We're not ready to leave."[3]

EXPERIENCE KEEPS A DEAR SCHOOL

As these stories show, the road to selling your business is lined with pitfalls. Leo Mullen found that, with careful planning, it can sometimes succeed beyond your wildest dreams. Other times it can plummet to depths beyond your worst nightmares. As the owner of the business, you often just have to hang on for the ride. The entrepreneurs in these stories learned a lot from their experiences. These lessons were sometimes expensive, very expensive. As Ben Franklin once said, "Experience keeps a dear school, but fools will learn in no other."

On the following pages, you will have an opportunity to learn from the experiences of these entrepreneurs. We'll share more of their experiences, as well as the insights of subject area experts in organizational psychology, law, wealth management, and other fields. They'll offer a multidimensional view of the complex challenges of selling a business. Their insights will help you maximize the value of the sale and minimize the pain and confusion. You'll learn ways to get good advice and save money in the process. This will help you be clear about what you want from the most important deal of your life—and how to go about getting the most out of it—however you define your goals. You have one shot at selling your business successfully. You need to do it right.

NOTES

1. While his name and some identifying characteristics of the business have been changed, the numbers, dates, process and other facts of Bill Chambers's story are his actual experience.

2. Linton Weeks, "Biography of a Bookstore: In an Era of Big Competitors, an Independent Needs to Stand on Its Prose," *Washington Post*, December 28, 2000, p. C-1.

3. Jeffrey A. Trachtenberg, "Succession Plot at Bookstore Took a Surprise Twist," *Wall Street Journal*, March 21, 2005, p. A1.

CHAPTER 2

WHAT DO YOU WANT?

Be Clear About Your Goals

GOALS FOR THE SALE

In the three cases presented in Chapter 1, the owners had different goals for the sale and this led to different outcomes:

Homeland Designs: Bill Chambers wanted to maximize his price, but he became too greedy and let the deal drag on too long. The buyer walked, and he needed to rescue the business, which had been neglected during the deal-making process. He failed to reach his ultimate goal of selling the business.

Iconix: Leo Mullen wanted to maximize price and ultimately chose to maximize cash. He brought in a professional CFO and shifted the business online to make himself more dispensable. He found a strategic buyer that would roll up the company with other businesses, and he walked away with a $26 million

We are grateful for the expert insights of Michael Kennedy of PricewaterhouseCoopers on structuring the inside sale, John Fruehwirth of Allied Capital on mezzanine financing, and Lou Diamond of Buchanan Ingersoll in Washington, D.C., on Employee Stock Ownership Plans (ESOPs).

deal. The downside was employee turmoil and watching his business torn apart.

Politics & Prose: The partners were more concerned about preserving the business and protecting employees than extracting the most return. They chose a buyer who they felt would continue the business and allow them to continue to be involved. But they didn't pay enough attention to the legal and financial side of the deal, particularly the escape clauses needed if things went south, which they did.

When Bill Chambers acquired Homeland Designs from the founder in 1986, he negotiated what turned out to be a very attractive deal. Chambers was president of the company at the time, which had revenue of about $15 million. The owner had two key goals, to keep the company operating as it had been and to continue to work for the firm after the sale. Chambers and the owner hammered out an agreement for a sale price of about $1.5 million with interest. The deal required Chambers to put up only $100,000 up front, with the rest paid off over time. Chambers's lawyer even negotiated for a two-year hiatus in the payments if necessary. With a downturn in the industry in 1988 and 1989, this proved to be a lifesaver.

According to the deal, the owner had to stay on at his current salary. He didn't want to run the business day-to-day, but he wanted to stay involved. Why was this so important? When the owner had sold his previous company to a competitor, he had an agreement to work for the company for five years. At the end of that period, they tossed him out. It had always left a bitter taste in his mouth to be booted from the business he had founded. He was determined that it wouldn't happen with Homeland Designs. The owner's daughters held most of the stock. While they expected an eventual payoff, they were in no hurry to cash out. They were happy to be paid over time. It worked out well for everyone, particularly Chambers.

The owner might have received a higher price on the open market, and certainly more cash up front, but he got what he wanted out of the deal. He could stay involved in this business as long as he wanted, without the headaches of owning it. Since the owner was like a father to Chambers, it was a good deal all around. While Chambers's lawyer and financial adviser both cautioned against having the former owner involved, Chambers ignored their advice, trusting his own gut. The founder would sometimes challenge Chambers's decisions, but it was done in a measured way, and Chambers found that the insights of the founder were very often right on target.

Of course, when the market and business bottomed out in the late 1980s, Chambers did ask himself a few times what he had gotten himself into. But when the business kicked back into gear in 1991, he knew it was going to be a good deal. He made the final payment in 1993 and gave a big party. By understanding the owner's goals for the sale, he had ensured that they both made a good deal.

Chambers continued to build the business, living through downturns again in the late 1990s that forced him to take out a second mortgage on his home. He then fired up a comeback, building the business to $66 million in revenue and more than $11 million adjusted EBITDA by 2001. Clearly, his $1 million–plus investments had paid off well. His success was something he never expected. He had just wanted to earn a decent living, support his family, and be able to serve as a financial backstop for his extended family.

THE ONE THAT GOT AWAY

When it came time for Chambers to put together his own deal, as discussed in Chapter 1, he had several offers. One offer was for $30 million in cash plus a $10 to $15 million earn-out, from a large corporation. A second offer, from an entrepreneurial competitor, came in at $40 million with a $5 to $10 million earn-out. Chambers reviewed his options in more detail and considered their impact on achieving his goals for the deal. When he calculated the payoff for other family members who had shares of his business, he didn't think the $30 million would be enough (he realized only later that he could have easily given them a gift from his own $15 million share). He knew it might be a little more of a wild ride with the entrepreneur but decided that the added upside made it worth the risk.

When negotiations started with the entrepreneur, his aggressive advisers got hold of the process. They drove hard bargains. Too hard. The buyer, a volatile CEO, wasn't going to be pushed around. Instead he found an excuse to walk. The deal cratered. "I learned some hard lessons," Chambers said. "If I did it over again, I'd create a more competitive situation to find out what they were going to do before signing with one of them. I'd also make sure my vision was the dominant one on our side of the table."

Should he have taken the $30 million? A large company might have been a more stable buyer, even though the earn-out would have been in the form of the company's stock, the price of which would be largely out of his control. Still, he'd have been able to retire with the money in the bank.

Most of all, he needed to be clearer about what he wanted from the deal, from the company and from life. That was perhaps the biggest lesson of all. He decided to get this right the next time around. Now he is clear about his goals. He wants to get cash out of the business and retire. It would take a few years to get the business back into the position he'd like.

To throttle back on his operational responsibilities, Chambers brought in a professional operations manager, who was named president and COO in July 2004. Chambers is now working on new growth areas, such as expanding European markets. Within a couple of years, he expects to go back to the deal table again in a strong position.

He learned much about deal making, and also about his own goals. "I have learned a lot from the process," he said. "This company and making money are not what life is about. It is learning and, if the lesson is important, it is an end in itself. All these things taught me who I am, what I can do, and how important people are to me. Many of my closest friends have come from this business. Those are life lessons this company helped me to learn. Whether I reach a financial pinnacle or something less, I've gotten a lot out of this."

WHY ARE YOU SELLING?

While you may want to get the best price, there are many other goals that could be priorities in the sale, as summarized in Table 2-1 below. Being clear about your goals will help in finding the right buyer and avoiding "seller's remorse." What are your goals for the sale? How can you best realize them?

Trade-Offs: Payoffs vs. Disruption

In weighing the different goals, an important tradeoff is between maximizing financial payoff and minimizing disruption to the business, as illustrated in Figure 2-1. A sale to a strategic buyer will usually give you the best price for the company. Compared with financial buyers who are only looking at the business as a way to earn a return on their dollars, the strategic buyer actually knows what to do with the business after the sale. This type of buyer, often a rival

TABLE 2-1. GOALS FOR THE SALE.

Potential Goals	Issues
Maximizing price	To maximize cash payout or price, you might need to find a buyer who would be likely to strip out parts of the business or sell off pieces of it.
Maximizing cash	Taking the payoff in cash can be a sure thing in the short term, but might sacrifice potential upside if the business is still growing.
Staying personally involved after closing	This can give you a say in business decisions and ease the transition into retirement. This can be achieved by staying on the board or selling only a minority stake. But some sellers (and buyers) want to make a clean break.
Keeping family involved	This might involve a sale to children or other family members. It helps to maintain the legacy, but can be complicated if there are no viable candidates or family relationships are tangled. Would they be better off with cash or stock?
Taking care of employees	At the extreme, the owner could sell to employees through an ESOP, or make arrangement to take care of employees through payouts or guarantees as part of the sale. This may mean sacrificing a higher price.

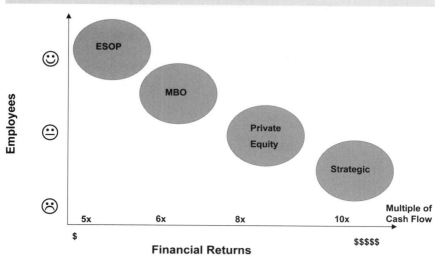

FIGURE 2-1. BIG SMILES VS. BIG BUCKS.

firm, might be able to combine the acquired company with its existing business, making them both more efficient. The strategic buyer might also be a customer who is backward-integrating, or a supplier who is forward-integrating.

You will likely get the best price from a competitor because they have the opportunity to reduce overhead, but you can expect that they will significantly restructure and disrupt the business. Stripping out overhead usually means employees, so what the buyers gain on the financial side may have a high human cost. Some buyers are extremely aggressive in cutting staff, wiping out most of the employees but leaving the customer base standing. Suppliers or customers expanding their businesses would be much less likely to do massive downsizing of the business. If you know there is going to be a lot of breakage, you might pay out a bonus from the sale to employees or extend severance from three to six months as part of the deal.

A financial buyer, on the other hand, will be looking at improving the existing business so there will be more limited disruption. A management buyout (MBO), in which the company's current top managers join with private investors to take control of the company, will ensure more stability, since the existing management will continue (although managers may have aggressive plans for reshaping the business). The ESOP represents the least disruptive path, since employees will still be in charge. The goals for the sale will have a direct impact on the outcome.

Table 2-2 offers a more detailed comparison of the upsides and downsides of each approach, as well as a ballpark for financial returns.

Becoming Clear About Your Goals

Examining these trade-offs can help you become more clear about your own goals and how to achieve them. As with any complex process, selling a business successfully requires very careful thought and preparations. It is easy to get muddled and lose your way. *Every single situation is different.* There is no formula for success. But I believe there are a series of important steps that should be taken to maximize the likelihood of a big win. Start early, and revisit these questions often.

We will discuss some of the specific issues to decide and prepare for in the following chapters. But for now, let's look at the decisions about where to begin in clarifying your goals. Here are some useful first steps:

1. *Get advice early and often.* Discuss the idea of the sale with your kitchen cabinet or trusted advisers. This group should include your board of directors, your spouse, your lawyer, and your accountant. Have a separate lunch or breakfast with each to get input on every single angle. What price makes sense to them? Who would be the right buyer group? What structure makes sense? What can go wrong? What's their gut feeling about your plan to turn the business over to your son, daughter, or top manager? Of course, do it all in strict confidence.

You should also start expanding your circle of advisers as quickly as possible. As examined in Chapter 5, it is never too early to have discussions with lawyers, accountants, psychologists, and other key advisers with specific experience in selling businesses in your indus-

TABLE 2-2. WEIGHING THE TRADE-OFFS.

Option	Multiple	Upside	Downside
ESOP	5-6x	Employees buy the business, so they are in charge. This is very employee-friendly and tax-friendly. The owner will take a lower price but will have the satisfaction of knowing that the business will continue and that there is a high likelihood the owner can continue to be involved.	Many ESOPs are not successful because there is a lack of leadership and too many interest groups. United Airlines discovered this. There are often too many chiefs and not enough Indians, particularly in entrepreneurial businesses that are used to the strong leadership of the founders.
Management Buyout (MBO)	5-7x	Very employee-friendly and strong continuity, this also offers a smooth transition from current owners to current managers.	This requires high leverage; there is no new blood, so few new perspectives on the business, and no new resources to grow the business.
Private Equity	6-8x	Strong management partnership and fresh insights on improving the business. Maintains the continuity of the company.	High leverage and limited resources.
Strategic Buyer	8-10x	Highest payoff, new resources for the company that can help in expansion and yield a higher upside. The buyer has strategic knowledge and synergistic businesses that can increase the value of the deal.	Usually layoffs and restructuring of the business are needed to realize synergies and unload underperforming parts of the business.

try. If there is one big lesson from our Politics & Prose story, which these two highly intelligent business owners are the first to admit, is that they really blew it all by using the approach of "ready, fire, aim." To their own amazement today, they did not even tell their board they were turning ownership over to an outsider. The owners didn't discuss their plans with one another or establish explicit goals for their business. If they had, they probably would have brought employees into the process much sooner.

In what is not an unusual situation, the founders of Politics & Prose were experts in running their business but had no experience in actually *selling* a business. They simply were too darn busy running their bookstore to spend a lot of time on this. Since they had never had the experience of successes and failures in selling businesses, they didn't fully appreciate what was at stake in forging a successful deal.

Now they have gained this experience the hard way. The deal also emerged organically, so they didn't really think through how they wanted to approach it. They felt good about the buyer and plunged ahead. It is to their great credit that they were wise enough to quickly unwind a bad deal. But as they would be first to tell you, "Don't do what we did!"

2. *Set the stage.* Owners should make out their wish list for the sale. This could address any of the following factors:

  a. Price?

  b. Cash at closing?

  c. Willingness to finance the sale?

  d. Keep it in the family?

  e. Owner's postclosing role?

  f. Selling 100 percent or keeping a piece of the business?

  g. Postclosing office space needs and role of assistant?

  h. Continuation of owner's perks—cars, boats, planes, etc.?

  i. Spin-off of company-owned real estate?

  j. Timing of closing?

k. Any special provisions (e.g., special allocations for long-term employees, including family)?

l. Willingness to come back to the company if things go poorly?

m. Willingness to sign realistic sale documents with their standard representations and warranties to the buyer?

This is just a small sample. Once you've read through this book, you will have dozens more questions and detailed ideas about how you want to proceed. Put down your entire wish list—everything and the kitchen sink. Next, take that list to your trusted advisers to get their input and make sure your list is sensible. Most of all, get unvarnished input on your price expectations (we have much more on valuation in Chapter 6). I love business owners, but to their fault, their passion for their babies often clouds their judgment on price, making a deal impossible. If you really want to get something done, you must be realistic.

3. *Retain a point person.* Even with an inside sale, I believe a third-party point person is essential. This may be your CPA, lawyer, or perhaps a director. You do not have to pay this person a huge fee, and this can normally be done on a fair hourly rate. (We'll discuss lining up your dream team in Chapter 5.) But no matter what, this will be an emotional process with sticking points (particularly the documents) and it is *worth every penny* to have this *buffer* or *honest broker* standing constructively between buyer and seller.

In terms of compensation, every deal is different, but perhaps you can hire this person for $250 to $300 per hour, and ask them to let you know every time they are at a cost of $5,000, so you can track costs carefully. Be sure this person has lots of relevant business sale experience! Do not hire your friendly divorce lawyer or cousin Alfred! This may disappoint professionals with whom you have worked for many years, but it is better to ruffle a few feathers at the outset than later lack the advice that you will desperately need to complete a successful sale.

4. *Timing.* In addition to deciding what you want to do, it is also important to consider *when* to do it. The best time to sell is

when the business is doing well, of course, and when the market will give a fair price for the business. If the company is not at the top of its game, it could be well worthwhile to invest the time and money into improving the business before putting it up on the auction block. In this process, timing is everything.

Structuring the Payout

The goals for the deal also will affect how the payout is structured. Should the payout be in cash, notes, earn-outs, or stock? The choices in some cases are limited by the structure of the deal itself. But these choices can also be affected by the seller's attitude toward risk. Moving from cash to stock, the risk increases, but so does the potential reward, as shown in Figure 2-2.

Consider each of these options:

• *Cash.* Cash is green and ready. There is no upside. It is the bird in the hand, but there will never be two in the bush. It also means that you pay taxes right away.

FIGURE 2-2. DESIGNING THE DEAL: RISK VS. REWARD.

• *Notes.* These offer tax deferral and interest income. They have medium risk but a fairly weak upside, unless they are convertible to stock.

• *Earn-Out.* An earn-out is used to pay off the owner over a period of years. It is usually used by the buyer to ensure that the owner continues to support the business. It is high-risk and some reward, but can be tax-inefficient when compared to other mechanisms. (We'll discuss other problems with it later in this chapter.) Buyers also use consulting contracts to reward former owners and keep them involved in the business, but these also are tax-inefficient. They generate ordinary income rather than capital gains. It should be noted that it is possible to structure some forms of earn-outs as equity or debt where you can get capital gains, so consult your tax expert.

• *Stock.* Stock often offers the highest risk and highest reward. The tax is deferred as long as you continue to hold stock, but the risk can be high. If you sell the stock after closing, you pay your taxes at that time.

INSIDE SALES

The goals for the sale can lead to two very different paths: the inside versus the outside sale process. Do you sell to managers, employees, or family? Or do you find an outside buyer? Sometimes they can be combined—where both outside bidders and inside managers or family members are invited to participate—either on an equal footing or with preferential treatment. But this type of hybrid approach has its own pitfalls. For many companies, the best way to maximize value and options will be to hire a third-party adviser to conduct the sale to outsiders. This is called an outside sale. (Executing this approach is dealt with extensively in Chapter 7.)

But for many business owners, the best way to achieve value or other goals is to conduct an inside sale, basically selling the company directly to senior management, employees, or family members. For the time being, we will set aside the complexities of family relationships, but these are very important matters. We will consider the impact of the family drama and assessment of potential heirs more thoroughly in Chapter 4.

Many companies are excellent candidates for an internal sale. These would include very small companies, such as those with less than $5 million of annual revenue, where an auction just may not be an economic approach. Inside sales also may be the best approach for businesses that are highly dependent upon human talent, such as consulting firms or professional service firms. Sometimes the goals of the seller make an inside sale attractive, such as when the owner of Homeland Designs sold it to Bill Chambers. Another good candidate for an inside sale is Politics & Prose. Since preserving their legacy is more important than maximizing their returns, a sale to employees or managers may offer the best chance of preserving the distinctive character of the business.

Define the Internal Buyers

Even if you decide to do an inside sale, you need to define exactly which managers or family members would make the best buyers. Do you want to sell to one person, such as your COO, the senior team, or the whole company? Every situation is different, but as a general rule, I am a great believer in the idea that *less is more*. It might be a nice concept to sell to many employees, but then, who is in charge? There are too many chiefs. Generally, only a handful of key senior managers really drive results, and making fewer people accountable is better, in my opinion. Make the buck stop somewhere. In addition, of course, the fewer people in the inner circle, the less politics and turf-fighting—and thus the less hassle in pulling off the deal. But make sure that key people to the success of the business are included.

Caveat Emptor

Another reason to keep the circle of buyers small is that once you start discussions with *anyone* about a sale, be prepared for the entire world to know. As in so many situations, hope for the best but prepare for the worst. What happens when your plant manager, who is not included in the deal, finds out? What about customers? Just be prepared! And then, tell the truth. I strongly believe that the best way to frame the story is simply to use that old Wall Street adage (always delivered with a bit of Washington cagey diplomacy) that the owner is simply "considering all strategic alternatives." That is not a lie. It is really what is happening. Having "talks" does not mean a deal will be done. Will people be nervous about this? Yes, of course. Human beings just hate uncertainty. But that is life. Of course, if you tell them that you see no likelihood of layoffs in a sale, that will be helpful, but only if you honestly mean it.

Get Skin in the Game

Suppose your business makes $300,000 in pretax profits on sales of $2 million, and you have agreed to sell the business for five times pretax, or $1.5 million. So you have an appropriate price and handshake with your buyers.

Now you need to get the money! The big problem, of course, is that normally your management team or family members *do not have the money to do the deal.* In fact, they normally are only able to contribute a very small portion of the sales price. When Bill Chambers bought his company, he had almost no capital. In such cases, the owner will need to provide most of the financing. This is not atypical. In fact, it is totally common.

Wall Street does its very best to make all of this sound very complex, to justify bankers' fees, but buying a business is in many ways just like buying a house. The buyer puts up as little money as possible, borrows the rest, and pays the debt down over time. That, folks, is all that a Leveraged or Management Buyout ("LBO" or "MBO") is: a business purchase just like the purchase of a home.

Whatever the case with the inside buyer, however, I believe that having some "skin in the game" is essential. They just must cut some kind of check. If it is a $1 million check, great. If it is a $10,000 check, and that is meaningful to them, great. Make it a meaningful amount, but do not make them take out second mortgages on their homes to do it. You don't want overly leveraged, stressed-out, risk-averse managers making short-term decisions to keep a roof over the heads of their families.

How would an inside sale to managers be structured? As discussed above, most inside sales are structured a lot like a house sale, and every deal is different. But suppose we use the $1.5 million example. In a good case, the management team might put up about $300,000 of equity capital. Then, perhaps, the company's bank will lend $600,000, or two times cash flow, to help finance the deal. That leaves a gap of $600,000 (or likely $650,000 to $700,000 when considering all closing costs), which nearly always needs to be financed by the owner in the form of a note.

These components are different on every deal. Perhaps management has only $100,000 or less and the bank will lend only $200,000. Now the owner must finance $1.2 million. Or perhaps the banks will do nothing, and the owner needs to finance $1.4 million, or over 90 percent of the price. This is not atypical. The seller of Homeland Designs financed 100 percent when he sold to Bill Chambers. He took his money over time in an earn-out. This is generous, of course, but is often the best way for the owner to get reasonable value on an inside transfer.

Let's put a bit more meat on the first example. Suppose the managers put up $300,000 of skin and the bank puts up $600,000. How will all of this work? We use the simple "Sources and Uses" table below to clarify:

Sources of Capital		Uses of Capital	
Equity from Management	$300,000	Cash to Seller	$850,000
Bank	$600,000	Fees	$50,000
Seller Financing	$650,000	Seller Note	$650,000
Total Sources	$1,550,000	*Total Uses*	$1,550,000

And what is the cost for each piece? It's all a negotiation (there is a lot more in Chapter 6 on this topic), but in today's markets the bank piece will have a 1 to 1.5 percent fee attached and charge interest of 8 to 9 percent per annum, or approximately $50,000 per year. And the bank will have a *first lien* on all the assets, which means that if the deal goes badly, they will own the company.

The seller note is always a matter of negotiation, and has many possible permutations. It is literally an open canvas. But a typical approach might be a seven-year note with 8 percent interest and some small amortization or pay-downs starting in year three. Perhaps there is accelerated payoff of this note if cash flows are strong. There are other creative notions, which we will discuss below. But largely this note will have a *second lien* on the assets of the company in case the deal goes badly. This means that, as seller, you will have to stand behind the banks in getting money back if things go south.

Seller financing of this type should dictate that the seller have covenants on the loan as protection. These would normally be simple cash flow covenants such that if the business falls off, the owner can take actions to protect his or her interests. It again is open to discussion, but an owner who takes back such a large piece of financing should normally maintain a board seat until most of the note is paid off.

Earn-Outs and Equity

As mentioned, a partially or wholly seller-financed approach is the typical route to an inside sale. It also is sound tax-wise, as the seller pays capital gains tax on only the cash portion of the sale, and the tax on the note piece is deferred until payments on the principal of the note are made. Also, it can allow for some nice current interest income on the note in the meantime (sorry, you must pay ordinary tax on this interest income).

Earn-Outs

The earn-out can be married with the note structure or used alone to facilitate a payment. The earn-out simply means paying some piece of the future cash flows for the business to the seller. For example, a sale could be made by the seller agreeing to sell 100 percent of the stock in exchange for a payment equal to 100 percent of the pretax profit in each of the next four to five years. After that point, the buyers would own the company free and clear. This is essentially what Bill Chambers did on his original purchase.

Or the earn-out could be combined with the note. As in our example above, perhaps the seller, as a "sweetener" or "kicker," will receive half of the pretax profits in excess of $400,000. Thus, if the business really takes off, the seller gets an additional bonus. There are literally infinite permutations of the earn-out approach, and it can be very effective.

I am not a fan of earn-outs, however. I much prefer the clarity of seller notes, for several reasons. First, it means that the seller must have careful oversight on the business income statement, as this is his driver of value. This can be a big problem and nuisance for the buyers, and it puts the buyer and seller at cross-purposes. An earn-out structure, by definition, is driven to maximize profits. But suppose in Year Two after a sale, the right long-term move for the company is to open a new plant. This may curb profits in the near term but be a big winner long-term. However, as this may kill the earn-out, the seller may say "no" to a potentially great growth plan. Thus, the lousy conflict of the earn-out.

The note is much cleaner. Buyers either make their payments or they don't. If the new owners can both open the new plant and pay off your notes, they do it. If they don't make their note payments, they are in trouble. But at least the long-term decisions for the company rest with the new owners, so they will not be henpecked by the seller. There are additional burdens and complexities for children who use an earn-out to buy out a parent, as will be discussed in Chapter 4.

Another big problem with the earn-out is what happens if the new owner wants to pursue a merger or acquisition or sell the firm postsale. In both scenarios, the earn-out payments create huge problems. How do you protect the first income statement in a merger? Which costs go where? Who is responsible for synergies? It is simply a quagmire. Again, notes are crisp and clean for the most part.

Equity Kickers

Suppose the seller would like to maintain an equity stake in case things take off or to be able to show an ongoing interest to current customers? This is fine and can be structured quite simply without an earn-out. The interest, and the seller's future role (board seat, etc.), are all a matter of negotiation. A simple way, as mentioned above, is to let the seller buy a piece of management's equity. In our example above, management takes $300,000, so if the owner wants a 20 percent stake going forward, he can fund 20 percent of the equity ($60,000) on the same basis as management and participate in the upside.

A smart accountant like our friends at PWC could help you structure this equity piece as a tax-free equity exchange. Such equity kickers also can offer greater price comfort if the seller perceives the price of the business is too low. By retaining equity, the owner can participate in the expected upside.

Home Run Warrants

A home run warrant is a fancy feature wherein the seller receives a bonus if the business is sold for a huge profit later. For example, suppose you sell your business for $1.5 million but the buyers hit a "home run" in the next five years, selling the company for more than $5 million. You could have arranged at the time of the deal to receive 25 percent of the amount over $5 million, which would provide some insurance against selling too cheaply.

This seems like a remarkable gift—having your cake and eating it too—but you'd be surprised at what you can get from a motivated seller if you think to ask. It is very easy to sign away a small part of a hypothetical home run before it materializes, but impossible once the ball is out of the park. Part of the interest on the notes can accrue (this used to be called *payments in kind*, or PIKs) rather than be paid in cash.

Keep It Simple

Of course, if we want to be financial wizards like Michael Milken, we can marry or interchange many of these elements. The deal could have notes, earn-out levels, equity kickers, and home run warrants. In addition to disliking earn-outs, I am a huge fan of simplicity in deal making. First, plain vanilla structures are easy to understand for all parties, including your banks and yourself (sellers can be too smart for their own good). *Simple structures will dramatically simplify your documents.* This means less time and attention on your part and lower legal fees. In our heavily lawyered times, I believe the last point alone makes a simple and straightforward approach the preferred route. Every time you add something to the deal, ask yourself if the gains will be worth the added burden created by the increased complexity.

Simplicity also makes it easier to focus on achieving your goals. You'll be better able to see what is happening and make sure your own goals for the deal are achieved without being so caught up in the details of a tangled deal structure that you lose sight of the big picture.

These are just sketches of how an internal deal might be structured. We'll explore some of these aspects of the deal in more detail, but this gives a sense of the possibilities for how a deal might be structured, so you can better think about these possibilities in your own business and how you can achieve your goals.

ESOP Till You Drop

If your goal is happy employees above a higher immediate return, then the Employee Stock Ownership Plan (ESOP) might be your best bet—and it offers some tax advantages. The ESOP, a tool that is available to small and large business owners, is a tax-qualified employee deferred compensation plan. It is similar to a profit-sharing plan, but is designed to invest primarily in the stock of the sponsoring employer. An ESOP can also represent a proactive exit strategy because of its tax-advantaged treatment. It's quite surprising to me that the ESOP is not used more frequently, because the tax advantages are very powerful. It may be because ESOPs are highly complex, and you need to have an independent valuation done every year, so the ESOP requires that you retain very experienced advisers.

An ESOP is also a good choice if there is no external market for the business, or if you want to reward employees who have not been adequately compensated for their role in building the company. If the business depends entirely upon its employees, who might walk if a new owner comes in, an ESOP might also be a good choice for retaining and motivating the talent needed to sustain the business. Finally, as in the case of Politics & Prose, selling to employees might be the best way to preserve the character of the business (although a sale to a few managers also should be considered).

The biggest challenge of this structure is, of course, that now the employees as a group are large stakeholders in the corporation and must be considered in go-forward decisions. Governance is the tricky part, particularly for majority purchase situations. As noted above, turning the business over to the whole tribe instead of a few chiefs can lead to complicated decision making. Failed ESOPs such as that of United Airlines demonstrate how difficult these situations can be. When the going gets tough, who takes the hits when the employees are in charge? It's difficult to make the tough calls in that situation. Finally, ESOPs are very difficult to unwind, so go carefully. But if it fits with your goals and the nature of the business, you should definitely take the time to consider this option.

The leveraged ESOP is particularly powerful as an exit vehicle. In a leveraged ESOP, the company obtains a loan from a commercial lender (there are many ESOP–specific lenders) and then lends this money to the ESOP, which uses it to buy stock from either existing shareholders or the company itself, thereby creating a liquidity event. This can be executed for a minority or majority stake in the company. The most powerful and compelling part of this strategy is that not only is the interest on the loan tax-deductible, *but the entire principal amount of the loan is deductible*. This represents a massive tax savings and should be explored. For S-corporations, the ESOP literature suggests that there are even greater tax benefits. For this reason alone, this approach may be worth discussing with your advisers.

Family Insider Sales

The approaches used above would work perfectly well in a family context, assuming that the owner is selling an interest in the business to family members for some consideration. However, in a family situation, many times the owner or owners want to transfer interests to family members for the lowest possible considerations to create minimal taxes. The laws here are very complex, and the family must seek expert tax and legal estate advisers to make sure they plan these transfer events well in advance and avoid landmines. There is an extensive discussion of some good gifting and transfer options in Chapter 9, including an overview of various charitable and other trust structures that may be pursued.

Consider a few of the obvious points. Large interest in successful companies cannot be transferred without consequences. If you give someone a $5 million interest in a business, they will have to pay meaningful taxes. But there are numerous methods to reduce this tax burden. Many have been referenced in this book, but the only way to fully understand your options is to visit with our friends at firms like PWC, Goldman Sachs, or Hogan & Hartson. In Chapter 4, we also discuss some of the relationship issues that often can be more of a challenge in family sales than the actual financial details.

The Outside Sale

You may have decided to go for the whole kahuna and sell your business to an outsider. There may be no family members or managers qualified to take the helm, or you just want to be free and clear with the most cash in your pocket. You've set your goals, you know where you're going, and you have long since reviewed all of your tax, legal, estate and philanthropic issues. You have discussed this with your kitchen cabinet and have a terrific team of professionals to support you, including expert counsel with substantial deal experience. Preparing for the outside sale, including cleaning up your financials and hiring professional managers, is discussed extensively in the Chapter 3. We also consider how to find relevant buyers and to structure the deal. While much of this best practice may be applicable to family sales or insider sales, this thorough approach is particularly relevant in outside sales.

DO YOU REALLY WANT TO SELL? GETTING CASH WITHOUT GETTING OUT

Finally, in the process of examining your goals, you also need to consider whether you truly want to get out of the business at all. Do you just want to reduce your responsibilities and time commitment? Do you want to bring in additional cash to grow the business or allow you to take cash out? You can do both of these things without selling your business. You might bring in professional management, as discussed in the following chapter, but use the management to reduce your time in the business without giving up ownership. If you want to bring in an infusion of fresh capital, you might do this through strategies such as selling a minority stake, obtaining new financing (such as mezzanine financing), or initiating an IPO. Some of these strategies ultimately can be steps toward selling the entire business by putting one foot out the door:

• *A Minority Stake.* While a minority sale is typically used to gain access to the capital to run or expand the business, it might be used as a gradual step toward exiting. A partner may be given a minority stake with the option to purchase more of the business in the future. This can, however, draw out the process (or prolong the agony) and muddy the waters if your true goal is to get out. Selling a minority stake may be a good first step toward a sale, or a way to liquidate some of the value of the business.

• *"Mezzanine" and Other Financing.* There are literally hundreds of ways to finance growth in this complex financial world. With interest rates at historically low levels over these past several years, the debt markets have boomed, and bank debt and "mezzanine debt" have become much more viable alternatives. One of the sectors that has experienced tremendous growth is the area of BDCs (Business Development Companies). These are essentially large and powerful investment firms that finance corporate growth through debt and equity instruments. But they are more than lenders. They act as constructive corporate partners to build value. The granddaddy of BDCs is Allied Capital, based in Washington, D.C., operating for over 40 years with a market capitalization of over $4 billion. There are pros and cons to going the debt route to finance your potential liquidity, of course, as explored in the case below (see box), which describes a successful entrepreneur who financed growth and liquidity through Allied Capital.

Joe Wesley and Allied Capital: The "Mezzanine" Growth Capital Strategy

Joe Wesley had a problem. He was growing his business too quickly for his banks to keep up. Joe runs Tradesman International, a tremendously successful $200 million construction contracting company that is a leading U.S. supplier of talented workers to construction companies.

In 2004, Tradesman was doing too many things well. First, it was growing too rapidly, which required cash. Second, it was doing too good a job of managing its accounts receivables. Tradesman was collecting receivables so well that its days receivable were going down. This seems like a good problem to have, but the standard bank practice is to secure the company's bank facility based on its receivables. This means lower receivables reduced the company's ability to borrow to fund growth. No good deed goes unpunished.

Between the rock and a hard place of rapid growth and declining bank borrowing capacity, Joe knew he needed longer-term financing to augment his banks. But what kind of financing? He started looking at all the alternatives for permanent financing, the main two being direct equity investment from a private equity firm or some "mezzanine" debt. His approach to this challenge not only illustrates an effective way of finding financing for growth but also for researching and weighing other decisions about selling or financing the business.

"Mezzanine" is a bit of an awkward term for someone who doesn't live in the finance world. It does little or nothing to describe what it actually is, which is just more permanent, longer-term debt. It's called mezzanine because the world of financing is primarily broken into three or four pieces and is always drawn like a building, as shown in Figure 2-3.

The theory of the tower or building schematic in Figure 2-3 is that the least risky money—the "senior" or secured debt—is on the top, and that the levels below represent more "risky" or expensive capital. The senior debt represents Joe's typical bank lending, nearly always secured by most or all of the company's assets. Second, or the "mezzanine" level of the

FIGURE 2-3. LEVELS OF DEBT.

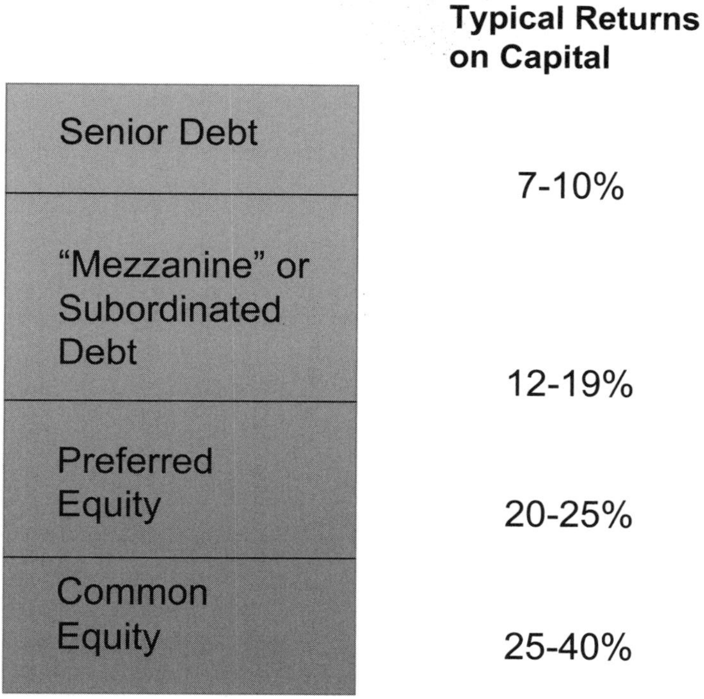

	Typical Returns on Capital
Senior Debt	7-10%
"Mezzanine" or Subordinated Debt	12-19%
Preferred Equity	20-25%
Common Equity	25-40%

building (thus the odd name), is the debt that is subordinated to the senior debt. This is more risky because it has bank debt above it and typically has little or no asset support (just "second" liens), and below that comes the much more risky equity levels. As you can see to the right of the building, the different risks carry different returns—or costs to the borrowing company.

The mezzanine debt is an interesting hybrid of debt and equity, usually having a ten-year life, limited annual amortization, and interest rates of 10 to 14 percent (in today's market). It frequently has some equity options, or warrants, attached to it (particularly for smaller deals), so its "all in" yield to the investor, and cost to the company, is in the range of 12 to 19 percent, with a likely target of 17 to 18 percent.

The good news with mezzanine is that it is clearly less expensive than equity. The bad news is that it *is* debt, and does create additional leverage, and thus risk, for the company. And this was exactly the dilemma that Joe Wesley faced as he looked for $10 to $15 million to grow his business. Should he go with mezzanine, which is much less costly but more risky (because it is debt, and if things go badly, these guys will own the company), or should he get in bed with the "vulture capitalists" and give them a permanent piece of his company?

This is never an easy call, but Joe went about the quest perfectly. He did the very smart thing of bringing in some investment bankers to give him all kinds of free advice (which we will discuss in Chapter 5). He brought in one bank to look at the mezzanine option and one bank to present him with equity options. This gave him a broad range of input and meant each option was explored thoroughly.

Joe first evaluated the costs. After talking with both of his advisers, it became clear that the cost differential was very large. The mezzanine folks wanted a 12 to 14 percent annual coupon *and* warrants to acquire 3 to 5 percent of the company. Based upon future projections, this would cost him at least 16 to 17 percent. The banks also wanted part of his "excess" cash flow (is there really ever any of that?) to pay down the loan, which would drive up returns to the lender over time. And he would be taking on more debt! On the private equity side, the costs were even higher. His bankers were telling him that the private equity firms would want 15 to 20 percent ownership in his company in exchange for their investment. If things went as well as Joe expected, the returns on these dollars would be 30 to 35 percent per year. And, of course, the equity folks wanted a seat on his board.

Joe's decision hinged not only on risk and cost but on good old "value add." If he is going to take a big chunk of cash from these folks, what can they do for the business? He believed he could get good strategic and financing advice, as well as Wall Street relationships, either way he went. He also knew he would encounter smart and experienced professionals with either option.

Now Joe faced the same decision faced by entrepreneurs every day: Go with the cheaper but riskier option or the more expensive but less risky approach? In the end, such decisions largely rest on the owner's confidence and view of business risks going forward. If it looks like the business is safe and thriving with a big upside, the much cheaper mezzanine alternative is likely the way to go. If there could be big bumps in the road or if the business is very cyclical, the safer but more expensive equity route is the way to go.

Joe Wesley had a high degree of confidence in his future. He also was running a service business with high variable and low fixed costs, and he knew from past bumps in the road that if things turned down he could cut his variable costs. Thus, he decided to go down the mezzanine path.

Upon making that decision, he made another astute one: He retained one of his two bankers to shop his financing to six major mezzanine shops. Allied Capital ultimately won the business, but it had to compete for the opportunity. As with any smart bank auction, it got Joe the best terms the market could offer.

After offering the deal to the six mezzanine players, he got strong proposals from two and played those two against each other. At the end of the day, the terms were very close, but he decided to go with Allied for a handful of important reasons. First, their pricing was very competitive. Second, he liked and trusted the people from the firm, such as John Fruehwirth of Allied's Chicago office. Third, his adviser told Joe that having a very strong brand name like Allied as a partner would reflect well on the company down the road, should it pursue other financing or an IPO. Lastly, Allied was not demanding a lot of control, just some covenants on their debt and a right to "observe" at board meetings. Both of these provisions were fair requests. So Joe picked Allied, got the deal closed, and could not have been happier. He has been paying down debt and growing his company, and only gave up a few points of ownership to get this deal done.

Joe also negotiated one or two other provisions of his deal,

which *every* owner should go for. He was able to get a performance agreement with Allied on their equity, such that if Joe
hit certain high performance targets, Allied would need to give
back part of their equity. A smart move, very much to Joe's
benefit, and an incentive for him to make his growth strategy a
home run.

One additional important piece of counsel that Joe Wesley
offers to all entrepreneurs: Watch those lender covenants very
carefully. Too many entrepreneurs do not look at them at all
critically. They can really come back to bite you. Look at them
carefully, run financial sensitivities, and negotiate every one
hard. Great advice from a successful entrepreneur.

• *The IPO.* Another way to begin to cash out of the business is
through an initial public offering (IPO). An IPO can sometimes
have a significant upside. It gives the company a public valuation
and currency that can be used in acquisitions. An IPO can offer
significant cost of capital advantages for a company that has a high
PE ratio. The IPO allows you to offer options to employees, and
ultimately provides a liquidity path. But it comes with many significant strings attached—investor relations, lawsuits and Sarbanes-
Oxley, to name a few. It also can take a long time for the owner to
actually leave the business and liquidate the investment. Although
the IPO is often discussed as an "exit strategy," technically it
doesn't represent an exit. It is a pre-exit strategy, not a liquidity
event. Investors are still up to their necks in the deal after the IPO.
It is only after selling the stock that they actually have made their
exit, and this usually takes at least two years. The owner will probably have to hold stock for a period of time after the deal and will be
subject to SEC restrictions on sale of the stock. The IPO might
facilitate an exit later, but it isn't an exit in and of itself.

There are only certain businesses that would even consider an
IPO. To do a successful IPO, you need a very strong story that can
be communicated quickly to potential investors. When you are on
the road shows, you must differentiate yourself from similar businesses and have a strong plan you can execute. The pitch also has to

have a certain pizzazz. A company making auto supply products or HVAC equipment, unless there is some unique angle, probably isn't sexy enough. You need a strong story of growth and a lot of differentiation in the marketplace. Management also gets extra points for having strong communications skills. A CEO with some punch can drive the story home.

Timing the IPO is extraordinarily challenging. You have to go when the ducks are quacking, but there is a high price to pay for going to the market prematurely. If you can't accurately predict business income for the next two or three years, you will get crushed by the market. In any event, it will take a lot of management time. There will be $250,000 to $500,000 just in printing, legal, and accounting expenses. In addition, today's investors and IPO markets are unforgiving. If you miss your numbers, you will get permanently hammered by the market. Finally, you need to look at the strategic issues involved. Don't do an IPO if it runs counter to the strategy of the business. Is it an industry in which business cycles of more than a year will create conflicts with the short-term demands of investors? Will uneven cash flows or business seasonality cause problems? Will going public make it harder to make needed investments that could hurt earnings in the future? How much of management time will be diverted to dealing with shareholders? On the other hand, you should also consider how having a public stock will help the company in funding its further acquisitions and growth or attracting employees. There are no simple answers to these questions, but you should raise the strategic issues as you work with partners to consider an IPO or a sale.

ACHIEVING YOUR GOALS

There are many ways for you to sell your business and to realize good value for your company. The financing and structuring part is, frankly, easy. The harder part is deciding what you want to do. Do you want to sell the business at all? What returns do you expect? What disruption to your employees and organization are you willing to accept? Given these goals, should you pursue an inside sale or outside sale?

After seeing his $40 million deal go bust, Bill Chambers refocused himself on his goal of selling the business. He is working on his next exit strategy, which he expects will be much more successful than his first time out of the box. He has learned a lot. He is carefully preparing the company. He has hired a professional manager. Like an athlete, he has been knocked down, but he's back on his feet and training the business into peak performance. From his experiences with his disastrous last sale, he knows what he doesn't want to do. He also knows what he wants and how to get it. He is clear about his goals. There is still much work to be done, as we will consider in the following chapters, but he has his eyes on the prize and knows how to get there. What are your own goals for the sale of your business? How can you reach them?

FIRST, GET YOUR HOUSE IN ORDER

Prepare for the Sale Years in Advance

PREPARING FOR THE SALE

The owners in the three cases presented in Chapter 1 made different preparations for the sale of their businesses:

Homeland Designs: On his first attempt, Bill Chambers took a deliberate approach to preparation, but after the collapse of the first $40 million deal he redoubled his efforts. He brought in a professional manager and is focusing on growing the business in preparation for his next trip to the deal table.

Iconix: Leo Mullen, as discussed in this chapter, transformed the business to make it more independent of him and his wife, bringing in professional management, tightening financial statements, and transforming the business to make it more marketable, with great success. By the time he sold, the business was in excellent shape and he received top dollar.

Politics & Prose: After drifting into a sale agreement on the first try, with little or no advance preparation, the owners took a more careful approach as they prepared for their next move. They hired an adviser and are consulting closely with their advisory board and employees.

Helene Patterson had hired her husband, Leo Mullen, as a graphic designer back before he was her husband. For twenty years, they had built their graphic design business and later digital media business into a multimillion-dollar firm. They had raised two daughters together. He was CEO, and she was CFO. She was the glue that held the company together, and one of the few people who could stand up to him if he was headed in the wrong direction. It was a true partnership—right up to the day they decided one of them had to go.

Neither Leo nor Helene had an accounting or business background. While she could find any number associated with the business, and never made a mistake on an invoice, the company's entire financials were on a series of legal pads. This was an $8 million company and growing. As they began to tidy up the business for a sale, they both recognized that they needed to bring in a professional CFO. Helene helped find a former finance executive with Marriott and brought her into the organization. Helene stepped aside as CFO but stayed on as chairman of the board, second-guessing decisions of the CFO. Leo and Helene both knew they had to do something, so they met one day to discuss it.

It was an awkward meeting "I love you enormously, and our family and kids are the most important thing in the world to me, but it's time for you to shift from an operational role to an advisory role," Mullen said. "We've put in motion this strengthening of our professional management, and we have to see it through. It's like we are the Flying Wallendas and we have spun off the trapeze. We can't go halfway."

Intellectually, Patterson understood the reasons to step aside from her operational role, but it was very hard to do. "We both understood the rational reasons for this change, but Helene had put twenty years of her heart and soul into running the business," Mullen said. "She was every bit my equal. We couldn't have had this business without her."

Just because they both knew it was the right decision to prepare their company for sale didn't make it any easier. "It took a long time for both of us to get comfortable with the new operating structure. We had collaborated so closely for so long on every aspect of the business, it was difficult for me not to have Helene's insight into all the management details," Mullen said years later.

It took them seven years to pull off their plan to get the business ready for sale. In addition to transforming the graphic design firm into a digital strategy consultancy, they had brought in professional managers and an external board. It was the kind of tough decision making and advance planning that is needed to queue up a successful sale. They took a business that might have sold for $2 million and walked away with more than $26 million.

RISK AND THE BUYER'S VIEW OF THE WORLD

To prepare your company for a successful sale, you have to put yourself in the shoes of potential buyers. You have to understand risk from the buyer's perspective and mitigate that risk. Unaudited financials are going to raise red flags for buyers, as would financials on legal pads. So would having the CEO's wife serving as CFO. The more these risks can be eliminated or mitigated, the higher the multiple that buyers should be willing to pay. To understand how to increase the value of your business, you need to be able to see risk through the buyer's eyes.

In this chapter, we examine a variety of risks from the buyer's perspective and strategies for eliminating or mitigating these risks. These approaches will reduce the perceived risk for the buyer and enhance the value of your company in the buyer's eyes. In this game, you often need to think ahead. Strategies for risk reduction often need to be implemented years in advance of the sale. If you find problems or just need to get your flabby books or operations into fighting form, it can take a few years to put your house in order.

The value of your business will be based on the risks that the buyer sees there. The buyer is taking a risk on your business, and the buyer's overall risk assessment is the primary driver of valuation.

Reducing risk is the most important thing you can do to affect the value of your business. If the business has few perceived risks, and a decent rate of growth, you will (and should) receive a high multiple. As much as possible, you want to make buyers feel like buying your firm is as attractive as settling their heads on a down pillow at the Hilton. As with selling a house, if there are noisy neighbors, leaky water pipes, or a toxic waste site out back, you are going to knock dollars off the sale price.

All Will Be Discovered

Before examining some examples of the major risk assessment areas, here are a few general comments. First, every business has risks. You do not have a risk-free company, and you should not attempt to portray it as such. In fact, a selling memo for a business that does not identify risks actually throws up all kinds of red flags for buyers. Such a memo shouts "Risk!" "Buyer Beware!" or "Iceberg Ahead!" It is essential to clearly and fairly delineate all the risks in the business. A selling document that presents the company as risk-free will attract more chuckles than dollars.

The corollary to the existence of risks, but more important, is that *all will be discovered*. I'll make this point several times in this book. All will be discovered. All buyers are smart and very diligent. And if they aren't, their lawyers are. And if they aren't, their investment bankers are. Don't try to hide or finesse your business risk. You will only hurt yourself and the transaction. If you are playing poker with someone and they find out you've got a card stashed under the table, what will they think? If they don't kill you on the spot, they are going to think: What other cards are being hidden? And they will walk away from the table. If it is a significant oversight, it can easily blow the whole deal.

You can mitigate risks, you can eliminate them, but you can't ignore them. You may need to drop the price to reflect the risk. If you've got an environmental issue, it will be discovered. If your largest customer is shaky, it will be discovered. If your inventory is bloated with out-of-date stuff, it will be discovered. If your son or daughter in management is a weak link, it will be discovered. If your largest competitor has a new product that will hurt your company, it will be discovered.

You get the idea. All will be discovered.

Disclosing the risk doesn't just make you a better Boy Scout. It helps everybody. You sleep easier, of course, but the buyer respects you more, trusts you more, and may be willing to pay a higher price. Remember, it is all about risk, and having a partner you can trust reduces that risk. This trust can also help later in the deal if you need the buyer to work with you when you hit bumps in the road. You may need the buyer to give you the benefit of the doubt.

The important thing about the risks is getting them out there and telling the buyer what you are doing about them. If there are competitive threats, what actions are you taking? What are you doing about management holes, or needed new products? That's the explanation that is essential. And if you don't like having these conversations, try as hard as you can to make these problems go away before inviting the buyers in. Find the management you need. Acquire or develop the new products. Knock the competitive threat out of the box. Then sit down with whatever risks remain and lay your cards on the table.

SIX TYPES OF RISK

To mitigate or reveal risks, you need to know what they are. In the following sections, we examine each of the major risks that a buyer evaluates when assessing the value of a business. There are six primary risk areas. If a business owner can successfully address each of these factors, this will do a lot to maximize the value of the business:

- Financial statement veracity
- Customer concentration
- Management stability and motivation
- Competitor behavior
- Industry change
- Company growth prospects

Other important, but less essential, risks include supplier concentration, obsolete inventory risks, tax risks, and real estate risks.

All of these risks will be addressed below, and I will attempt to quantify the impact of the various risks.

Again, your goal is to do your best to 1) to mitigate as many risks as you can, and 2) demonstrate to the buyer that there are good days ahead (without seeing the world through rose-colored glasses). A positive outlook is essential to the sale process.

Risk #1: Financial Statement Veracity

Relying on a company's financial statements is, of course, critical to any sale. You, as a seller, will be asked to sign a legal, binding document, with recourse, which says your financial statements are true and correct. It's a serious burden.

This may seem to be a no-brainer from the seller's perspective. ("Of course my financials are correct!" shouts the seller.) But there are several reasons why buyers view this seemingly obvious area as one fraught with risks. First, every seasoned buyer has been screwed by bad financials at least once. Sometimes, it is pure fraud—like the tile company owner who changed labels on inventory to fool auditors before a sale. Other times, the finances have been finessed through some creative bookkeeping. Of course, you would never do that, but if the buyer sees some rough edges on your financials, the red flags will go up.

A second reason why financials are so important is that we live in a Sarbanes-Oxley world. The massive financial meltdowns of Enron, MCI, and Fannie Mae have only heightened prior concerns. Sadly, now most buyers probably assume that financial statements are wrong on their face, and it will take years to correct this skepticism. Given this predisposition, you need to give them as little as possible to worry about when they are looking over your company's books.

Carefully Track Add-Backs

A third reason why buyers are concerned is that the financials of family-held companies have always been tricky. All seasoned buyers are aware that private companies often manage their financial statements to minimize taxes, not to maximize profits. This is well known, fully legal, and is not an obstacle from the buyer's point of view. The natural consequence of this approach, however, is the famous "restated" financials replete with the list of "add-backs."

This is well-understood ground. Whenever buyers look at financials from a family-held business, they fully expect to see a healthy list of "add-backs," which are costs in the income statement. These add-backs will no longer exist once the business is not owned by the family. These are traditionally in the area of above-market compensation to the owner, owner's perks such as a car or club memberships, excess compensation to family members who may or may not be working full-time, and potential above-market real estate lease payments to other family-held companies. In sum, these add-backs normally are of great consequence to the financial statements, turning a marginally profitable statement into a highly profitable statement.

The careful and consistent treatment of add-backs is essential. The seller should make sure all these "family-associated" expenses are tracked carefully every year so the buyer can have comfort that once the business is transferred, these costs will no longer exist. Everyone knows they are there. They just must be disclosed in a consistent and documented manner.

You may also want to dispose of real estate owned by the company. This is an essential discussion to have with your tax adviser, but it nearly always makes sense for business owners to spin off the company-owned real estate into a separate entity prior to the sale. This is dictated by simple economics, moderated by current economic times. With today's low interest rates, real estate is often valued at ten to fifteen times cash flow upon sale, which is normally much more than the business will fetch. As such, it is usually more productive to transfer the real estate to a separate entity prior to the sale. But when you do this, you can do two things to smooth the way for the sale of your business: make the lease at or close to market rates, and make the lease long enough (at least five years) that the new business owners can make long-term plans for the business and with their bankers.

Get Audited Financial Statements

The other critical way to bolster the credibility of your financial statements is to get audits for three years prior to the sale. We're talking about *audits* here, folks, not just a review. As an aside, I have been shocked in my many years of looking at family-held companies at how many owners do not get audits. Forgoing an audit because of the extra $30,000 or $50,000 of expenses and the associated hassle is the most penny-wise and pound-foolish decision I have seen owners make. Do you expect the buyer to take your word for it that your financials are accurate? Do you expect the buyer to check them all out? You've just increased the buyer's risk, and reduced your price—almost always by much more than the cost of the audit.

Audited statements are particularly important in this crazy business world where nobody believes anything. Not only have you reduced your price, but you've also scared off some potential buyers who don't want to be bothered with the deal at all. There are too many business investors and buyers, the author included, who will not invest in or buy a company that does not have audited financials. And this requirement will only grow more prevalent.

Further, just to make it an easier decision, realize that every serious buyer will require that sellers go back at least two years and get audits done on the financials. The buyer usually bears the cost of this process, but it creates a massive and time-consuming financial burden on the seller. Make it easy on yourself and hire a well-known, highly respected auditing firm and bite the bullet. You can pay now or pay later. Get your financials audited three years before you sell, and ask the auditors to separately quantify the "family-held" business expenses, or add-backs, each year. This will improve your quality of life dramatically at the time of the sale.

One other financial statement element to avoid if possible as you lead up to a sale is dramatic changes in your margins. Slight annual improvement is always good (and, of course, to a certain extent the margins are what they are), but it's always a big red warning flag for the buyer if profit margins have magically doubled in the year before the sale. This hurts credibility. The buyer immediately discounts those numbers and begins to worry that the business has been so carefully groomed for the sale and that things will never be as good as they are today. Some owners throw out ballast and adjust the business to boost margins, thinking it will please buyers. It gets their attention, all right—like a red cape waved in front of a bull.

Make Credible Financial Projections

All buyers base their diligence partly on validating the past but also on looking to the future. Your future projections for the next two or three years are essential to the buyer. There are a couple of key points about these projections. First, they must be *credible*. If the business has grown at 5 percent annually for the last three years, do not project 10 percent growth in the future, unless you have the orders in hand. This type of jump will only hurt your sales prospects. Buyers like good news, but they don't care much for fairy tales.

Second, your projections must be *supported by facts*. The way you arrive at the numbers is as important as the final answer. As your grade school math teacher probably told you, be sure to show your work. Support your projections with the key analytical metrics that drive sales and margins. These projections will be heavily scrubbed by the buyer. Do not just put your finger in the wind. Produce robust, thoughtful, and supportable plans. The detailed planning you do up front will pay you meaningful dividends on the sale.

Risk #2: Customer Concentration

Customers are a significant source of value to the business, and can be a source of risk. Your customer base will undergo enormous scrutiny in the sale process. (We'll discuss strategies for communicating with these customers later in the book.) How has your customer base changed? Who are your twenty largest customers? What are the margins on your largest customers? Which customers are most at risk? Are there long-term contracts? Most important, is there a "dominant" customer? This is of great concern to buyers, of course, because if that customer has financial problems, it can have a huge impact on your company. This risk came through in spades in the case of Bill Chambers, where the bankruptcy filing of one of his largest customers nearly killed his business.

If you have one customer that represents more than 12 percent of annual sales, you have a customer concentration issue. If you have a customer who represents more than 30 percent of annual sales, you have a customer concentration problem. In many small companies, it is hard to avoid this problem. If you do have a 30 percent customer, it will certainly impact your sale price for the business. The bigger question is: What can you do about the problem? It is a hard one to fix, but if you can address it, it will pay big dividends in your sale value.

The best shot, as with many of these matters, is to start working hard on the matter two to three years before you sell. Recognize early that any customer above 12 to 15 percent of sales is going to hurt your value and start working like mad to add new customer names. These new customers will dilute the concentration of the dominant customer. Of course, this is easier to write than to do. It is hard work, but worth it.

Beyond that, the best you could do would be to get the largest customer to sign a long-term (2 to 5 years) contract. Again, easier said than done, but very helpful. If you can't get the contract, any type of assurance from the customer that reduces the risk for the buyer can help your case. Recognize that your buyer will rightfully demand to speak with and likely meet with your largest customers later in the process. No customer risk issues can or should be concealed. Again, all will be discovered!

It's important to mention an issue that is particularly relevant to family companies. Often, the business owner has very close personal relationships with customers. The buyer will be looking for this relationship and will view it as a big business risk. If the owner leaves or no longer owns the business, how will his departure impact the customer base? If in due diligence the buyer finds that the owner is a golfing buddy with all his customers, this is a problem that will reduce the price.

Therefore, the goal should be to make the business owner's personal relationships with customers as small an issue as possible. Personal sales are often inevitable, but work as hard as possible in the two to three years before the sale to make sure that customers buy your product or service because it provides the most value to them, not because they've known you for twenty years. Otherwise the business hangs by a thread that will be snapped once you're gone. Make sure your customers have relationships with your professional managers who will be there after you have left. Personal contacts, rather than market-based sales, will adversely impact the sale price.

Risk #3: Management Stability and Motivation

At the end of the day, every buyer knows that it is management that makes a business go. As such, buyers will spend days concerning themselves with management risks and motivations at the company. Is the team strong enough to take the company to the next level? Do they need a new CFO or head of marketing? Are there strong managers below the founder? Once we buy this company and the CEO steps down, will managers have what it takes to step up to the task of running the company? Will the business continue to grow and prosper? Will the management team be motivated or are they getting too rich from the deal? Will they still have the "eye of the tiger"? Are other family members in the company helping or hurting it?

This complex equation of management motivation and capability is the most difficult one for any buyer. This is one of the reasons that the acquisition game is not for the faint of heart. The most successful investors tend to be very experienced. They need to have lost money on bad deals, assessed hundreds of management teams, and seen winners and losers. In essence, they have watched the "Management Dynamic" movie many, many times, memorizing every possible fumble or dream play.

No matter how many books are written on this subject, they can never get it entirely right. The assessment of the quality of the team is largely personality-based and can never be fully measured. Therefore, decisions about management will always be subject to the risk of good judgment. This is a massively idiosyncratic process, and the ultimate assessment is nearly entirely subjective or up to the judgment of the buyer. But sellers can take actions to increase the perceived stability of management.

One objective indicator of management capability is consistent historical performance. If a company generates consistent results, there is obviously a strong team. With good numbers, it is up to the buyer to assess the role of the founder and other managers in these results. The buyer also has to assess which members of the team have been central to the results and make sure that these individuals are highly motivated to ensure the future of the company.

One major concern that many buyers have (or should have) is whether any of the key managers are getting rich at the time of the transaction. Regardless of what any manager says, if a $5 million wire is hitting his or her account, the manager will act differently. Like the lottery winners who say the money won't change them, they may go back to work the next day, but they probably will be gone within a year. Maybe it will be the pursuit of new passions or travel, or the influence of a spouse or other family members. In nearly all occasions, less energy will go into the business. It is just human nature.

Making sure managers have some skin in the game is one way to ensure their sustained attention. There are many investors who will not invest unless senior managers are rolling over at least 50 to 75 percent of their after-tax proceeds from a sale into the newly acquired company. It all goes to the core of management motivation in the NewCo world, and many buyers will require this. Be prepared. Also prepare your managers to avoid surprises, who otherwise may feel that money is being put into their pockets only to be taken out again.

For family members employed in the business, as we'll consider in Chapter 4, the guiding principles should be to make sure they are compensated at market rates and are constructive in the business. As in the case of Leo Mullen, you sometimes have to "move family out" to maximize the value of the company. In general, it is sad to say that most outside buyers will assume that even very competent family members are not key to the business and will probably not last long in the new structure.

Family members imply some risks to the buyers (and a reduced price for the seller). If there are family members on the team, buyers will assume they will need to recruit new, untested managers to replace them. This adds costs for recruiting and creates team risks to bring new people on board. If family members do go forward with the business after the sale, you need to take extra effort to make their competencies and contributions clear.

Overall, the best management planning that any business owner can do in advance of the sale is to build a highly professional and motivated team that can run the business successfully, even if the owner goes on vacation for three months. Nearly all buyers will rightfully assume that the owner will not be around for long. (As soon as they are reporting to *anyone,* they normally "get out of Dodge.") Buyers will look to the next level of management for leadership in operating and growing the business. Buyers need to see that there is enough bench-strength at this level to keep the business going strong. This is why succession and development planning should begin years before the sale.

One essential action that selling owners should take is to be sure that the senior management team is highly motivated to make the sale itself successful. The buyer will be able to smell in a nanosecond if senior managers are not on board. I strongly advise all owners to put in place a "stay bonus" for key managers. This can be structured in many ways, such as stock options, phantom options, or pure cash. (The latter is always a great motivator!)

The plan goes like this: You sit with your senior managers and let them know (as part of a carefully crafted communications plan discussed in Chapter 8) that the company may be sold and that their support will be vital to the process (which it will be, by the way, as this is a ton of work!). Tell them that you want to align your interests with theirs. As such, you are allocating 5 to 10 percent of the sale price for the management team. (This number may vary widely depending upon the deal and the owner. Leo Mullen, for example, set aside 20 percent for his team. Some owners even give a piece of the action to every employee, although this is rare. It just needs to be an amount that is meaningful to each player, and it can be allocated in any way the owner sees fit.)

This is not just an act of loyalty or generosity to the folks who helped you to get to where you are, but it is just plain smart business. It benefits the seller as much as it does the team. It assures that managers will be pumped up and constructive in the process and amiable to buyers. Don't you think that could add 10 percent to the sale price?

Do you need to disclose the sale bonus to the buyer? Not up front, but if asked, you should reveal it. It's standard, and no buyer should be surprised or concerned by this fact. (With the caveat noted above that the upside should not be so large or immediate that it demotivates the managers after the sale.) As I've said, it's just smart business.

Risk #4: Competitor Behavior

One of my favorite varieties of humor is found in the "Competitors" section of most business plans or selling memos. Many times you'll be lucky to find this section at all. Even when there is an analysis of competitors, these sections are typically very weak. There may be only a name or two. It's usually just a few lines, which point out that while there are competitors, they are weak and few. Our company just stands alone. This normally causes a chuckle and paper crunching noise as the plan slams into the round file.

All buyers know that *every* business usually has numerous, aggressive competitors. Therefore, you are only hurting your own credibility by failing to recognize them. Put the risks out there, and it will help your credibility and will actually help your buyer feel more comfortable. This will also give you the best possible price for the business, and avoid unpleasant surprises later on.

Understanding the shifting sands of the competitive landscape is key to both buyer and seller. A seller who recognizes competitive risk and defends against it aggressively is a credible seller who will build goodwill with the buyer. A seller who thinks he has little competition is a naïve seller or, worse, a seller in denial or in spin-mode. The point here is clear. In discussing the competitive threats in your marketplace, be open, honest, and complete in your assessment. No buyer wants to be the one to purchase Netscape just as the sleeping giant in Seattle wakes up and takes over the browser business. Again, the prospective buyers will identify all of your current and prospective competitors in their diligence anyway. You might as well come clean at the outset. Remember that all will be discovered!

It makes you look smarter and more open when you acknowledge the current prospective competitors and, just as importantly, delineate what actions the company is taking to diminish the threat.

This latter point is critical. We know you have competitors; just tell me what you are doing about them.

Risk #5: Industry Change

Along with risks from competitors, there are also risks from changes in your industry. If there are new entrants coming into the industry or new technologies and customer shifts that could change the playing field, these changes will increase the risks for buyers. For example, if you have a print or advertising business that has not adequately recognized the impact of the Internet, this shift in the industry will hurt the sale price. If you run a company that supplies automobile companies and haven't addressed the rising concerns about environmental impact (seen in hybrid cars), this will be a concern to the buyer. If you are in a technology or customer service business and haven't moved to outsourcing, or at least addressed it, this will be a problem for investors. They don't want to buy a U.S. business in a market that will shift to India or China.

This risk factor is much more germane to certain industries, such as computer technology or telecommunications companies, than others. Of course, the very rapid change and viciously short product life cycles in technology are what make those sectors so risky, and why investors must be so cautious and knowledgeable to put money there.

But some normally changing conditions affect every industry. Are there any new materials being used? Is foreign manufacturing having a big impact? Are retailers like Wal-Mart, with their onerous supply chain requirements, forcing you to dramatically change the way you do business? Are customers finding substitutes for your product or service?

All of these risks should be carefully assessed by the seller and disclosed to the buyer through the process. Again, this will not scare off any buyer: Buyers are aware of these risks. But thoughtful planning here will build the seller's credibility and help the buyer assess the business more quickly. One of the benefits to the seller of all this careful self-analysis, putting oneself squarely in the shoes of the buyer, is that it will give the seller a clear-eyed view of the company's prospects and what might hurt a sale. Of course, for the buyer, it is better to smoke those risks out early, to know whether there will be problems with a sale before spending many months and hundreds of thousands of dollars on a tiresome sales process.

Risk #6: Company Growth Prospects

As we've discussed, the future is everything for the buyer. They want to make sure the past is robust and fact-based, but their opportunities all lie in assessing the future. That leads to one of the key points of this book, which, while being quite obvious, is often missed by sellers. The seller should sell the company when things are going well and when the picture of the future is bright, not when the business has reached its peak and is about to decline. If the business has reached its crescendo, the buyers will quickly figure this out and either walk away or dramatically lower the purchase price to reflect a down or flat future. The purchase multiple will collapse.

It is critical that the seller make a very strong case for the company's growth prospects. In fact, it is absolutely essential. No one knows exactly what will happen. But this future-growth story, fact-based and numerically supported, is essential to a successful and fruitful sale. Which new customers do you hope to add? Which new industry sectors are you pursuing? What is your market share in the various sectors, and how quickly are unit sales in those sectors growing? What is your new product pipeline and what are the prospects? Where are you getting improved margins through scale or cost reductions? How many new stores can you open, and where will you put them? When will you put price increases in place, and will they hold? What about the online marketplace? Is your business growing there? What about overseas markets? Are you growing there? Can you really compete?

As you can see, there are many considerations, but the case must be made forcefully and early in the presentation of the company's prospects. This section is normally called "Investment Considerations" in your selling memorandum.

THE CHALLENGE OF FIRING YOURSELF

Many of the risks from customer relationship to management strength are connected to the central role that you as owner play in the business. Sometimes before you can sell the business, you not only have to fire your wife, but also fire yourself. You want to bring in professional management to remove yourself as the linchpin of the operation. You've decided to try to make yourself dispensable.

It is harder to replace yourself than it looks. First of all, you know that all entrepreneurs are one-of-a-kind, so replacing yourself is impossible. Second, at this point in the development of the business, what is needed is not a clone but a person with the ability to take the business to its next level. Finally, you need someone who can live in the shadow of your overlarge ego and ambitions for the business, yet still have the creativity and drive to take it where it needs to go. And the new leader will have to able to withstand any family crosswinds affecting the business.

Despite the obstacles, for any one of a number of reasons, you are looking for a "professional manager." It could be that you are preparing to sell the business or otherwise make a graceful exit. Or it may be because you would like a better lifestyle or quality of life (since most entrepreneurs have none!) or because the company has grown beyond your comfort level and you want more some managerial talent. Think of yourself as Bill Gates stepping aside and bringing in Steve Ballmer. Is this easy? Never. Like most entrepreneurs, you're probably a control-hound and will have a hard time letting go (more on this later). But you've decided to do it for the good of yourself and the company. So, how do you undertake this process?

The Costs of Failure

First, most entrepreneurs really do not take the process of finding the new CEO seriously enough. They do not focus on the stark fact that if you hire the wrong person, the costs are simply enormous. Let's ponder this for a second. If your new CEO will make $250,000 per year, you have likely paid a recruiting firm at least $90,000. That's down the drain. It probably will take you six months to figure out that it is not working, and another six months to get up the guts to admit your mistake and make a change. Price: $250,000 in salary and the $90,000 fee down the drain. On top of that, add the severance: six months' minimum, going nowhere. Price: $125,000. So now you're out a galling $465,000 for your bad hire—and we are just getting warmed up.

The hard costs are actually the less painful part. Morale is probably low, and you have lost a few key people. Price: high! Worse, your customers may be upset, and you are losing sales. Price: Literally $1 million in equity value. Then you personally step back in to take the wheel and right the ship. Price: high! Massive stress!

And just when you've gotten to the end of this disaster, like in the movie *Groundhog Day*, the alarm goes off, and you start the process all over again with a new recruiter. Another hundred grand sails out the door. The total costs are well into the millions by now, topped off with that new pacemaker you had to get when you were about to strangle your recruiter, or even better, strangle yourself, for not hiring the right person. And then there's the hair loss! Now that is a real cost!

I think you get the idea. You cannot afford to botch this hire! It will cost you a bundle, and all the peace and serenity that you expect to get out of having a professional manager on board will be turned into bitter agony and a sinkhole for your time and energy. You cannot take this seriously enough. Make sure you get it right.

Finding Your Jack Welch

Fortunately for you, you will not botch this hire. You recognize that the cost is high, and you take a disciplined approach. You have this book, and tons of new technology and tools, to gather insights on hiring managers. Of course, this is the human-choosing business, and though we may like to think we are perfect, we are not. Even with all the best approaches and judgment, we can still get it wrong. (That's the reason pencils have erasers and contracts have escape clauses.) This is because personality always matters, and it is just so hard to assess. But there are even tools for this.

While the process is never perfect, you can improve your odds of success in hiring a CEO or president to manage your company by learning from the venture capitalists.

Learn from the Venture Capitalists

Venture capitalists have made their entire livelihoods on picking good managers and leaders. That, in fact, is really their entire job, and they will tell you that. If they get it right, they make money. If they fail, they will likely lose money. In real estate, it's location, location, location. In creating successful businesses, it's management, management, management. Some of these venture capitalists develop quirky habits and superstitions, to be sure. There is a successful Silicon Valley investor who simply will not back a CEO whose last name is the name of a vegetable. He probably has backed too many losing ventures run by guys named "Carrot," "Broccoli," or "Bean." Others won't back managers who wear pinky rings or whose suit shines like an Elvis outfit (presumably having learned the hard way that they are "nothing but hound dogs").

But these quirks aside, there is much we can learn from the rules used by VCs. Some of these may appear to be common sense, but it is surprising how often such good sense goes out the window. They may seem so obvious that we overlook their Zen-like simplicity. But read them carefully and apply them in your thinking about your own hires. They have been tested over many years by the real pros.

• *Back a Winner.* Most venture capitalists will not back a manager unless they have had a *proven, identifiable success in the industry being proposed.* This means reviewing the manager's track record carefully. Did revenue and profit grow on the manager's last watch? Did shareholders make money? Many investors require two past successes, which helps rule out dumb luck. A fancy resume showing Ivy League schools is never enough. Venture capitalists want executives to "show them the money." What have they done? Where are the results? Just the facts, ma'am. If they are not there, it's a pass. No further questions needed.

• *Proven P&L Experience.* No venture capitalist will back managers unless they have proven profit and loss experience. The manager must have controlled revenue and costs, and the buck must have stopped on his desk. Professional VCs do not hire marketing managers, regardless of their success as marketers, to run their companies. Being a CEO is hard, and it's just not worth the risk. We need no test-drives.

• *Relevant Industry Experience.* It sounds quite obvious, but it has been a consistent surprise to me that companies are willing to hire a CEO without relevant industry experience. The strong success of Lou Gerstner as CEO of IBM, arriving with no computer industry experience, is a rarity. (Remember that John Sculley tried to make a similar leap when moving from Pepsi to Apple, with somewhat less spectacular results.) Each industry has special characteristics that take years to understand and internalize. The retail world is so very different from manufacturing, which is so very different from media.

One of the biggest mistakes my investment firm made followed on the heels of the acquisition of a bike manufacturer with $600 million in annual sales. We needed a new CEO and brought on a prominent recruiting firm to lead the search. The bike company owned many of the industry's best known brand names, so the recruiting firm included "brand managers" in their search. We quickly found a young executive with a brilliant reputation in the brand world. He had worked for one of the big soda companies and at that time was president of a huge beer brewer. He was articulate, very smart, and wanted the job!

After doing reference checks, we hired him. He seemed great at the start but had never before managed a large manufacturing concern. Our bike company had plants all over the world. His inexperience with manufacturing and inventory management quickly led to disaster. Inventories became bloated, and it turned out that we weren't making the bikes the customers wanted. We ended up losing over $100 million, all because we ignored the simple advice of looking for relevant experience. *Don't take a risk on an unusual hire.* Hire someone who leads a strong competitor or perhaps comes from a customer or supplier. At a minimum, make sure this experience lines up—manufacturing for manufacturing, etc. It is an obvious principle, but it's surprising how many folks miss it.

• *Cultural Fit and Founder Fit.* Fitting in with company culture is essential and is often underestimated in the mix. *Every* company has a unique culture that must be considered in the CEO selection. In the case of Politics & Prose, the company was founded and run for many year by two women who had a very collaborative and nurturing management style. In picking their successor, they chose a guy who was the proverbial bull in the china shop. They might have done better to choose a woman successor who would better integrate into the culture and provide consistent management. If your company is run hard by the numbers and is rough-and-tumble, perhaps you need a General Electric–trained manager.

Speaking of General Electric, the company highlights the delicate balance in choosing a successor. When Reg Jones made his inspired decision to appoint Jack Welch as new CEO, he wasn't looking for a clone. The two men were very different in their approach. Instead, Jones was looking for someone who could meet what he perceived as the future needs for the business. Similarly, the manager you hire may be nothing like you in many ways, but should be consistent with the culture of the organization.

Further, and crucially, the new CEO must fit with the founder. Of course, the founder is often a very strong character with lots of strengths and a few blind spots. A successor should possess a great deal of humility and an ego that is comfortable living in the background behind the founder. Ideally, a successor would also be able to cover some of the founder's blind spots. Overall, you are looking for someone who can carry the company through the sale process and its next stage of growth.

Use Today's New Tools for Assessment

But how does a company assess its culture and identify the qualities needed in a new leader? There are many advanced tools for corporate assessment, and I am a big advocate of taking advantage of these tools to get this critical decision correct. One of the most powerful and enlightened steps to take before ever launching a CEO search is to hire specialized assessment professionals to conduct an overall assessment of culture and what the company needs for a leader to get to the next level. One such firm is The Global Consulting Partnership (TGCP). We spent many hours speaking with them in preparation for this book. The TGCP leaders are extremely experienced in assessing corporate leadership through their "leadership audit." They are also professional psychologists who have deep skills in assessing management, culture, and the vast nuances of the dynamics in a family-held enterprise, as discussed at length in Chapter 4.

TGCP's method of assessing the needs of the company and the qualifications of potential hires illustrates a thorough process. Before embarking on a CEO search, TGCP conducts an assessment of needs and makes recommendations on the CEO hire. TGCP then works with the company to interview candidates and also stays close to the founder and CEO posthiring to make sure that the integration works seamlessly. The initial assessment of the firm and its needs usually involves a team of two professionals conducting twenty to thirty interviews of company employees and family members.

They conduct one- to two-hour interviews with all senior managers. In addition, they interview key administrative assistants (if you *really* want to know what is happening at a company, talk to the top admins! They know it all!), and family members, including the Chief Emotional Officer (usually the founder's spouse). This process also has the great benefit of involving your senior team in the search process and soliciting their input, a step that should be taken regardless of whether you hire a consultant.

This process normally takes about two weeks. After completing the interviews, the team prepares a detailed report of its findings about the company, supported with direct quotes, and holds an offsite meeting with the owner to discuss the results. These analyses, which might typically cost $30,000 to $40,000, will be the best money ever spent on a consultant. Remember, when we tallied up the cost of mistakes, we had a price tag that ran into the millions in hard dollars even before "pain and suffering."

This process will help you learn things about the strengths and weaknesses of yourself, your organization, and any family relationships that could affect the business and the success of your new hire. These sessions may uncover all sorts of hidden tensions and weaknesses, so they may not be easy to go through, but they will be worth it. These tensions are likely hurting the company and will certainly hurt the sale process. They will need to be dealt with eventually whether or not you hire a professional manager. Why not do it now?

If you don't do this kind of homework, you might bring a great new manager into a minefield. Or you might hire someone who seems to have good chemistry but is entirely the wrong person to lead the business forward. This is what TGCP refers to as "hiring by design, not chemistry."

Should You Hire a Recruiting Firm?

Armed with this insightful assessment, you are now ready to move on to the recruiting phase. Most entrepreneurs do not like to hire professional recruiters because they are so expensive, generally costing 33 percent of the executive's first-year salary plus out-of-pocket expenses. Business owners believe they can find someone themselves if they just "put the word out." This is generally a failed strategy, though, as the owner normally already holds what seems like three full-time jobs. Taking on a critical hiring assignment is just way too much. Thus, this essential task falls by the wayside or is done in random fashion, by "getting names from friends."

In addition to a shortage of time and attention, the CEO also has many psychological reasons to avoid the task. It represents threats to control and a reminder of mortality, making it easier to procrastinate. Remember, again, how important this hire is to the company. While expensive, the 33 percent recruitment cost may still be peanuts compared to a mistake in finding the wrong person or failure to complete the process at all. Therefore, I strongly advocate engaging in a professional assessment and hiring a professional recruiting firm to conduct a full-on search.

In addition to bringing in a team with lots of professional recruiting experience, a recruiting firm brings a large Rolodex of candidates and often deep industry experience. It is for the latter reason that I normally advocate hiring one of the big firms, such as Hedricks & Struggles, Korn Ferry, SpencerStuart, or Russell Reynolds. They have large resources, big lists of contacts, and industry groups—and usually cost about the same as the smaller firms. There are also, of course, high-quality niche firms that can run a wonderful search process, particularly when their focus on a particular industry or region is a good match for the company. Smaller businesses also sometimes may get more attention from smaller search firms than the big players.

To kick off the process, you provide the search firm with the detailed criteria you have developed. They then mount a search to find the perfect person, making calls on your behalf. We all must recognize the obvious conflict in the search: It is in the search firm's interest to get this done as quickly as possible. Therefore, they may quickly surface a strong handful of candidates directly from their database. These might well be qualified candidates, but the best hire is not always sitting in inventory. You as the entrepreneur *must hold their feet to the fire* to make sure they hold fast to your criteria. Just because you have hired a professional doesn't mean you should sit back and relax.

After you've narrowed the field to serious candidates, be sure to go through all the essential steps, such as a full background check, litigation search (trust me, you do not want to hire a litigious leader), credit review, arrest review, and resume verification. You can work with an outside partner such as TGCP on assessing candidates; or most large recruiting firms have their own professional attribute assessment teams. For approximately $10,000, you can put your candidates through a battery of IQ, leadership style, logic, and other assessments of strengths and weaknesses. These are excellent tools to further push toward the right candidate.

The Reference Checks

I have several strong biases when it comes to reference checks. First, *the only reference checks that really matter are the ones that are not on the reference list.* I have made literally thousands of reference calls, and I guarantee you that I can write the script of the calls to names on the manager's own list before I make them: "Terrific leader," "sterling reputation," and "unquestionable ethics." Then, my favorite comments, when you are begging for just one weaknesses: "Well, he does work too hard," "She travels too much," "Sometimes he neglects his family," or "She's tough on subordinates."

All of these so-called weaknesses are actually strengths. To get the real scoop, you must ask each of the original references for names that are not on the list. Probe! "Who else would you recommend I speak to?" "Anyone who doesn't like this person?" Ask candidates for their own list of two or three people whom they have terminated in the past. I can guarantee you that these people will have no trouble coming up with a list of real weaknesses. (You need to weigh the source in deciding how seriously to take these points, but they will certainly help you to surface all the black marks.)

Also, on reference checks, do not delegate! Make as many calls as possible yourself! This critical task should not be left to the recruiters. You are the only one who can pick up on the hesitation or a nuance that could mean success or failure for the hire in your firm. No one knows your company better than you do, and no one cares as much about the outcome.

My experience with recruiters' reference checks is that they tend to be a bit soft. Remember, they want to serve their client as their first goal, but they also want to get this search finished so they can make some money and move on to the next one. And they want to protect their Rolodex. In total, for a serious hire, I would complete at least ten reference checks with *people not on the list.*

Hiring a Recruiter

Since finding a recruiter may be the first step to finding a good leader, how should you look for the recruiter? As noted above, look for someone with lots of experience in your industry. Also, as in so many matters, interview several candidates. Ask several recruiting firms to pitch you on the business and make them compete for the work. You will quickly find out what they are made of and see the good, the bad, and the ugly. You will also be able to drive the best terms. While you are unlikely to get a price cut, you can often get other good terms, such as a "free next search" if the current one proves unsuccessful within one to two years. This not only can save you money if things go sour, but also aligns the recruiter's interests even more closely with your own.

Senior hiring decisions are crucial to the company and to a sale. They are also massively expensive if they fail. They can derail your opportunity to sell the business or keep you involved long after you'd like to retire. They can destroy value that you worked so hard to create, as well as goodwill with customers and employees. There is a lot at stake in this work. You've spent a lot of time and sweat and money building your company. Be careful. You cannot do enough work in pursuit of getting it right.

The recruiting tools available to companies have improved dramatically in the past ten years and should be used to your full advantage. Also, while it may not be most entrepreneurs' inclination (as they normally like to keep things pretty private and feel they know what is going on), a full corporate assessment by professional corporate psychologists can only be beneficial in understanding how to build the company in the future.

With a strong and effective process, good partners, and a little luck, you may be able to pass the baton of the business to a strong leader. This will make it easier for you to exit when you sell your business. It will also reduce the risk for the buyer, raising the value of the deal.

SEE YOUR BUSINESS THROUGH THE BUYER'S EYES

Unless you can see your business through the eyes of the buyer, you will have a hard time selling your business effectively. You need to be able to understand how your business will be perceived from the outside. If you were buying the business, what would concern you? What can you do about these concerns? You need to recognize how factors that may mean nothing to you create huge red flags and are seen as incredible risks from the buyer's view. These are often enough to ditch the deal or significantly reduce the price you receive.

While you need to disclose everything, you also need to work diligently to make sure you have less to disclose. Identify and address your competitors. Press and starch your financials. Clean up your audits. Build a broader customer base. Put the company into fighting form. Begin early. Keep at it right up until the sale. It could be worth millions in the sale price. That should be motivation enough to get it right.

TAKE CARE OF YOUR OTHER CHILDREN

Family Is Family, Business Is Business

FAMILY MATTERS

Family issues did not play a major role in the three cases presented in Chapter 1, but they had been considerations in developing the business and the sale.

Homeland Designs: A few years before the sale, Bill Chambers had brought his daughter and son-in-law into the business with an aggressive growth plan, but they had unraveled the deal by the time he was ready to sell. His concern about the size of payouts from the sale to family members was part of his decision process for taking the larger, riskier deal, so family issues did influence the deal process.

We are grateful to Mark Brenner and David Pellegrini of The Global Consulting Partnership for sharing their insights on family dynamics and their methodology for assessing and addressing the family issues that can have a tremendous impact on the value of the business and the process of a sale—either internal or external.

Iconix: The biggest family issue Leo Mullen and Helene Patterson had to deal with was keeping their personal lives from being impacted by trying to manage the intensity of a fast-growing business where the changes never seemed to stop. They didn't want to burden their children with responsibility for the business, so they struggled to keep business and family separate.

Politics & Prose: While Carla Cohen's son had the capabilities to run the business, the two partners decided that they didn't want to saddle their heirs with "the family farm." They turned to an outside partner, but it proved more difficult than they had expected.

John Sampson had a problem. The scrappy, hard-driving entrepreneur had built a successful chain of retail stores in a very competitive industry. At first, he had felt fortunate that two of his sons had followed him into the business. But now, in his seventies, he didn't feel he could turn it over to either of them. It wasn't because they didn't have the skills. Both sons, in their late forties, were highly competent.

The one, vice president of operations, was on the floor and knew the operations and 1,000 employees of the business inside and out. The other, vice president of administration, was sharp as a razor and knew the inner workings of the company's finances, strategy, and real estate holdings. On paper, it looked like a match made in heaven, but the reality was that the sons were barely talking about the business. When they did speak, they were at each other's throats. It would be like turning the business over to Cain and Abel.

As the owner reached retirement age, the strong morale in the organization began to weaken. Employees were nervous about the future. Several employees said that if this succession issue could not be resolved successfully and soon, they would leave the business. There were positions that were not filled, and the company's growth strategy was stalled because the two sons could not cooperate. Worse yet, were this situation to continue and the business put up for sale, it would be a fire sale. Each son stated emphatically that he would leave the business if the other were named CEO.

John Sampson had built a very successful business, but this family crisis could undermine everything he had worked so hard for. As much as he wanted to continue the family legacy, he felt that he had to go to an outsider to run the company. After a professional search, he placed a general manager over the two warring sons, with a hope that this new structure would help stabilize the organization and allow him to retire. Perhaps this outsider could even encourage the sons to develop the leadership skills needed to break their impasse.

A FAMILY LEGACY

Sampson's business had always been in the family since it was founded by his immigrant parents during the Great Depression. Sampson's father had lost his job. His mother set up a small shop in her garage to make ends meet. The store grew after the end of the Depression, and her husband eventually joined the retail store. The company was passed down to two sons and two daughters, but John Sampson and his brother bought out their sisters. When his brother died, Sampson took over the business. He aggressively expanded the chain of stores and revenues, building it into a regional enterprise with more than $150 million in revenues. But the black-and-white photos of Sampson's parents still hang in the corporate offices. His mother is in her apron and his father behind the cash register. He had expected that the same photo would hang in the offices of his sons, but now he was not so sure.

Sampson hoped the new GM might serve as a "nanny" who could bring the two sons along. It wasn't a perfect solution, but the best they could do. When the GM developed health problems that caused him to step down, the father went back to the search firm to hire another general manager. The search firm executive, who had known Sampson for many years, suggested they take a closer look at the situation. Instead of throwing another outside executive at the problem, he suggested that Sampson examine the family and organizational dynamics more carefully.

That's where Mark Brenner, chairman of The Global Consulting Partnership, and his colleague David Pellegrini came in. They conducted extensive interviews across the organization, including managers, the owner, his sons, and, just as importantly, their spouses (who are the real "CEOs," the chief emotional officers). Brenner and Pellegrini reached an unexpected conclusion: There was a possibility to work out the relationship issues and allow the two sons to take over leadership of the business. "Sometimes it may look bleak," said Pellegrini, "but when you have the firepower and the business skills in the family, you can often make it work. You just need to get a handle on the emotional issues."

The results of the interviews were summarized in a 70-page report, laying out the challenges of the relationship between the sons, the impact on the business, and the potential for improvement. "Everyone could see how destructive the relationship between the two sons was," said Brenner. "It was taking a material toll on the business." In an emotional, daylong meeting, the owner and his two sons met with the consultants in a hotel room to discuss the results.

One of the turning points was a particular question that Brenner and Pellegrini had asked each son during separate interviews: *Would you want to go it alone?* In answering this question, both sons realized that they had complementary abilities and that neither one would want to continue to run the business without the other. With this new appreciation, they began to visualize a way to work with each other. "It was a seminal moment," Brenner said. "They realized they needed to form a rational business partnership. It just happened to be between two brothers."

Both brothers, while very competent in their areas, needed to build the emotional intelligence to be successful leaders. They engaged in an ongoing period of individual executive coaching with TCPG, as well as coaching sessions together. When Brenner and Pellegrini met with them a year later, the difference was profound. "The year before, there had been a cold chill in the room," Pellegrini said. "They didn't acknowledge one another. You could cut it with a knife. When we met with them a year later, we marveled at how they did with one another. There was much less stress in the room, and it was a real business meeting."

TRANSFERRING OWNERSHIP

The general manager position went unfilled. The sons were named COO and CFO, with the understanding that they would share operation of the business. They began taking more responsibilities from their father. But it was also clear to both of them that one of them needed to be the "go-to" person. From their discussions, it became apparent that it should be the COO. Employees, vendors, and other partners already looked to him as the face of the business. While John Sampson is still CEO, he is transferring more of the responsibility for the business to his sons. He even managed to take his wife for a long-anticipated trip to Europe. But Sampson's own favorite destination is still the floors of his own stores. As one son says, "The day he doesn't show up at the office will be the day he is dead."

But the sons are on track to take over, and the plan for succession is now clear. The owner had already transferred ownership of the business to the children. There is less uncertainty for employees, and the brothers can focus more on the strategy of growing the business and less on the emotions of the family relationship. They are now concentrating on developing the bench strength of their own managers. They are happier, and the business is healthier. The business can continue to be run profitably and successfully, as they expect to do, or it could be sold in excellent condition without the baggage of internecine battles.

IT'S BUSINESS

This case demonstrates the importance of addressing the family issues that are inextricably intertwined with a family business. While some family transitions have succeeded wonderfully, such as the transition in the Roberts family at Comcast, most have failed miserably. Complex or destructive relationships, which take their toll on a business at any time, come to the fore in discussions about selling a business or transferring ownership to the next generation. Bad blood can precipitate a sale. It can undermine a sale. Or it can make it impossible to keep the business in the family. Sometimes, as in the case of John Sampson, these knots can be unraveled productively. But these "soft" issues are sometimes overlooked. Addressing them is every bit as important, and as complex in its own way, as dealing with financial, tax, and legal implications.

Whether the business is to be transferred internally or sold externally, owners have to deal with the complex family issues involved. "One of the big obstacles to succession planning is if the family has leadership and relationship issues," Brenner said. "It often raises the question for owners of whether it can be done. Can they change the way they have related to each other for fifty years? We can't always convince them that they can do it, but we can convince them to make a run at it, for the sake of the business."

Most family business owners expect to leave the operation of the business to their children. It will be their legacy. But most businesses will pass to an outsider, if they survive at all. As noted in the preface, only about a third of businesses make into the hands of second-generation family members. Sometimes, as in the case of Sampson, battles between the children in the business undermine the goal of a family legacy. Sometimes the children really are just not competent to run things. These family problems are so difficult to deal with that they can make powerful CEOs tremble. So these owners may put off considering succession or dealing with persistent issues that may be undermining the success of the business. But these issues need to be addressed to meet the challenge of succession or a sale. "In understanding family dynamics, you need to recognize that it is like an iceberg, 10 percent is above the surface and 90 percent is below," said Pellegrini.

As discussed in the preceding chapter, the more the business looks like a family—particularly a dysfunctional family—the less it will be worth. This recognition can be a sobering moment for the family and the business. Family relationships are crucial if the business is passed on to children or other family members, but these relationships are also important in the deal process. It is time to bury the hatchets (and not in one another's backs). After the sale, family members can take up any old grudges they may have. But during a sale, like a wedding day, it is time to gather together, smiling for a family photo. This, of course, is easier said than done.

UNHAPPY FAMILIES

As Tolstoy wrote in his famous opening line of *Anna Karenina*, "All happy families are alike; each unhappy family is unhappy in its own way." There are as many ways that families, and the businesses they found, can go wrong as there are families. But there are some common patterns and pitfalls identified by Brenner and Pellegrini in their work. These include:

1. *Rules of families are egalitarian while businesses are hierarchical.* The principles that operate in a family may not work well in a business. "Families are egalitarian but businesses are hierarchical and differentiated," said Pellegrini. "Responsibilities vary, and market rates vary." For example, three sons were employed in one family business. One managed fifty people with full P&L responsibility, the second had more limited management responsibilities, and the third worked in operations. All three were paid the same salary. Their compensation was not based on the hierarchy of the organization but rather the egalitarianism of the family. What do you think the son with the most responsibility thinks of the fact that his brother in a much more limited role received the same compensation? What do other employees think? In some companies, family members draw a salary without any role in the business, or the company may bankroll family members in a new venture. These types of arrangements can create many resentments and strains on relationships within the family and with other staff. But they become particularly problematic when it comes time to sell the business. Will the new owner really want to retain an operations employee at the same salary as a senior manager? Very unlikely.

Family firms commonly pay both family members and non-family members below market rates. The idea is that if family members stick it out, they will inherit the business. Owners think about all the blood, sweat, and tears they put into the business. They remember how they took little or no salary in the early years. They had paid their dues, and the next generation should do the same. But it can take a very long time for family members and other employees to see the payoffs, if ever. The deflation of salaries for other staff makes it harder to retain good people. With this "suppression of talent," the best employees, inside and outside the family, tend to go outside the business for opportunities.

Sometimes family members may have unrealistic expectations or assessments of their own capacities, and founders are reluctant to confront their children. The children may aspire to leadership, without the necessary skills or aptitudes, but they can cut the legs off everyone else in the organization who threatens their position. To create the best conditions for a successful sale, the business needs to be run as a meritocracy, and the family principle of egalitarianism needs to be saved for working out inheritance. If this hasn't been done in the past, it should certainly be done in advance of a sale. If owners are not able to confront these issues alone, they should bring in outside consultants to address them.

2. *It is difficult to attract and retain professional managers.* The Center for Creative Leadership has estimated that, across all businesses, 40 percent of new CEOs fail within the first 18 months.[1] The number is very likely much higher for family businesses. In addition to below-market compensation, as discussed above, outside managers have to deal with the cross-currents of family meddling, founders' egos and many other forces. There may be sons or daughters who feel they can tell the manager what to do, or a family-dominated board. Professional managers also have to be comfortable playing second fiddle to the founder, not stepping on the toes of other family members, but then be able to assume leadership when the founder heads off into the sunset. This requires a rare set of capabilities.

Sometimes professional managers are hired to play interim roles. One successful professional manager returned the business to growth, stabilized operations, but made sure not to receive too much recognition, so as not to offend the second-generation family members. Then the manager turned the business back to a son who was designated to take it over. This role as a turnaround artist can work, as long as it is clear from the outset. It needs to be spelled out whether the manager is a place holder until the family members are ready or is expected to step into the leadership role. If the family is clear about the role of its professional managers, they can be tested and screened to make sure they have the necessary skills and cultural fit to work. "Hire by design, not by chemistry," said Brenner. Some strategies for these outside hires are discussed below.

With careful planning, outside managers can be very successful. The 2003 *American Family Business Survey* found that while relatively few family-owned businesses (13.6 percent) hire outside CEOs, of those that did, 31 percent rated the experience as "extremely successful," and 40 percent rated it as "very successful." Taken together, less than a third (29 percent) rated the hiring experience as "somewhat," "slightly," or "not successful."[2]

3. *A founder infantilizes children.* A founder who treats the business as his exclusive enterprise and doesn't pay attention to the next generation will give insufficient attention to grooming children or bringing in professional managers. Everyone in the family and business defers to him, and they are infantilized. Founders often have trouble delegating. The owner looms so large in the business that other family members cannot escape his shadow. There is no strong management or leadership. The owner also can never see the children as anything more than the snotty-nosed kid or the 14-year-old who screwed up and was brought home by the cops. Finally, when he is in his late fifties, the founder looks around and sees: Babies! There is no one who can take over the business. How did this happen?

The infantilizing of children can be a self-fulfilling prophecy. The kids are kept in the business but are never given any real responsibility or training. The owner never feels they are ready for real challenges. In protecting them, he prevents them from gaining the experience they need to lead. So when it comes time for him to transition out of the business, the kids really are unprepared.

Brenner notes that "the founders will frequently reinterpret the situation as something like: 'My boys simply don't have what it takes, so I'm stuck having to go down with the ship; there's just no one to turn the helm over to.' So, the founder shoots himself in both feet this way, not just one! He retards the professional development of his kids and unknowingly places a 'curse' on his succession plan."

4. *Owners are unable to let go.* Because of this attachment, these owners often engage in a lot of tire-kicking in selling the business. They pretend to put the company up for sale, with no real intention to sell. They will never be able to let go. Or they have such unrealistic valuations for the business that they know it will never sell. Then they act surprised when they are unsuccessful. But they don't want to be successful! These owners plunge back into running the business and promise that they will revisit the question of succession later. Later never comes. Very often, unless they experience a serious illness or other event, they may postpone this decision until their deaths. They just can't bear the thought of letting go of their babies. "It's their firstborn," said Brenner.

Owners need to begin looking at the possibilities for life after the sale, as discussed in Chapter 10. While the thought of selling the business may be painful, the thought of having more time to pursue a hobby or public service, or to make up for lost time with grandchildren, may make it more appealing. They need to be able to see a life on the other side. These owners also need to get a little distance from the business. Bringing in a strong professional manager might give the owner this opportunity for greater detachment. Knowing the business is in good hands can make it easier to walk out the door. In this process, owners need to be brutally honest about the capacities of children who are involved in the firm. Often owners are forced to stay around to prop up a weak heir, and this delays decisions about moving out of the business.

5. *Founders have insufficient emotional intelligence.* Many founders who were brilliant in building the business are "EQ challenged." Their low emotional quotient (EQ) makes managing relationships a problem. In building the business, this may be less of a problem,

because their single-minded vision and force of will helped drive the business to succeed against the odds. Relationships are important in building a business, of course, but many relationship errors can be glossed over with healthy cash flow or a powerful business model. In selling the business, those relationships that were not addressed in the past have to be dealt with. There are relationships with family, with employees, with customers, with other investors, and with the new owners. Navigating the delicate negotiations required to pull off a successful deal is a serious challenge.

Although founders can be tigers in their business negotiations, they often are pussycats in family matters. "Big, tough, potent entrepreneurs often get the willies over their kids' interpersonal problems and will do anything to avoid addressing them directly," said Brenner. They are not self-aware about how they affect other people. Pellegrini and Brenner usually try to interview the spouse of the founder, who may have deeper insights into the emotional dynamics of the family—and their origins—than the owner. And they are more willing to reveal them for the sake of getting help. Understanding and controlling the emotional cross-currents is essential to setting up a successful sale.

You need to be honest about your ability to manage relationships. Bring in outsiders if needed. The value of the business will suffer if these problems are left to fester. If your goal is to help your family, getting top dollar for the business could be the best thing you could do for them.

6. *Owners lack clarity.* Sometimes, to avoid conflicts, owners give mixed messages to children. The owner of one successful business had four children. At one time or another, he had promised each of them individually that "someday this business will all be yours." He had brought in two daughters from outside in addition to the two sons already working inside. As he grew older, it became apparent that none of the children had what it would take to run the business (and some had less than others, even though they all received the same pay). The owner brought in an outside president but later had to fire him when he was caught smoking pot with

employees. So the aging owner was still in the driver's seat, with many heirs apparent but none capable of actually taking the reins.

He didn't have the heart to tell his kids that they didn't have the skills to run the business. Instead, he let them *all* believe they were in line to run the business. "He led all of them on that they would take over the business," said Pellegrini. "He was so scared he would lose his children." Instead, he ended up creating more problems in the long run. Being clear and direct from the outset is usually the best policy. Sometimes an honest recognition of the weaknesses of the children can create opportunities to build new strengths, or to create a smooth plan to transition them out of the business.

7. *Founders expect to beat the odds.* While founders know the low chances of sustaining family businesses across generations, they also know that they have already defied the statistics to create a successful business in the first place. Why should selling the business be any different? "They are charismatic world-beaters," said Brenner. "They've beaten the odds in every other way. When they see the statistics, they just think that they will do it again." What they may not recognize is that the personal qualities that allowed them to build the business may not be the ones that will lead to a successful sale.

It is a different game. Michael Jordan is a legendary basketball player but was stuck in the minor leagues when he tried his hand at baseball in the 1990s. Instead of wishful thinking, owners need to take a hard look at their own capabilities and what is needed to carry out a successful sale or transition to the next generation.

DO THE KIDS HAVE WHAT IT TAKES?

As noted above, the skill development of children can be a self-fulfilling prophecy. How do owners objectively assess whether their children have the capacity to take over the business, or the ability to carry the business forward? It is a rare owner who can set family relationships aside and look objectively at the situation. The professional tools for assessing outside hires discussed in Chapter 3 can also be used to test children and other family members in the business. These assessments tools are particularly valuable in family situations because they can help to penetrate the fog of emotions and relationships. Owners can take a hard look at what their family members can actually contribute to the business. This can help make an objective assessment of the best fit for the organization, and the results also can form the foundation for a candid and objective discussion of the individual's prospects in the business and other opportunities outside.

Such testing may be the best thing you can do for your business—and your children. It can help to clarify what skills are needed for the future success of the business, whether they exist inside the enterprise, and which skills need to be brought in from outside. This is vital information in preparing the organization for a sale or generational transfer.

There are some factors that can contribute to the skills of the next generation. First, it helps for children to have experience in the larger world. Even if you can proudly say that your kids will outdo you in running the business, it is still a wise move to send them out to work at other companies to see how other organizations are run. They will gain independent experience and a chance to show their capability. Otherwise, the other employees in the organization, or family members outside, may question their experience and authority. If they only work in the family business, regardless of their performance, there will always be nagging questions about whether they found their jobs through merit or nepotism. A trip out into the great world, when possible, can put these concerns to rest and bring valuable new perspectives to the organization.

Second, if family members are inextricably involved in the business, make sure the relationship is professional. Salaries should be according to market rates, and promotions should be based on merit. If you want to give children a part of the business for being in your family, give them a share in the enterprise that is separate from compensation for their work. It will keep things a lot simpler. Keep family as family and business as business. Your family will be happier, and your business will be healthier.

STRUCTURING THE DEAL: PRESSURES OF AN EARN-OUT

With an inside sale, the structure of the deal and the owner's role after the sale will affect the outcome. Since children usually don't have a lot of capital to put up for the sale, families often choose an earn-out to transfer ownership, allowing children to pay the founder over time. In Chapter 2, we considered some of the business implications of an earn-out, but there are also emotional issues involved.

While an earn-out may seem like a good solution for a child who doesn't have the resources to buy out the founder directly, it should be used with caution even if it makes financial sense. The earn-out will mean that the owner's retirement income will be affected by the decisions of the children running the business. This loss of control may be infuriating, and owners will not stay on the sidelines for long. Even if they might be able to restrain themselves from second-guessing their children under ordinary circumstances, they now have to protect their investment. This will give them more reason to meddle in the operations and decisions of the children—after all, it is their money at stake! It can be much harder for the children to take charge in such circumstances.

Even if the owner is able to bite his tongue and watch as the kids make their inevitable mistakes, the earn-out creates added pressure on the children. Children will feel the responsibility for supporting their parents and other family members. At the time when they are already assuming considerable pressure just in running the business, this is an added weight on their shoulders. It should be done with caution, and the family and emotional issues should be discussed explicitly.

This doesn't mean that it can't be done. Bill Chambers acquired Homeland Designs in an earn-out deal with the founder, who treated him like a son. It allowed Chambers, who was a senior manager in the business at the time, to purchase the company, even though his personal resources were limited. The owner maintained an office, and Chambers respected his advice. The relationship worked so well that the earn-out was a huge success. Clearly defining the postsale role of the founder is vital in this process.

PASSIVE OWNERS

Sometimes family members are not involved in running the business, but they are still owners who can rear their heads in the sale process. As owners, they have a stake in the fortunes of the business and can meddle with its operations or exert psychological pressure on the family members leading the firm.

For example, Mike is a business owner who inherited the family business from his father. His stepbrother and stepsister, Phil and Jen, are passive owners who are more concerned about their personal tax liability than the overall success of the business. While Mike tries to make the best decisions for the long-term success, he has to deal with the sniping of his stepsiblings pressuring for decisions that benefit their tax liabilities. This is not only uncomfortable during business meetings, but Mike also finds himself avoiding Phil and Jen at family functions. He feels like the bad guy, although he is only trying to make the best decisions for the business. But the issues often are far deeper than just financial interest. Mike's siblings might be angry that the business was given to him by their father. There may be emotional depths beneath what may seem a relatively straightforward issue on the surface.

These relationships with passive owners can become particularly important at the time of a sale. Siblings and other family members might have some direct say in the sale process and outcome. They might have to give their blessing to it. Even if they don't have a formal role, they could use back channels in the family to influence the outcome. It is vital to recognize these relationships and discuss the pending sale with these family members, clarify roles and goals, and look for red flags that could interfere with the sale process.

INVITING THE CHILDREN IN

While we have focused on the challenges of having family members involved in the business, some founders face the opposite set of issues: what to do when the children are not involved in the business at all. And at a certain point, the owner might wonder whether the children should have been involved. Many founders err on the side of caution. Perhaps they had overbearing parents in their own childhood and want to give their children the freedom to make their own decisions. They think they are doing the kids a favor by not pushing them to follow in their footsteps. But the children could feel that they are being shut out by not being invited to be part of the business.

It may be only after the business is sold that founders learn about the interest of their children in their business. "It is a hard issue for a lot of family businesses," said Pellegrini. "There is a thin line between pushing the business on the kids and the children not feeling invited into it. The father intends to give them room to be what they want to be. He doesn't want to overburden them with his dreams. But the kids feel like they are being kept out."

This is a discussion that founders should have with their children before the sale, if only for their peace of mind afterwards. This will remove nagging doubts and regrets for the founders and resentment that may be felt by the children. It also could be an opportunity for a successful next-generation transfer that never happens because the question is never asked. Or it could just make everyone more comfortable with the sale that ultimately results. If the children are not qualified but still have dreams of being asked to take over, this should be addressed head-on. It may be an uncomfortable conversation for both sides, but it may leave both founder and children better off, and ultimately improve the relationship. And it will certainly improve the business and its value for buyers.

DEALING WITH EXTENDED "FAMILY"

The same types of destructive relationships and soap operas that are seen in family relationships often also emerge in nonfamily relationships with partners or key employees. These relationships can have similar complexity to the relationships with family and similar negative impact on the sale price and process. A famous example that illustrates these points is Leslie's Poolmart. A bitter battle between the two founding partners, which made the Hatfields and McCoys look like high school sweethearts, undermined the sale of their business.

In 1963, Philip Leslie and partner Raymond Cesmat founded Leslie's Poolmart and built it into a $50 million business. While the business was booming, the partnership self-destructed. In the mid-1980s, Cesmat wanted to sell his interest in the firm to settle a divorce proceeding. Leslie wanted to buy, but the 50-50 owners couldn't agree on a price and had no exit agreement. Cesmat went to court to petition to dissolve the corporation under California law. The court appointed a temporary third director and proceeded with the sale. Leslie was livid.

He didn't just get mad, he got even.

When prospective buyers would come through the door, Leslie did his best to scare them away. He threatened to set up a competing company and drive them out of business if they bought the firm. With Leslie giving every potential buyer the evil eye, a company that once had a fair prospect for fetching a good price became a dog. It was sold at fire-sale prices to investors led by Hancock Park Associates for $17.5 million. (As half owner, this hurt Leslie just as much as Cesmat. But for Leslie, getting even was more important than getting richer. He cut off his nose to spite his face.)[3]

When the company was sold in May 1988, employees who were loyal to Leslie stayed off the job and even picketed company stores. Leslie called up retailers to badmouth the new management. For seven months, he waged war on the company, until he finally dropped his crusade under the threat of a $45 million lawsuit by the new management. But when his air war was brought down, he launched a ground war. He set up a competitor, Sandy's Pool Supply, Inc., and opened new stores across the street from Poolmart locations.

Somehow Poolmart survived this attack, but only after posting two years of losses, and with the help of a successful IPO. By 1997, shareholders approved a plan to take the company private. The company that was sold for under $18 million was now valued at more than $100 million.[4] But Leslie and his partner only earned headaches and pennies on the dollar from what could have been a very lucrative deal for both of them. The problems with their partnership undermined the value of their successful business.

CREATING AN ADVISORY BOARD

One of the best ways to maintain some perspective on the business and keep family issues from dominating it is to create an advisory board stocked with outsiders. A good board with expertise in key areas can be a great way to test ideas and keep the operation and governance professional.

This board is never more important than when the business changes hands or goes up for sale. The advisory board at this point will offer sage advice on whether the business should stay in the family or go outside. The board can also be a source of leads for buyers and advisers who can help in the deal process. Board members may themselves offer advice on the strategic, financial, and legal issues involved in a sale.

You don't need to be a public company to benefit from the advice of a board. You will need to compensate your board members, but it will generally be worth every penny. If your only advisory board is other family members, you will never be able to step back from the business to see family issues that need to be addressed for the company to prosper. Outside directors can play a vital role in offering this sense of perspective.

ASSESSING THE OVERALL RISKS

Like any other risks of the business, risks from family issues can be assessed and addressed. Brenner and Pellegrini have developed the following checklist (Figure 4-1) as a quick-and-dirty assessment of the overall emotional health of the business and family. It presents a set of questions that every family business should ask itself, particularly at a point when the business might be sold. One set of questions focuses on the business and another on the family.

Working through the questions in the checklist in Figure 4-1 can help identify the problem areas that might derail the organization or

(text continues on page 92)

FIGURE 4-1. CHECKLIST OF SUCCESS FACTORS FOR THE BUSINESS.

1. We have a clear and elevating Mission, Vision, and Core Values.

This has "cost" us ← → We have truly benefited from doing this well.

1	2	3	4	5
☐	☐	☐	☐	☐

2. We have created both a company culture and a set of people practices in which we all take pride.

This has "cost" us ← → We have truly benefited from doing this well.

1	2	3	4	5
☐	☐	☐	☐	☐

3. We agree on the most effective way to lead our people.

This has "cost" us. ← → We have truly benefited from doing this well.

1	2	3	4	5
☐	☐	☐	☐	☐

4. We agree on the most effective way to manage our company day-to-day.

This has "cost" us. ← → We have truly benefited from doing this well.

1	2	3	4	5
☐	☐	☐	☐	☐

5. We agree on our business strategy and how to execute it over the near and long term.

This has "cost" us. ← → We have truly benefited from doing this well.

1	2	3	4	5
☐	☐	☐	☐	☐

6. All family members in the business act as role models for one another and for our employees.

This has "cost" us. ← → We have truly benefited from doing this well.				
1	2	3	4	5
☐	☐	☐	☐	☐

7. As a business family, our teamwork is about as good as anyone's.

This has "cost" us. ← → We have truly benefited from doing this well.				
1	2	3	4	5
☐	☐	☐	☐	☐

8. We are fully aware of most of the challenges that lay before us in the future, and typically go straight at them—no heads in the sand.

This has "cost" us. ← → We have truly benefited from doing this well.				
1	2	3	4	5
☐	☐	☐	☐	☐

9. We've demonstrated that we know how to manage the succession process.

This has "cost" us. ← → We have truly benefited from doing this well.				
1	2	3	4	5
☐	☐	☐	☐	☐

(continues)

FIGURE 4-1. Continued.

Success Factors: For the Family

This has "cost" us. ←————————————→ We have truly benefited from doing this well.

	1	2	3	4	5
1. In and out of the business, we live by our *Family Code of Conduct*.	☐	☐	☐	☐	☐

This has "cost" us. ←————————————→ We have truly benefited from doing this well.

	1	2	3	4	5
2. We are quite skilled at handling intra-familial conflicts.	☐	☐	☐	☐	☐

This has "cost" us. ←————————————→ We have truly benefited from doing this well.

	1	2	3	4	5
3. We have no "difficult" family issues.	☐	☐	☐	☐	☐

This has "cost" us. ←————————————→ We have truly benefited from doing this well.

	1	2	3	4	5
4. All "closets" are clear of skeletons.	☐	☐	☐	☐	☐

This has "cost" us. ←————————————→ We have truly benefited from doing this well.

	1	2	3	4	5
5. We are quite effective at handling the toughest of issues: family rivalries, money, hurtful actions or attacks, addictive behavior, marital problems, differing abilities and career potential, etc.	☐	☐	☐	☐	☐

6. We take a long-term approach to how we bring our children into the business—we have a decades-long strategy, and we stick to it.

This has "cost" us. ←————————————→ We have truly benefited from doing this well.

1	2	3	4	5
☐	☐	☐	☐	☐

7. We are effective at managing FOB challenges: trust, fairness and equity, inclusion, privacy, performance, compensation, dissent, individuality, etc.

This has "cost" us. ←————————————→ We have truly benefited from doing this well.

1	2	3	4	5
☐	☐	☐	☐	☐

8. We've been quite successful at creating high-quality work experiences for family members, young and old alike.

This has "cost" us. ←————————————→ We have truly benefited from doing this well.

1	2	3	4	5
☐	☐	☐	☐	☐

9. In everything we do as a family, we walk the talk of FOB continuity and longevity.

This has "cost" us. ←————————————→ We have truly benefited from doing this well.

1	2	3	4	5
☐	☐	☐	☐	☐

10. We've demonstrated that we know how to prevent parental success and wealth from stunting the growth and development of our children (and their children).

This has "cost" us. ←————————————→ We have truly benefited from doing this well.

1	2	3	4	5
☐	☐	☐	☐	☐

undermine a sale. It can shine a light on the dark corners and offer a useful starting point for recognizing, discussing, and addressing these challenges. This can ensure that these "soft" issues—which might be avoided or overlooked given all the details involved in preparing for a sale—are carefully examined before they suddenly rear their heads in the middle of the sale process.

HEARTBREAK HOTEL

Families can present a very complex stew, with intergenerational conflicts, gender differences, birth-order baggage, black sheep situations, interfamily feuds, spouses, in-laws, and issues of power, control, and money. The impact can be huge. The Pritzker family offers a cautionary tale. After the death of founder Jay Pritzker in 1999, he had bequeathed the business to eleven family members, three of whom were put in charge. Within a few years, family disagreements over money led to a plan to liquefy the $15 billion empire and distribute the assets, including the Hyatt Hotel chain.

But even this plan didn't put the matter to rest. An 18-year-old heir, Liesel Pritzker, who contended that her trust fund was emptied, filed a lawsuit demanding $1 billion plus $5 billion in punitive damages. The suit filed in 2002 was ultimately settled by the family in 2005 for a reported $1 billion, which opened the way to breaking up the empire.

These soap operas can become very messy, very quickly, and can cost the business years of time and, in this case, billions of dollars. Owners need to pay attention to them before they get out of hand.

One of the things that can be most useful in keeping family focused on addressing such issues is to remind everyone of the stakes involved. It could mean millions of dollars in value for the business—or even its ultimate survival. This can sometimes get the attention of family members and allow them to focus on the hard work they need to do. Even if the situation has eroded to the point where individuals don't care about other family members, most will still retain an interest in the success of the business and their own financial stake in it. Making the business case for addressing family issues can be the best way to focus the family on the needs of the business.

NOTES

1. Don Ciampa, "Almost Ready: How Leaders Move Up," *Harvard Business Review* 83, 1 (2005), p. 46.

2. *American Family Business Survey,* published by MassMutual Financial Group and the Raymond Family Business Institute, January 2003, p. 13.

3. John R. Emshwiller, "Desire for Revenge Fuels and Entrepreneur's Ambition," *Wall Street Journal,* April 19, 1991, p. B2.

4. "Leslie's Poolmart, Inc. Shareholders Approve Plan to Take the Company Private," *Wall Street Journal,* June 13, 1997, p. B4.

BUILD YOUR DREAM TEAM (BUT REMEMBER, IT'S YOUR DREAM)

Competence and Chemistry—and a Freebie from an Investment Banker!

BUILDING THE TEAM

In the three cases presented in Chapter 1, the owners had different approaches to building their teams.

Homeland Designs: Bill Chambers found that his take-no-prisoners advisers ended up helping to kill his deal, and then sent him a hefty bill for the service. In the next deal, he'll be much more careful about not only the skills but the chemistry of the team.

Iconix: Leo Mullen carefully put together a team with the accounting, legal, and investment banking expertise needed to pull off the deal. They helped him identify and nail down a deal with a buyout firm to purchase his business.

Politics & Prose: The partners didn't have any team the first time around, but after their first failed attempt they hired a business adviser to help with their future plans.

One of your first tasks in moving toward a successful sale is putting together your team. The wrong advisers can do a lot of damage to your deal and your business. In Bill Chambers's deal, his advisers couldn't build rapport with the buyer and eventually lost the deal. On the other hand, remember how the lack of advice for the owners of Politics & Prose led to decisions that they later regretted. You need to find people with the right expertise whom you can trust with the most important deal of your life. You also need the right chemistry. When the winds come up and the ship is taking on water, you want to make sure you have all hands on deck. You also have to be able to trust the people you are working with and that they won't turn away potential buyers. Even if you and the buyer are initially aligned, it is not uncommon for alignment to shift over the course of the deal. If that happens, you don't want to find yourself sharing a bed with Jack the Ripper.

The professionals you've worked with in the past to build and run your business may not have the experience—or the reputation—to pull off a successful deal. This means you may have to work with relative strangers on one of the most important deals of your life. Hire carefully. This chapter examines the advisers you will need and strategies for identifying the people with the right skills and chemistry to make the deal successful. What are some of the problems to avoid? Where do you find good team members?

The interview process can be an education in itself, and we'll show how you can use your interviews with experts to gain free advice about your business and learn about the deal process and the potential of your own business. We also consider whether you should try to do the deal on your own and avoid giving away 2 to 3 percent to an investment banker. (This is often penny-wise and pound-foolish.) Finally, we look at how you can structure your deal with these partners to ensure that you receive their full attention.

TAKE THE TIME TO HIRE CAREFULLY

The advisers who took you to this point in your business may not be the best ones to carry you forward. You might have high levels of trust with them. You might have long relationships. But look long and hard at their records. Do they have experience in putting together the size of deal that you are considering? Are they experienced in working with the size of investments you will be managing? Do they have knowledge of the intricacies of tax laws involved in selling a firm? Will they be credible to potential buyers? Take a cold hard look at your current advisers and recognize when you need to move out of your current circle to make the deal a success.

You cannot give too much time and attention to selecting your partners. Owners sometimes accept the first recommendation of a friend or advisory board member. They may turn to their long-standing lawyers and accountants, even when they have no experience at all in selling businesses or putting together a deal of this size. Owners may spend more time interviewing for an administrative assistant than they do in staffing up for the biggest deal of their lives. This is just plain foolish. Part of the reason for this may be that owners feel a bit intimidated by this work. They don't know where to begin in assessing the skills of potential partners.

The best solution to this problem is to plunge in. Once you've met with three candidates, you'll know who is best. Do your reference checks. Trust your instincts. Think about how each adviser will contribute to or detract from your deal team. This may seem to be unnecessarily time-consuming when you have a business to run. But the time you spend on selecting the right team will be paid back many times over in the time and dollars you save as the deal progresses. Remember that there is so much money at stake in this deal, more than any other deal of your life, so small mistakes or marginal improvements can have a magnified impact.

We've already worked through the costs of getting this wrong. The price tag is just immense. The red ink bleeds out like the blood from a victim in a low-budget horror film. The sight is not at all pretty. Keep these risks in mind. You will trust these advisers with your most valuable possession, your business. Keeping focused on the risks will help make sure that you have the right team and that they are all moving in the right direction.

Some owners do manage to sell successfully on their own or with the advice of a longtime trusted accountant, but they may get less than they could have. They may face much more limited options than if they had skilled advisers with broader contacts. Most sellers will benefit from working with investment bankers, lawyers, and other advisers to put the deal together. Skilled advisers will offer insights into potential buyers, deal structures, and hidden risks that might not be apparent to the owner.

It is never too early to start discussions with potential advisers—and talk is cheap. Understanding if chemistry is right can often take some time. Understanding the expertise and ability of your advisers may only be clear after several interactions. Go visit them. Interview them. In the discussions, you'll learn more about what you need and what they can offer.

Start early in this process. The minute the vaguest idea of selling your business enters your head, you should be picking up the phone. It may take you some time to become well enough versed in the different areas of expertise to make an informed decision. Early discussions can shape how you are thinking about and preparing for the deal. You will learn a lot in the process. And as long as you are serious (not a tire-kicker) and appropriate to their area of expertise, good advisers usually will be happy to speak with you about your business and what they can do for you. It is virtually impossible to begin this process too soon.

In making your choice of advisers, two issues are fundamental: competence and chemistry. Competence ensures that they have the specific expertise that you need to bring to the table. Chemistry ensures that they, along with other team members, have the right fit to do *your* deal in a way that you are comfortable with.

Creating a Competent Team

Work with a strong and very experienced team. Find someone with experience in selling businesses and preferably in your specific industry. Ideally, they should be close by, because you'll spend a lot of time running back and forth to their offices. Make sure the partner you are comfortable with will actually have time to attend meetings and think about the project. Here's a list of the core set of advisers you should look at hiring and what to look for in each area:

• *Accountants.* For the accounting firm, you want a well-respected company. You obviously can't go wrong with one of the Big Four, but any strong firm with a sterling reputation that will be credible to your buyers could be a good partner. In fact, some middle-size firms with specialty in your industry or family businesses could be a great choice. Remember that the quality of the numbers you offer to buyers will be judged based not only on the reputation of your company but on that of your accountant. Make sure that the lead partner is going to have time to dedicate to the project and that the firm has experience in your industry. It is extremely important that they have conducted similar business. They also need the metrics to compare your business to similar companies across diverse dimensions.

• *Bankers.* Money may all be green, but the money you bring to the deal is not all the same. Bankers must have specific industry and buyer knowledge. Experience and trust are key. You will be trusting them with your business, and you may need a good relationship at some point in the future. Get a commitment on who will run the process. There are many bankers to choose from, so interview at least three, and drive a hard deal.

• *Lawyers.* You should interview three or four firms for the work. It is unbelievable how many inexperienced lawyers are hired to run multimillion-dollar deals and what crazy obstacles they can throw in the path of a good deal. Choosing the wrong firm can easily ruin the deal and cost you lots of money and years picking up the pieces. If you have any influence on choosing the lawyer used by the buyer, don't use it to stack the deck with one of your cronies. Instead, make sure they get someone competent and *experienced* in buying and selling businesses, not a divorce lawyer. The only thing worse than having a bad attorney on your side is to have one sitting across from you. If the buyer is uncertain about a choice of legal representation, you might give them the names of four or five good firms. Then it won't look as if you are trying to tilt the field in your favor, but you can still be assured that they will find someone competent.

Lawyers should have experience and also a soft touch. You don't want a lawyer at the table who is a deal killer, one who will knock down every proposal on the table or make it so hard for potential buyers that they will walk away. You want someone who can drive a hard bargain when necessary but still keep the deal alive. Look for personality and bedside manner, and, above all, trust your own gut.

• *Investment Bankers.* If you are planning an outside sale, I believe it is essential to have an experienced investment banker represent you. They are expensive but usually earn their fee. Sometimes they earn their fee tenfold. They act as sage counsel, uncover a large universe of buyers, run your auction, and take on the role of the bad guy so the business owner doesn't have to. They run great interference and know how to play buyers off against one another to get you the absolute best deal. And they normally can smoke out when a buyer is not real, which can save you huge amounts of time and money.

Can you run an auction without an investment banker? Yes. You could have a smart lawyer to help you, and you could try to do it yourself. But it is suboptimal, and nearly impossible to do when you are also trying to run your company. So go with a pro. Remember, their fees are nearly all success-based. They only get real money if *you* get real money.

• *Wealth Managers.* Even before the wealth comes in from the sale of your business, you need to start looking at wealth management advisers who can help you put it to its best use. Get the best advice you can and recognize that the issues you will be dealing with after the sale will probably be at a much higher level than those you have addressed in the past. A few zeros at the end of your financial statement can make a world of difference. Get the right advice for your new challenges. We'll consider this issue in more depth in Chapter 9.

These initial team members can help you find others that you will need along the way, depending on the type of deal you are doing and its structure. When the *American Family Business Survey* asked family business owners whom they regard as their "most trusted business adviser," a majority of respondents (69 percent) rated their accountant as one of the top three most trusted business advisers. Behind accountants in the one-through-three rankings are lawyers (54 percent), bankers (22 percent), and business peers (20 percent).[1] In the deal process, the investment banker and lawyer may play a more central role in the process.

Be prepared for this to shift, and realize that the accountants you have always used in the past may be out of their league for this deal. Also, recognize that like any professional, they may be the last to admit that they don't have the expertise to do the deal. It is up to you to recognize the skills you need and, while being fair to your current advisers, get the advice that you really need to pull off the deal successfully.

Who's on First

Which of these advisers should you bring on board first? There are two potential paths. In some cases, there will be a close, trusted adviser such as one of your directors or a longtime lawyer or accountant. This is an adviser whom you can trust implicitly. If you are lucky enough to have such a trusted associate, this person should be your first team member, and your investment banker would be second. If not, choose your investment banker first. There are two reasons for this. First, the banker is normally the quarterback of the process. Second, bankers often have numerous legal and accounting relationships with folks who have extensive experience in deal-making, so a good investment banker can help you assemble the A-team to get your deal done.

Better Living Through Chemistry

In addition to the tangible expertise these advisers bring, you also need to look at the intangibles. Are they trustworthy? Can you live elbow-to-elbow with these advisers? If you were trapped together in a snowbound cabin in the mountains, would you get out alive? Will they turn off the type of buyers you are looking to attract? Do they have commitment to your success and the deal? Are incentives aligned to keep them focused? What are the terms for retaining these different members of the team? How can you strike the best deal with each of them?

If you interview more than one adviser in each area, you'll begin to get a clearer idea about the differences in experience and approaches. Look over their records and then make your choice. Don't wait until you have a buyer making an offer or until you are wiring millions of dollars to an account. Then it will be too late to do a thorough job. Think about hiring advisers in the way you'd hire a top manager for the company. Spend the same amount of time on it. Give it the attention it deserves.

THE PROCESS OF SELECTING YOUR TEAM

How do you find good advisers? While the process is different for every advisor, we illustrate the general process by examining how you would go about finding an investment banker.

Selecting an Investment Banker

There are literally thousands of investment banking firms. There are international giants such as Goldman Sachs and Merrill Lynch and focused boutiques such as Legacy Partners and Edgeview Partners. There are regional niche firms and global players. There are firms that won't work on a deal that is less than $100 million and firms that specialize only in "forest product" deals. The entire landscape is available to you. In addition to industry and size, some firms also specialize in selling family-held companies. There is a big list of bankers in the back of this book, which can be a starting point for your explorations, but there are also several steps you should follow to find "your banker."

1. *Do your homework and find the right fit.*

The first step is research. The Web has made this relatively easy for you to identify firms that fit your needs. The primary specifics that you are looking for:

    a. *Deals in Your Size Range.* You want to be an important client, not a rounding error.

    b. *Significant Experience and a Track Record in Your Industry.* Industry knowledge matters. You can normally search records to see which advisers complete deals in your industry. It's important because it means they know all the players, their interests and their quirks.

    c. *Deep Partner Experience.* Sheer deal experience over many years matters greatly in this world. Deal-making is complex and takes many turns. Knowing how to read a bluff or spot a real buyer, or knowing how hard to push a buyer, are all matters of feel, born of experience.

2. *Hold a "beauty contest."*

Once you have identified five to ten firms that meet your criteria, you or a trusted adviser should contact them and describe your goals. Some bankers will be too busy on other projects to work on your deal. (Sadly, some won't even take the time to return your calls.) But if you start with a list of ten credible firms, you will surely get three or four who will want to advise you. They have been through this drill a million times and will be prepared to come to you to make a presentation on their skills and ideas. This is called "the beauty contest," where all of these Hermes-clad rich folk come and beg you for the chance to help you realize your dreams. This part is fun! Enjoy it while it lasts.

After a preliminary round of high-level discussions on your goals (majority/minority sale, potential price range, rough ideas of financial performance), you will need to share detailed information on your company with the bankers on a confidential basis. This prepares them to give you the best possible advice, which is what you are looking for. It is a normal process: You send them a simple Confidentiality Agreement ("CA" in banker-speak). An example that you could use is in Appendix A-2.

3. *Send them the data.*

Once the bankers execute the CA, it gives you cursory protection. Then, you send them several key items (which you have long since prepared, as you have been thinking ahead!):

- Three years of audited historical financials.
- Two years of future financial projections.
- A detailed business plan if you have it, or a strong three- to five-page executive summary of the plan.
- Product descriptions and product literature.
- A discussion of your primary competitors.
- A list of "investment considerations" or primary selling points (a list of the positive points that make your company unique). This would include your market share, product excellence, key management bios, and major plans for future growth.

4. *Listen to the pitches.*

Using this data, the bankers will be able to make a meaningful and detailed presentation on your options. Some business owners are paranoid about data floating around and so they prefer to spoon-feed their bankers. Avoid this at all costs if you can. Good bankers are used to working with highly sensitive data and treat it as such. If you give them very little to process, you will get a lightweight and pretty useless presentation. Remember, garbage in, garbage out. If you want a useful pitch, give them good data. If you have provided enough information, some pitches will be absolutely terrific.

The pitch will be composed of a lot of boilerplate stuff, like the pages describing how super the bank is and a laundry list of their historic deals. Push them to identify their specific skills in your sector and find out whether the folks sitting in that room worked on the relevant deals. You will smell real experience very quickly. But after this appetizer, the meat of any good pitch can be very illuminating. The two main portions are "valuation" and "sales process." The first is essential, of course: Valuation is their view of what your company is worth based upon their analysis of your financials. This should be detailed and thoughtful. They should know, for example, exactly what multiples of EBIT or EBITDA companies like yours have sold for. From this data, they will give you a range of values for your business. They will say, "To us, all of this means your company will sell from six to eight times EBITDA for a total consideration range of X to Y."

Don't just have your head turned by very high valuations. Check the work. Do a smell test yourself. Some bankers do dangle very high selling ranges just to prompt you to give them the mandate. They can be like overzealous real estate brokers, telling you that you can get two times market values just to get your house listed with them. Then you list it for that price and (surprise!) there are no buyers. You've wasted a lot of time and hurt your asset. Be careful and prudent. Don't believe your own press clippings! And if it seems too good to be true, it probably is.

The next most important section of the pitch is a detailed analysis of the prospective buyers by name. There should be *thoughtful* lists of industry buyers as well as prospective financial buyers. And I stress *thoughtful* for a reason. These people are smart, and the list of ideas should be smart. If you have a $50 million company, they shouldn't list KKR as a potential buyer. The time and thought applied to this list are telling.

There will be other boilerplate items on the actual nuts and bolts of the sale and the team that will be on your deal. This latter point is essential. It must be spelled out *exactly* who will be on your team and who the team leader will be. If you have a fancy, high-powered partner at your pitch but he's not going to lead your deal, this is pretty worthless. You don't want the most important transaction of your life relegated to some third-year associate. You need a committed, experienced partner to run your deal. If they can't commit to that, they're not your bank.

Another reason to know the faces is that chemistry with the lead banker, in particular, is very important. You will spend months with this person, and many stressful hours, working on your most important transaction. You must trust them implicitly and envision yourself spending lots of time with them in a positive way.

The Covert I-Banking Freebie

Investment bankers are not known for giving away anything. But this is one of the best little nuggets in this book. The "sell your company" pitch by the investment bank is the only terrific freebie you will ever be given. At the same time you are evaluating the bankers, you are getting views of your firm and deal from many different angles. Your goal should be to have at least three potential bankers come and give you their detailed pitch. These pitches are normally 40–50 pages and are mostly very thoughtful and chock-full of information. And every pitch will be different, so by reviewing all three you will be able to synthesize the best parts of each into a terrific whole. You will have learned a ton about your merger and acquisition market from many massively compensated professionals, and it will cost you nothing but a bit of your time. It's great!

Structuring the Deal with the Bankers

Of course, then the meter starts running. One item that will not be in their pitch is their fee structure. Don't be coy: Just ask them what their fees are. There's normally a retainer (around $50,000 for out-of-pocket expenses), a minimum fee (all over the map—$200,000 to $2 million for the big guys) which can be offset by a percentage fee (1 percent to 2 percent). Much more on this later. Also, be sure to ask them if they have room on their dance card to work on your deal when it needs to be done.

If these pitches go well from your perspective (and theirs), you should ask all the bankers to send you their engagement letter right away, so you can see the details. An example of a standard engagement letter is included in Appendix A-3. It lists their fees and many key facets of their engagement. There is a pretty traditional structure to these, so they are unlikely to vary widely. Your goal here, of course, is to get the best bankers at the best price. Strong, busy firms are unlikely to cut their fees very much, but they will not respect you—or you yourself—if you don't give it a try. The best case is to have three firms want your business so you can play them off against one another. Go back to each with your requests: lower up-front retainers, lower total fees, lower minimum fees, and shorter tails (this last is the part that obligates you to pay them for a year or 18 months if any of these buyers do a deal. It is standard and fair, but can be negotiated).

One way to potentially get a better deal for yourself is to ask them to shift fees to a greater success basis. For example, give them an initial fee at the low range and a higher fee as a reward for success. This can be highly motivating and powerfully align goals. For example, they might say they can sell your business for $50 to $60 million and they want a 1.5 percent fee. Suggest that you will pay them 1 percent below $50 million, 1.25 percent from $50 to $65 million, and 2 percent above $65 million. This puts your fees in their range but gets them a big home run if they knock it out of the park. It's a bit like the "home run" kickers we have discussed. On all of these, they may say no, but it will never hurt to ask.

Hiring Other Advisers

You ideally want to go through a similar process of a bake-off for hiring lawyers and accountants, or at least interview a series of firms in each area. With a law firm, you need to make sure you work with experienced securities lawyers, not estate practice, but people who have done extensive securities work in similar styles of transactions. If you have a public company, you need a securities lawyer with extensive experience in public firms. Again, look for chemistry, and also look for signs of attitude that can kill a deal that needs to be driven hard but can easily be driven to death. Is this someone who could wreck the whole deal environment because of machismo and too strong of a desire to win points for clients?

Once you select a law firm, how do you negotiate the best deal? You need to ask the law firm to disclose the hourly billing rate of all the people who are going to work on the team. You need to make sure the team is appropriately sized. Big law firms might give you a five-person team for a small deal if you don't carefully manage expectations. Make sure it is a partner or senior professional, or you might get a fourth-year associate. Ask for interim bills on a "clipping level" basis (when you reach $5,000 or $10,000 or other milestones). This can help to ensure things don't get out of control.

If you have a bake-off and interest from more than one law firm, you can also sometimes negotiate to dramatically reduce fees if the deal dies. For example, if the deal goes south, the law firm would agree to take 25 to 30 percent off your bill. This is a very important clause if you can get it. This helps to limit your downside risk of deal failure and also gives the lawyers a little added incentive to do everything they can to make sure the deal succeeds. There is an implicit understanding in such an arrangement that you will go back to them if the deal is revived or you set up another deal. You won't always get such concessions, but you don't know until you ask.

All of the same rules for lawyers apply to hiring an accountant. They need the right experience and should come from a good firm. It doesn't have to be a Big Four firm, although that doesn't hurt, but it should be a well-respected firm. As with lawyers, ask for billing rates, set "clipping levels," and find out who will be on your team. Also ask about overhead charges that will apply. These billings for copying, FedEx, messengering, and other small details can add up, leading to "death by a thousand cuts" if you are not careful.

MONEY WELL SPENT

Hiring your team may seem like a lot of time and energy just for the right to spend a lot more money to pay for their advice and more time working with them on the deal. But unless you have extensive experience in selling businesses, it is usually time and money well spent. (And even seasoned veterans have learned from hard experience the value of having good advisers on board. In fact, the more experienced they are, the more they recognize the value.)

Don't think of this process of hiring advisers as an expense. Think of it as an education. When you have a bake-off among different firms, you get to see what they are made of, and you learn a lot about their areas of expertise. You have access to some of the brightest minds at some of the best firms. They are offering you insights on your business and the deal process. This can be the best education you will ever receive in deal-making—until you actually put your own sale together.

Make sure you are getting good value for your advice, but most of all, make sure you are getting good advice. A good team can make a good deal even better. In a bad deal, a good team can pull your tail out of the fire to help you avoid getting burned. On the other hand, a bad team can run a sterling deal into the ground. Choose your partners with care and treat them with respect. It will be the best thing you can do to succeed in the biggest deal of your life.

NOTE

1. *American Family Business Survey*, published by MassMutual Financial Group and the Raymond Family Business Institute, January 2003, p. 21.

VALUATION

How Much Is Your Business Worth?

WHAT'S IT WORTH?

How might you go about valuing the three businesses we discussed in Chapter 1? Here are a few general observation:

Homeland Designs: Bill Chambers oversees a fairly traditional business, although it is growing quite rapidly. A business in such an industry might fetch five to six times cash flow, but with higher growth Chambers might get up as high as eight or nine times cash flow. It depends on growth rate and market.

Iconix: Leo Mullen had wonderful luck and timing, selling an Internet service business at a time when people were focused on eyeballs, not on cash flow or revenue. He was able to sell at a time when such businesses were selling at 20 times cash flow. When things get out of whack, it can be a good time to think about selling.

Politics & Prose: With a small but stable business, the multiple would be in the range of five to six times cash flow and could be impacted by local competition, since the business has fairly low barriers to entry.

What is your business worth? No question would appear to be more central to a sale, and yet no answer will be more elusive. Determining a fair price for a company is never a simple task. While it would be nice to have a neat mathematical formula to crank out a single number, math is not enough. While it would be handy to pull out a Blue Book, look up your make and model and then adjust for mileage and accessories, the value of a business cannot be pulled from a book.

VALUATION: SCIENCE OR ART?

Valuing a company is, in fact, part science and part art. The science is determining what similar companies are worth, where the industry is headed, and what kind of multiples a company of this size and shape could command. The art is then adjusting that mathematical number to reflect the characteristics of the actual firm. The science part is well known, and there are many good books on valuation that can help you refine your approach. Many of them, however, utilize esoteric valuation techniques that are not very useful in practice. These approaches may be useful if you want to enhance your reputation as a financial wizard, seeking to make the process as complicated as possible. (Astound your friends!) But smoke and flashing powders are not necessary to pull off the basic trick of valuation.

This is not to denigrate complex analysis, spreadsheets, and higher mathematics. They can be useful, and if you like to play with advanced mathematics, go for it. There is probably no limit to the gyrations you can go through to calculate the value of a firm. But if you are interested in closing a deal, most of the time a fairly simple analysis can give you a good ballpark estimate for what your company is worth. As with most things in life, simple and straightforward is the best approach. If you want to know what the weather is like outside, you can pay for a fancy weather satellite and tracking system, or you can hook up a thermometer and barometer—and look out the window—to come up with a pretty good idea of whether you'll need your overcoat and umbrella. Still, as with reading the weather, you have to know what to look for. This is what we'll cover in this chapter.

THE SCIENCE OF VALUATION

Just as you comparison-shop for prices on cars or houses in an overall automotive marketplace, there is also a "market" for companies that determines overall value. In most cases, this is the public stock market. These markets drive the science for corporate valuations worldwide, and they will shape your valuation of your own firm.

The science piece of valuation is based upon getting your hands on the research analyzing trends in similar companies and across your industry. Companies in an industry usually trade in public markets along certain valuation lines, and many in specific sectors tend to have similar characteristics. Some break out of the pack due to terrible performance, in which case their multiples will be much lower. The multiples of other firms soar above the crowds, usually because of excellent growth or performance beyond the norm. It is important to look at the metrics for firms in the industry and to decide which are the important multiples.

In general, the multiple that is watched most closely is the ratio of overall enterprise valuation (value of equity plus interest-bearing debt) divided by the company's latest annual earnings before interest, taxes, depreciation, and amortization (EBITDA). EBITDA represents pretax cash flow before maintenance capital expenditures. It provides a measure of the cash flowing out of the company before the capital expenditures required to be made on equipment, systems, and facilities to maintain the business's market position. It is a primary focus of commercial banking, investment banking, and Wall Street research.

It is important, however, to look beyond EBITDA to EBIT multiples (earnings before interest and tax but after depreciation).

From the buyer's perspective, cash flow after maintenance capital expenditures (EBIT is normally a proxy for this figure) is also critical. Other multiples such as revenue multiples and net income multiples are useful but supplementary. Usually, you will want to track all of these metrics for 24 months of trailing EBITDA and EBIT. You'll also want to look at projections for 12 to 24 months ahead. The core EBITDA multiple used in valuation is based upon actual trailing 12-month EBITDA generated by the business. Sellers often attempt to get buyers to pay multiples based upon *projected* EBITDA—and if you can pull this off, more power to you—but it's the historic EBITDA that really matters to most buyers.

If you find out that all the companies in the sector are trading at seven to eight times EBITDA or nine to ten times EBIT, this is the range you would expect to fetch for your company, unless there are extenuating circumstances. For example, a company that finds its comparable industry multiples are six to eight times with an EBITDA of $17 million would look for a sale in the range of $102 to $136 million. The owner might propose an initial price at the top of that range, or farther down (now we are getting into the art), but you'd expect the final price to be somewhere in that range. In the normal course of negotiations, with a basic business, you might start at the high end, the buyer at the low end, and you end up somewhere in the middle. Makes it sound simple, doesn't it? It is very serenely simple in concept and diabolically difficult in practice.

Do Your Homework

Here's the first challenge: Where do you come up with those industry multiples? It used to be that any manager with a half-decent stockbroker could access the industry research analysis pretty easily. With the Internet, it is literally at your fingertips. Anyone with a connection to the Web can come up with the information you need to evaluate the metrics of the industry. (Of course, this means you will rarely meet a buyer who doesn't have access to the same information.)

Most investment banks have a strong research department where a bunch of very smart propeller-heads immerse themselves in the details of specific industries to produce research reports. These research analysts are the rock stars of the investment world, earning millions of dollars per year. They are poached by other banks for multimillion-dollar signing bonuses. Their word literally moves billions of dollars in the market. They are hardwired into their industries, making recommendations on whether to buy, hold, or sell stocks in those areas.

Institutional investors trade based on those recommendations (which means trading, investment banking, and M&A fees for the investment banks). If you decide to take your software company public, you will want the leading software industry analysts to write research reports on your company. To do that, you will need to do investment banking business with the firm where he or she works.

But right now, what you need more than anything is the reports these analysts produce. Everything you need to know about the industry sectors you're targeting is in these reports. They will give you an understanding of industry trends, an overview of competitors, and an understanding of how Wall Street values these companies.

How do you get your hands on this valuable information? It is really quite simple. Start by looking at the annual All-Star Research issue of *Institutional Investor*. This report will give you a list of the top research analysts, sector by sector. Review the list to find the best minds in your part of the world and identify where they work. These reports will also give you a view of how the financial world views your business. This will be invaluable in being able to look at your own firm through the eyes of potential buyers or bankers.

The next challenge is getting your hands on these reports. This research is so valuable to investment banks that you can't simply call Goldman Sachs blindly and ask them to pop the report in the mail. Start with your own stockbroker. Brokers often can get you some research generated by their own firm or others. If you're lucky, the broker might have just the reports you are looking for. If you know someone who has access to a Bloomberg service, you can often get research there. Just keep plugging away until you get your hands on it. It will greatly enhance your own understanding of your industry, strengthen your strategy, and increase your credibility in presenting your ideas.

While getting some of the more impressive analyst reports may take a little finagling, getting the multiples and other numbers you need will take almost nothing. All this information is available on-line. Many investment sites offer industry analysis and metrics. In a matter of minutes, you can have a fairly good sense of what companies are trading at in the sector.

When obtaining this research, look at several important issues. First, look at the date of the research. Wall Street research that is more than a year old is probably of limited value, particularly given the blistering pace of change in the economy. Second, research generally comes in three different forms: "macro" surveys on overall trends in the economy, company-specific reports, and industry analysis. The macro analyses generally cover economic trends or policy, and are interesting to read, but are not the most useful information for valuation or competitive analysis. The company-specific reports are quite helpful, and you should seek out pieces that analyze the largest and most direct competitors to your firm. These reports not only tell you the competitive context in which you need to make your case, but also may indicate the factors and issues that will be of key concern to buyers.

The most useful pieces are the industry analyses that evaluate all the major trends in a specific sector, such as Internet services or corporate training, analyzing the prevailing growth rates, margins, and valuation multiples of the primary competitors. Most analysts put out significant competitive compendiums like this once or twice a year, and when you're calling your friends or surfing the Net to get research, request some competitive industry pieces, even if they are six or nine months old. These are very valuable, and you should study them carefully and commit key industry metrics to memory so you can blow your buyers and bankers away with your knowledge.

By the way, not doing this level of research is simply not an option. This research, the financial metrics and competitive analysis, provides the basis for your valuation of the company and will be key to demonstrating to your partners the credibility of your effort. You must do it and do it well.

Why go to this trouble when investment bankers will be doing the same thing? If you have a bake-off, as discussed in Chapter 5, you'll get multiple perspectives on the value of your business. It is still important to do your own valuation, because you need to understand the core process of valuation so you can follow the often more complex arguments of the investment bankers. You'll be able to ask intelligent questions about their valuation process. Your own work also gives you a starting point for identifying and hiring bankers and other advisers who can handle a transaction of your size and putting together other aspects of your deal. As a seller, it is vital that you have some familiarity with the process of valuation, even if you hire experienced advisers to help you with the deal.

Preliminary Valuation

As I've mentioned, valuation basics do not need to be complex. To get you into the ballpark, consider that in the heady times of the 1999 and 2000 buyout markets the average purchase multiple for all buyouts completed was approximately 7.5 times trailing EBITDA. As it is an average, it reflects deals done at the high end and low end. Some deals in areas such as radio and other media were as high as ten to eleven times EBITDA, reaching such lofty heights because of their growth characteristics and because they are generally extremely stable and predictable businesses. The more predictable (and thus less risky) the cash flows, the higher the price one can pay. So a good target for a more normal operating business with traditional risks is six to seven times EBITDA. This doesn't tell you anything about what your specific business will be worth, but it does give you a frame of reference for what to expect.

You also can put this in the context of other investments, and it makes sense in terms of rates of return and risk. U.S. Treasury bonds are perceived to be the least risky of any entity and generate an essentially guaranteed rate of return today of about 5 percent per annum. So, a $1,000 Treasury bond yields $50 per year. To buy the bond, you're paying 20 times the cash flow of $50. That's your cash flow multiple. Now, think of the risks inherent in purchasing a living, breathing, operating company. Customers come and go. There are industry shocks, and people come and go as well. Well, this is normally a risky situation, and your cash return on your purchase should reflect that risk.

There was once a rule of thumb that one should never pay more than six times EBITDA for a company. This rule has long since been broken in this highly competitive investment environment, but it was a rule that made sense. If a risk-free rate of return was 5 percent, or 20 times cash flow, paying six times cash flow for a much riskier asset makes sense, as this implicitly generates an unleveraged yield of 16.7 percent per annum.

If buyers then put 50 percent leverage on the transaction (thus reducing equity capital required by 50 percent), they would see future equity returns of 30 percent per annum. As you can see, these numbers work and are sensible as risk/reward ratios go. Most buyout firms target a leveraged IRR of about 30 to 35 percent, and so should you. The 30 percent target makes sense because on an all-equity basis, you get a 16.7 percent return, which reflects the underlying operating company's business risk. Then, you layer a high level of debt, creating substantial financial or balance sheet risk, and you have a risky situation for which you should be paid a higher rate of return to commit capital. That moves the figure up from 16.7 percent to 30 or 35 percent, depending upon the overall level of risk.

That's why, for most businesses, it makes no sense for a buyer to pay ten times EBITDA (the exceptions to this rule are extremely predictable and extremely high-growth businesses, which can justify the higher multiples). This implies an unleveraged return of 10 percent on your capital, which to me is not enough return to reflect the risk of buying and managing an operating company. Remember, the buyer can purchase many corporate bonds in stable companies that yield nearly 10 percent and are much less risky than the cash flows from an operating company. If you somehow end up asking for more than ten times EBITDA, you better have one hell of a story to tell.

THE ART OF VALUATION

Once you have done the research, you will have gathered a range of multiples on comparable firms. You have defined the bounds of the universe, but you still don't know where *your* specific business fits in this universe. You need to look beyond generic features to see what makes your business more or less valuable. This is where the art comes in, of course. Now that you've crunched the numbers, you turn your attention to the critical nonfinancial issues to determine where you should sit in the range of multiples (or outside of it). Among the issues that might adjust the multiples are:

• *Pretax Margins.* If your company has lower margins than the industry average, you should likely discount the multiple. If it has higher margins, it may command a premium.

• *Growth.* If all companies are growing at 12 percent and your company is growing at 20 percent, it should receive a higher multiple. Buyers will be careful to see that the growth rate hasn't been artificially inflated (for example, by special selling programs implemented by the company) and that it is sustainable. If it survives these tests, the company should fetch a higher price.

• *Future Prospects.* If the company has some tremendous future events coming on line, such as the award of a large contract, you might boost the multiple. You don't want to create too glowing a picture, but if there is a realistic argument for a rosy picture, you should make it. If you just landed a multiyear government contract that will double your business, this has to be factored into your price. Strong future prospects will allow you to extract a higher price.

• *Customer Diversification.* As noted in the discussion of risk, if half the company's business comes from a single, dominant customer, this increases risk and decreases value.

• *Scale.* If the company is generating revenues of $200 million or higher, buyers should expect to pay public market multiples. If it is a $20 million firm, the purchase multiple will be discounted by 15 to 30 percent from public market multiples to adjust for the smaller scale (and therefore more risky company). A smaller firm typically doesn't have the quality of management, systems, customer relationships, or clout of a much larger company. But to the extent you can demonstrate that you do have this high-quality management—and bringing in professionals and brand-name advisers can help in making this case—you can bump up your multiple a bit.

• *Control.* Sellers of private firms sometimes will argue that buyers should pay a "control premium" because the buyer gains operating control over the company, rather than just a financial investment in it. Sellers contend that buyers should pay extra for this, but it is usually countered by the fact that the investment, unlike stock in a public firm, is an illiquid security. It can be a catchy argument and sometimes will bump the multiple a tad, but today's markets are so competitive, buyers generally pay multiples very close to the public market. Besides, as every business owner knows, controlling a company can be a double-edged sword.

• *History.* As noted above, buyers will look for several years of history in growth and earnings to make sure they are not just sleight of hand. If there are tarnishes on this record, that will reduce the price. Buyers don't want to set the value from peak earnings. If the company has earned 6 percent historically, and the year before the sale the earnings spike up to 10 percent, they will be very skeptical and are likely to set the value based upon the 6 percent historical earnings level.

• *Seller's and Buyer's Motivation.* The motivation of the sellers and buyers also affects the price. Are you desperate to sell or do you need cash quickly? Do the buyers have tax consideration or strategic imperatives that make them want to get into the deal quickly? Will your company allow them to reach a segment or market they desperately want to add to their business? This added motivation could increase the price.

• *Rival Bidders.* The psychology of rival buyers also plays a role in determining how much a business is worth. In one deal, a management team competing against an outside buyer was surprised at how high the outsiders were willing to go. It turned out that the CEO who was bidding for the firm had lost out on a previous deal and decided he *had* to have this one, no matter what. It was a point of pride—so reason took a holiday. While such a rival can be hell for a more level-headed competitor, there is often nothing better for a seller.

All these factors, and others that may be idiosyncratic to the deal, are used to adjust the value of the firm. How much of an adjustment should be made for each? That is the art. In addition, some of these factors will interact with one another. A company with a dominant customer may also have lower margins due to this customer, and these issues should compound a reduction in value against prevailing market multiples. You just need to systematically identify the issues, look at ranges for comparable firms, and then adjust your initial "scientific" estimates accordingly.

The outcome of this process is never a single price but rather a range. You decide at the outset what the top dollar and bottom dollar are. When you reach top dollar, you can smile. If you reach your bottom dollar, you need to be able to walk away.

The Balance Sheet Matters Too

Most business valuation analysis rightfully focuses on the income statement. This is appropriate, but sophisticated buyers will also carefully evaluate the company's balance sheet. They won't just look at the most recent balance sheet. Just as with the income statement, they'll expect to see the last three years of historic data and analyze the key working capital accounts to see how they've been changing. Have the days of accounts receivable outstanding been getting longer or shorter over time? If the receivable days outstanding are getting much longer over time, you may have a collections issue. If they've gotten much shorter in recent months, it might mean that you have accelerated the collection of receivables in advance of a sale. This may indicate that there was some kind of financial hole to fill.

These are the kinds of questions savvy buyers will ask about your business. You owe it to yourself to ask them—and answer them—first. Otherwise you may not have the right answer when they come, which could be an expensive mistake. Many dollars have been lost by sellers who have been caught flat-footed by a sharp question from a buyer. In the ensuing embarrassment, you can almost see the value of the business bleeding onto the pavement. It can even spook the buyer and kill the deal.

Inventories and accounts payable also will be scrutinized. Have the inventory days lengthened or shortened recently? If they've gotten much longer, perhaps there's lots of old inventory there that the new buyer will have to eat. If inventory days have gotten much shorter, perhaps it means that you've been tightening inventories to take cash out of the business. Same with payables. Are they stretched? If so, you may have some angry suppliers out there and a financial gap to fill. If the payables are very short, perhaps you have an *opportunity* to generate cash by extending the payables.

Buyers also will be wary of capital investment deficits in a company that's for sale. Just as it's natural for a seller to try to optimize the cash on the balance sheet prior to a sale, it's natural for a seller to underinvest in capital equipment Sadly, it's a little bit like selling a car. Maybe you left on the tires with just enough tread or put off changing the coolant. In looking at your business, you can bet buyers will have their "mechanics" crawling all over the place to see that capital expenditures match historical levels. If they identify concerns, you should have an explanation.

Buyers will also look at debt outstanding. They expect to purchase a balance sheet with certain working capital accounts. There's a natural working capital level for any business, and that's part of what they are buying. They may also be buying a company with some existing bank debt on the balance sheet. This is fine, but certainly impacts valuation. Remember the old, simple formula:

$$\text{Total enterprise value} = \text{equity value} + \text{debt value}$$

You need to be clear with the seller how this debt will be treated. A $10 million deal where the buyer assumes $5 million in bank debt is quite different from a deal in which the debt is excluded.

Balance sheet analysis is complex, and it will pay to have a good finance person on your team. Other issues that may arise are the seasonality of the balance sheet. Many companies have highly seasonal working capital needs (like a swimming pool company or a florist), and it's important for you to understand these seasonal fluctuations. In general, buyers will use a twelve-month *average* working capital and debt level as a baseline. If they can buy the business when the balance sheet is at its fullest, that's fine, but they will be wary of buying in the quiet months. If you are in a seasonal business, your best time to sell may often be heading into your busy season.

Debt raises some more esoteric questions, such as how to define debt. Are leases debt? Should leases on the balance sheet reduce the purchase price? In general, the answer there is no. Most leases can be rolled over in a sale and behave more like working capital. But all forms of bank debt and subordinated debt are clearly *debt,* and are a dollar-for-dollar reduction on equity proceeds in a transaction.

Of course, all these balance sheet anomalies have logical explanations. Look *carefully* at all the metrics. If they're consistent over time, you're probably in good shape. If they're bouncing around, you've got lots of issues to analyze and questions to ask. Again, seek out industry comparables to see where competitors' inventory turns, days of receivables, and days of payables are set. There is always both opportunity and risk in balance sheet management, but in my experience, buyers will normally see more risk than opportunity.

Why Not Use P/E Ratios?

The P/E ratio is the ratio of the price of the stock of a public company to its net income per share. It is also equal to the total equity valuation of the company divided by its net income. Buyers will certainly consider net income in their valuation review, but it is not often the driving multiple because the net income at the bottom of the income statement does not equate to cash flow. Net income comes *after* noncash charges, such as depreciation and amortization and taxes. These metrics may be different at each company and not useful because they may be wildly affected by old acquisitions or irrelevant amortization. Also, tax rates for all companies differ.

Cash flow is what matters. It's cash that the buyer will use to pay the piper, not net income. That's why buyers use EBITDA minus average capital expenditures to value their companies. As always, cash flow is king.

What If There Is No EBITDA?

We've talked a lot about valuation based upon EBITDA, but what if the company is losing money or is currently a not-for-profit business and there is negative EBITDA? In this case, naturally, you rely on metrics other than EBITDA to value the business. As always, look at all the industry comparables to see which metrics make sense. Do most companies in the sector trade at some multiple of revenue, such as 50 percent of annual revenue? If so, that's a guideline that can be useful. One rule of thumb in a situation where the company is not making money is to go to the balance sheet for valuation guidance. In this case, the net worth or net equity line on the balance sheet is a good guide for valuation. You might also look at liquidation value of all the assets and liabilities as a guide.

There are some businesses that simply have no value or negative value. With any luck, your business is not one of them. But if it is, there still may be opportunities to create a "sale." If the company is losing money and has a poor balance sheet, perhaps you will have to *pay the buyer* to take the company. Believe it or not, there are hundreds of deals done that way every year.

If the business happens to be a not-for-profit company that is converting to a for-profit model, the same rules as above apply, such as looking at comparable multiples of revenue as indicators of value. In this instance, though, other matters than financial issues would be of paramount importance, such as asking whether a previously not-for-profit company has the mentality, human resources, and capital base to venture into the for-profit world to compete with long-standing for-profit competitors.

NEGOTIATING STRATEGY

While we've discussed the science and art of valuation, the actual value of your business is what a particular seller is willing to pay. So the price that will be paid for your business is a process of negotiation. If you have done the valuation described above, and perhaps some more detailed analysis with the help of your advisers, you are armed with the information you need to go to the bargaining table. Then, the real art of valuation begins.

Every negotiation is different, but a general strategy is to begin by testing your value against the buyer's expectations. Now that you know what the company is worth, you don't just march into the buyer's office and put the numbers on the table. There are better ways to approach the deal. If you can, you want to always make the buyer put a price on the table first. Discuss the deal informally, and get a ballpark figure. If you know from analyzing multiples that the business might be worth $15 million to $20 million and the buyer is looking at $5 million, you know you have a long way to go. In fact, you may not even have a "willing" buyer. (Any buyer is "willing" if the price is low enough.) Perhaps you should use your crucial time wisely and walk away at that point, knowing you'll never find a point of agreement.

You might start this process of probing informally. Set up a lunch with the buyer and say, "I haven't looked at the numbers as much as I'd like, so can you give me a range of what you are thinking about?" Get the buyer to talk first. Sometimes, you can find a bluebird—a wildly favorable deal that lands on your shoulder like the bluebird of happiness. Don't let it fly away. These bluebirds fly in when the buyer overestimates the value, hasn't done his homework, or very much wants to get into the business. But use some caution. If the buyer appears to be way over market, the first question to yourself should be: Why? Is there some hidden reason why the business may be more valuable than you thought? If you've gotten a high offer and it all tests out, though, close the deal fast and thank the stars.

An unsophisticated buyer is the exception, however, because

usually a prepared buyer has a pretty good idea of what the business is worth. Most of the time, the buyer will be willing to talk at pretty close to market metrics, and you know you are dealing with a rational person. Whatever the outcome, these preliminary probes can be very useful in framing your later discussions.

It may help to use a good cop–bad cop approach in negotiations. One person maintains a close and friendly relationship, while the other plays the heavy. If there is a silent partner, this makes it easier to say, "I ran this by my partner, and these are the five things he has problems with." In other words, you love the deal but these tough partners are throwing up roadblocks. This approach often makes it much easier to develop and maintain a good relationship, which makes the work much more constructive. If you are a sole owner negotiating, your lawyer or a friend in private equity could play this role. Even a tangentially involved lawyer or accountant can act as your negotiating foil.

That foil is so important. When you're making a deal, always begin the negotiations 10 to 20 percent higher on all the parameters than where you want to finish at the end of the day. If your target price is $20 million, start at $24 million. Never lead with the deal you want to make. Start at a level where you know you won't insult the seller, thus losing the fight before it gets started, but start above your best deal.

Some straight shooters just want to cut through the "negotiating crap" (a technical finance term!) and put their one and only deal on the table. This is a nice concept in a perfect world, but in our world this loses 90 percent of the time. The reason is that it's human nature for people to want to win a negotiation or improve upon it. Believe me, even if the buyer seems to want to cut to the chase, his lawyer or banker will want to extract some pain from you. It's a well-honed game, and everyone likes to play. You should play too and make sure you are good at it.

Give the buyer some points to win, and be prepared to lower your price to make him feel like he's winning some big points. A term sheet always has a lot of points on it, and there are some that are critical to you and some that are critical to the buyer. It is certainly possible that one term critical to both parties may blow up a deal. But when you go through all fifteen to twenty terms on the term sheet, decide which three or four you want to win. Present a couple of straw-man points on which to lose, and then complain like crazy when you give them up. (This is going to kill me! But, OK.) Then hold tough on your "must have" points, and you'll have created a true win-win.

VALUE AND VALUES

At the end of the day, these negotiating points will address issues beyond dollars and cents. What is the owner's role going forward? How will managers and employees be treated? What will happen to customers? What will happen to the business? Think about all the goals you have for the sale, as discussed in Chapter 2. They should be addressed explicitly in the deal so you don't win on price and lose on everything else.

Valuation seems to be a precise science, and in some respects it is. There is also an element of art in just coming up with a solid number, as discussed above. But, after all this number crunching, value is inseparable from values. You want to maximize your returns from the sale of your business, but you also want to maximize every goal that is important to you. Many times there is no conflict. But think carefully about these other goals and keep them right in front of you. It is very easy in the heat of the moment, or at the urging of an adviser, to set these other goals aside and focus on ending the game with the most points on the scoreboard.

But there is more to winning the game than this. Of course, extra zeros on your payout always come in handy, but don't lose sight of the bigger prize. Your life will go on after the sale, so make sure you really have gotten what you wanted out of the deal. There is value in being able to move forward without regrets. This is a calculus that all the complex valuation equations in the world cannot work out. Just like you were the only one who could build this business, in the end, you are the only one who can determine what you want to take out of it.

CHAPTER 7

BRING IN THE RIGHT BUYER

Market the Company to Achieve Your Goals

FINDING THE RIGHT BUYER

What can we learn about finding the right buyer from the cases presented in Chapter 1?

Homeland Designs: Bill Chambers found two buyers, one an entrepreneurial peer and the other a large public company. He took a larger offer from the riskier buyer, and later regretted it.

Iconix: Leo Mullen found a buyout firm interested in rolling up a set of similar businesses. He helped in the process and successfully sold out his company.

Politics & Prose: The buyers came to them. By not actively identifying and pursuing buyers, however, they limited their options.

Where do you find buyers? Any business with a pulse has probably received a few calls over the years, or even the past month, with interest in buying the business. This isn't usually the way to find the best buyers, as the experience of Politics & Prose demonstrated. It can be flattering to take these calls. It can be tempting to say yes. After all, you might avoid all the time, effort, and expense of putting the business on the market. But the chances of the right buyer showing up on your doorstep are pretty slim. By not actively seeking buyers, you will end up with fewer options and likely get a lower value for your business—or worse. If you need any convincing, think about the cost to Barbara Meade and Carla Cohen for inviting their new partner into the business, as described in Chapter 1.

Sometimes a match made in heaven does wander in—and some people are actually struck by lightning—but it doesn't happen every day. It is always a good idea to identify a pool of potential buyers. But where do you look for a qualified buyer for the business? Do you advertise? Trust a broker? How wide a scope do you need to find a good buyer? How narrow? Should you ever take the first offer that comes along—even if it is a good one?

If you are pursuing an internal sale, you actually do have an easy search. You've already found your buyer, right there in front of you—in a manager, family member, or other insider. We've already discussed strategies and structures for inside sales in Chapter 2. But even with a management buyout or ESOP, you might want to put up the inside offer against outside offers to ensure that you get the best value all around. It sounds like a lot of work but can help avoid buyer's or seller's remorse after an uncontested inside deal.

This chapter examines strategies for seeking out the right external buyers—either strategic or financial. We consider the types of buyers who might look at your business and the advisers who might lead you to these buyers. We also look at ways to find elusive or counterintuitive buyers who could turn out to be ideal buyers for your business.

THE BUYER UNIVERSE

There are two primary classes of buyers for your business. The first are *strategic buyers,* who are interested in the business as an operating entity, and the second are *financial buyers*, who see the business as a financial investment that will generate returns. Your investment bankers or other advisers will have views on the best buyers, and we've discussed in Chapter 2 about how the different buyers help you achieve your goals for the sale. But no one knows your sector better than you. So you should have your own list, to be shared with your bankers near the time that you retain them. The buyer list can be very large, encompassing thirty to forty financial buyers and twenty to thirty strategic buyers. Whether you go very wide or very narrow is a strategic matter to be discussed with your banker. Ultimately, your goal is to set up a real horse race among three to four enthusiastic bidders. Then the bankers can get them all revved up to get you the best possible price.

Of course, ultimately, the strength of the sale will be built upon a strong buyer universe. In today's massively funded private equity markets, there will nearly always be a strong group of financial buyers, such as private equity firms, who would like to own your company. They should likely be in the mix, but you must choose the ones who do deals in your industry and size range. The strategic, or industry, buyer market is much trickier. Be thoughtful. Which competitors, suppliers, or customers would really like to own you? Which big companies outside of your industry may have an interest in a new or similar sector? Which conglomerates make sense? What about overseas competitors that want to enter the market?

Strategic Buyers

As we have noted earlier, strategic buyers will generally offer the highest price and the most disruption, since they have the opportunity to knock out overhead by consolidating your business into their existing business. The strategic buyers for your business might come from the following groups of companies:

• *Competitors.* Competitors are usually a good fit, and they can sometimes offer the best prices, but they have their risks. The sale process will require you to reveal sensitive information to direct rivals. If they purchase your firm, these competitors will also be most likely to dismantle your business and integrate it into their own. You probably know the difference between your lethal competitors and the nonlethal variety. Stay away from the nasty competitors if you can. It is almost guaranteed to end badly, no matter what the price. But get something done with your nonlethal competitors if you have the opportunity. They can be among the best prospects for buying your company if they are in the market to grow.

• *Suppliers and customers.* You also might find a buyer among other players in your industry, who understand the business and may be able to benefit from synergies with your business, even though they are not direct competitors. Sometimes a customer or supplier will want to integrate, either forward or backward, and your firm could be the path to expanding the scope of their businesses. If they are current suppliers or downstream customers, you probably already have a working relationship, so if they are interested, this could help in closing the deal. They also are close enough to really understand your business and industry, if they are in the market to buy.

• *New entrants.* New entrants into your industry, perhaps from a related industry or from a different region or country, may want to enter the market through the purchase of your business. For example, a Chinese manufacturer may want to purchase a business to gain access to the U.S. market. These can be some of the hardest buyers to find because they are not on the radar screen, but they can be some of your best prospects. They are not direct competitors, so you don't have to worry as much about giving away your company secrets to a rival. And they often will pay a good price for the business because of a strategic purpose, such as offering access to a new geographic market. This could make your business more valuable to them than to other buyers. Strategic buyers from adjacent industries may also be interested in purchasing a minority interest in the company. Although this is not a sale, per se, it can be preliminary to an exit, or provide needed capital to expand the business.

Financial Buyers

The universe of financial buyers has become huge. There are probably 750 to 1,000 U.S. private equity firms with between $150 billion and $200 billion in funds to invest. This is a great avenue to consider, and an investment banker can help you identify the best buyers for your particular firm.

Although private equity firms differ according to their particular character and investment strategy, they generally have told their investors that they will generate a minimum 30 percent annual rate of return. A deal that comes along that falls well short of this level is likely to go quickly into the dustbin. Most firms are also looking for a credible management team and the ability to get their money out within three to five years. They are looking for money makers and good leaders with a proven P&L record and a prior record of success, who have run all facets of a business. Above all, they are looking for people they can trust.

It's important to understand the mechanics of private equity firms so you can understand their motivations. These firms raise funds primarily from large institutional investors, particularly corporate and state pension funds, huge funds made up of retirees' pension dollars. They put most of their assets into stocks and bonds, but generally are allowed to invest 5 to 15 percent of their funds in "alternative assets." These alternative investments include LBO funds, venture capital funds, and real estate funds.

These institutional investors are the masters to whom the private equity firms must answer. When a private equity firm sets up an $800 million fund, each of the institutional investors in that fund has made a commitment to invest at a certain level (usually $20 to $50 million) for a five-year period. They realize these riskier investments can have their downside, but private equity firms must generate returns for their investors in order to guarantee continuing investments. Thus, they face intense pressure to invest their large sums of capital at high rates of return, or they will be put out of business.

Private equity firms pay their own overhead and deal expenses through a management fee of 1.5 to 2 percentage points per year charged to the investors for managing the capital. The professionals at the firm generally get 20 percent of the profits (the "carry," or "carried interest") generated by the investments they make. This piece of the action is the investor's Holy Grail and provides a massive upside incentive for them to do successful deals. You'd be surprised, but private equity firms generally have fairly small staffs, usually ranging from ten to fifteen. KKR, the biggest in the world, might have a staff of forty or fifty people. Everyone is extremely busy managing the existing portfolio of companies and looking for the next big winners.

This means that whenever a new potential deal comes in, there are probably thirty to fifty other deals sitting on the table. Professionals are highly compensated, very busy, and have short attention spans. Owners who want to put together a deal need to be very tenacious in contacting partners. It behooves you to have a very tight presentation. On paper, it should be boiled down to a few pages. On the phone or in person, it should be a direct ten-minute pitch. If the partner isn't interested by that time, it means he is already thinking about the next deal.

The primary reasons for their potential interest in a deal will be location, size, and industry. Location is obvious. Firms like to work on deals that are nearby, so travel times can be minimized. For the same reasons, you should seek out local firms so you don't have to travel as much and have a more accessible partner. Second, on size, most firms will only work on deals of certain ranges. This is typically driven by the amount of money that the firm has under management. A firm with over $800 million under management will need to do deals that require at least $20 million of equity and preferably $50 million. If your deal requires $5 million, be sure to target suitable funds. If it requires $200 million to $500 million of equity, you can now get Henry Kravis's or Ted Forstmann's attention.

Finally, many equity firms specialize in investing in particular industries, typically where the firm's partners have expertise. Some firms specialize only in information technology, health care or consumer products, or even low-tech industries. Some firms, but only a few, focus on turnarounds. Others target industry consolidation plays, backing teams in a series of acquisitions. Check Appendix B-6 and company websites to see which sectors they target, and align your interests with theirs.

During your search, you will want to look at how these firms treat their acquired firms. Are they constructive with employees? Are they overly tough on management? Will they try to change the deal at the end of the day? By talking to people involved in past deals, particularly if the deals were unsuccessful, you should be able to surface these problems. A week before closing, the buyer has much more leverage because it may be hard to unravel the deal, and some buyers will use this leverage to their advantage. So don't just look at the money; look at the chemistry and track record. Go to dinner with the partners to understand where they are coming from. As they become more serious, do reference checks and ask them specifically for the names of CEOs they have fired. This is where you will be able to see what they will really be like as partners in this transaction.

OPTIONS IN THE BUYER UNIVERSE

In addition to looking at financial and strategic buyers, there also are some specific options for selling that are worth considering. For example, some companies sell their business as part of a roll-up, as Leo Mullen did, which sometimes makes them part of a bigger business before they exercise their increased liquidity to make an exit. Sellers also have to consider whether to sell to a large or small firm, and be on the lookout for "lethal" buyers.

Participating in a Roll-Up

In a roll-up, a buyer draws together a number of small businesses in a certain area into a larger firm. Some of these have worked, but historically they have not had a good track record. Given this reality, don't be blinded by the potential upside. It is very hard to integrate a set of different businesses, not only from a financial and operational perspective, but particularly from a cultural perspective. You remember how hard it was to get your own business to work well. The same challenges face the roll-up, but over a much shorter period. Look for people with management experience and a good record of success. If you can get out with cash, as Leo Mullen did when he sold Iconix, it could be a good thing, whether the resulting business is successful or not.

In general, however, the roll-up means turning over control of the business for a stake in the new company. The value of this stake, painted in a glowing picture at the outset, often turns out to be much less than your business is actually worth. You also might continue to be involved in an operating role in the new business. One silver lining to the roll-up for some owners is that in a couple of years, when the business has cratered, they have an opportunity to buy back their old businesses for 10 cents on the dollar. But you can't bank on this strategy, and the pain is often not worth the gain. The moral is to proceed with caution.

Choosing a Big or Small Company

Is it better to sell to a large or small company? There are trade-offs. The large corporation offers stability and, if you take paper, a more predictable stock price. The large company has good resources and a large customer base. The large company will be less price-sensitive and may offer you a better price. But large corporations often are bogged down in bureaucracy, so it can be frustrating. The new business also will have to be absorbed into the large acquirer's culture, which can be a painful process.

Selling to a comparable-sized company may not bring as high a price but may be a better cultural fit, and it may be easier to get the deal done with less red tape. Resources will be more stretched, so the deal might fall apart along the way, as when, for example, financing doesn't come through. As for selling to a private equity firm, that is like selling to a small company, because they tend to be lightly staffed. Look for good management that really understands the business.

Which Buyers to Avoid

There are some buyers you probably don't want to do business with at any price. We've already mentioned the "lethal" competitors. There are also buyers that have reputations for changing the deal close to the time of closing. You also want to avoid litigious buyers if at all possible. Have your law firm do a litigation search on any prospective buyer. Some of them will sue at the drop of a hat. Unless you want to spend all your time in court and all your money on attorneys' fees, you should generally steer clear. Above all, don't be afraid to trust your gut and walk away from a deal that seems right financially but feels wrong. There is very often something you are picking up that is below the surface now—but it will come out in the course of the negotiations.

FINDING BUYERS

Now that we have explored the buyer universe, where do you find the best buyer for your company? As in any other business activity, you can work your own networks to track down the perfect buyer, either through your existing network in your industry or through investors and other channels. Once you get the word out that your business is on the block, deal opportunities start to flow in. The clearer you can be about what makes your business attractive, the more qualified buyers you will find.

You want to start with accounting firms, business brokers, investment bankers, and lawyers with whom you have worked, particularly those with knowledge of your industry. Some can even help you refine your approach to the sale at the same time they are connecting you with potential buyers. They will be in touch with buyers who are looking for opportunities. Each of these sources of deal opportunities has different strengths and motivations for helping you in your search:

• *Business Brokers.* Business brokers are the matchmakers of business world. As the young daughters of Tevye in *Fiddler on the*

Roof discover, however, sometimes these matches are not "the per-fect match." If you want to market your business without paying any fee, brokers are your choice. The buyer pays the fee. In a certain sense, you get what you pay for.

Brokers perform functions similar to investment banking M&A departments but focus primarily on much smaller companies (gener-ally below $50 million revenues). Brokers provide little or no service beyond pure brokerage—bringing buyer and seller together and col-lecting a fee. They are generally small or one-person firms with no research coverage or other investment banking services. Typically, larger firms will seek out a full-service investment bank that will be able to provide research and analysis.

Business brokers typically cold call family-held private compa-nies, and get the owner on the line. They tell the owner they repre-sent buyers interested in companies such as theirs and ask if the owner is interested in discussing a sale. If the owner says no, they are off to the next lead. If the owner says anything that sounds direc-tionally like yes, the broker has a fish on the line. He then calls a handful of potential buyers, normally private equity firms, to say the company is available for sale. When these potential buyers sign a fee agreement, the broker sends them information about the company, and the introduction is made. The broker collects the fee if a sale is consummated in the next year. The broker will normally attend the first meeting or two, but in general the heavy lifting on the deal will be up to you.

Given this process, it is easy to see that many of the businesses offered through brokers are not seriously for sale. Owners have nothing to lose, and so they may test the waters to find out about the sale process and see what their business might be worth. As a buyer, I've sat through many lunches with these tire kickers only to find that they have no intention of ever parting with their compa-nies. Maybe if they could receive three times what the business is worth, they might think about it. As a seller, if you go through a broker, realize that you have done nothing to signal to the buyer that you are serious about nailing down a deal. In fact, using a broker signals just the opposite. Assuming you are not a tire kicker, you need to do everything in your power to let potential buyers know you are serious about selling.

And even though you might not pay anything up front for a broker's services, you could end up paying in the long run. Buyers generally factor the broker fee into their offering price. So when you are weighing using a broker against the expense of an investment banker, don't let price be the primary factor in your decision.

Brokers are sometimes characterized as the used car salesmen of the deal business because they do almost no work in qualifying the buyer or seller. Without checking under the hood, they get the business on the lot and work hard to move it off again. If you have a great business, you'll probably have lots of interest even without a broker. With these caveats, however, brokers can be an important source of buyers that are worth looking at. You can sometimes sell your car on the used car lot and take home the cash! Brokers can sometimes play a very valuable role in bringing buyers and sellers together. In its early days, KKR bought several companies from a business broker in Los Angeles named Harry Roman. Harry did very well, and KKR built the foundation for its empire on these early business-broker opportunities.

• *Accounting and Law Firms.* For most business owners contemplating a sale, the first two people who will hear about it are the company's accountant and lawyer. They might know of potential buyers. Of course, you can also look beyond your own accountants and lawyers to contact other firms that serve the same industry. As close tax advisers to business owners through their auditing and consulting practices, accounting firms may have a direct line on other companies in an industry or buyers looking for opportunities in a particular area.

When contacting an accounting firm, start by searching out audit partners and M&A partners. Most firms now have highly specialized groups in areas such as technology or retail, so be sure to locate the group that specializes in your industry. In addition to the industry experts, the M&A group will see many potential deals.

Contact them next. If you close a deal based on a referral from an accounting firm, you need to find a way to compensate them. Often an advisory fee is acceptable, but more often the best reward is post-transaction audit work. If you need an auditor anyway, hiring the firm that made the suggestion makes sense.

Law firms are generally not a prolific source of contacts with potential buyers, but they occasionally can be, and are therefore worth contacting. Seek out the partners in the firms who focus on corporate work such as securities law and financing issues. If they refer you to a successful deal, you should find a way to compensate them in fees and follow-up legal work for their firm (with the caveat discussed earlier that you need to hire advisers who have experience in the type of deal you are putting together).

• *Consulting Firms.* Because consulting firms are also in close contact with senior executives at large corporations, they can be a good source of leads on potential buyers for your firm. Some large firms such as Bain have set up their own successful private equity groups. Smaller, niche-oriented firms may also have contacts with potential buyers. When approaching consulting firms, contact people as senior in the firm as possible, use personal introductions where you can, and target people in your area of interest.

• *Investment Bankers.* Once involved in the sale process, investment bankers can be a great source of potential buyers. An investment banker who is well versed in your industry will know the heads of corporate development and professionals doing deals for large corporations. The investment banker would know who would be looking to purchase a firm like yours, and the decision makers who can make it happen. This can help you cut to the chase in putting a deal together at a company where you might have trouble getting past the secretaries. They know who really wants to do deals in this space. This is why hiring an investment banker, particularly if you are setting up an auction, can save you a lot of money and time in the long run.

All investment banking firms have specialty groups that focus on specific industries. Be sure to get in front of the group that is focused on your part of the world. Some of them may be working with buyers that are looking for opportunities in your industry. The primary motivation of an investment banker to work with you is the collection of fees from buyers derived from the completion of the transactions. Fees vary widely depending upon the financing or nature of the transaction, but net closing fees usually range between 1 and 2 percent, depending upon the size of the deal.

Also, while you're there, be sure to ask them for their research in the industry you're looking at. They'll give it to you. Further, ask to be put on their research mailing list for paper and electronic distribution. They'll often do it, and it will be extremely valuable to you, now and in the future. They are very busy, so you will likely not get much time with them unless you have a personal relationship.

• *Active and Retired Senior Executives.* Other executives in your industry are often a good source of opportunities. Even former executives continue to be well connected and usually have fewer conflicts in recommending potential buyers. Use your networks in the industry, and ask your contacts for suggestions of other executives to talk with about potential buyers. This can be a great source of inside information specifically targeted to your business area.

• *Industry Associations.* Industry trade publications and trade shows also could be a source of potential buyers. You are probably looking at these anyway, but you might see them through new eyes now that you have a business to sell. If not, go on their websites to see when and where the leading trade shows take place and learn the names of the leading trade publications. You'll make contacts that could lead you to buyers. You might also look to the trade publications and trade shows of your customers and suppliers.

COUNTERINTUITIVE BUYERS

So far, we've rounded up the usual suspects. These are the buyers that are most likely to purchase your business. But the universe is filled with possibilities, so don't be afraid to look a little further out.

Particularly if you are having trouble coming up with a strong pool of buyers, you might need to think more creatively about potential buyers.

This is where your banker's contacts may come in especially handy. In some circumstances, for example, there may be foreign or domestic corporations that are simply looking to acquire a new line of business as a way to diversify their holdings. They could be building an old-line conglomerate, and your business may fit into their puzzle somewhere. While the building of conglomerates is less in vogue, it still happens. It will normally be your banker who has broad enough contacts to know about corporations pursuing a new direction, which can present such an opportunity. There also may be companies that are engaged in some kind of strategic diversification that could make them a potential buyer for your business, even if they are not a current supplier or customer in your current value chain. For example, a print publishing business might seek to acquire an online publishing firm for strategic reasons. An investment banker can be the best place to make such creative leaps across traditional boundaries. However, you too might think more broadly about what types of businesses, related or unrelated, could find your business valuable.

Finally, there are many individuals with very high net worth, who are looking to acquire companies or positions in companies. Like the corporate buyers above, these folks are normally not easy to identify, but they are out there. They often have hired bankers or accountants to help track down deals, and they may have idiosyncratic patterns of investing, so that is another good reason to be out there networking.

MAKING A DEAL

You now have an overview of the buyer universe and where you might find buyers for your business. If you've worked your own networks and other sources, you probably have a good set of financial and strategic buyers who have an interest in buying your firm.

You may also have a group of insiders making an offer. Now you need to narrow the field and put together a deal.

How do you make the best agreement and handle all the diverse details needed to pull off a successful deal? The next chapter discusses the process for handling the many details on the way to a successful sale, as well as keeping your business running and communicating with employees and customers.

NAIL DOWN THE DEAL

Drive to a Sale Without Taking Your Eyes off Your Day Job

NAILING DOWN THE DEAL

What can we learn about handling the details of the deal from the cases presented in Chapter 1?

Homeland Designs: Even after lining up a successful deal, Bill Chambers found that a lot can go wrong on the way to the bank. His buyer exercised an escape clause and left him holding the deal costs.

Iconix: With professional advisers and management, Leo Mullen worked through the details and completed the deal of his life.

Politics & Prose: Many details of the deal were not carefully worked out in advance, which exacerbated problems when the deal went sour. The most significant omission turned out to be the lack of an exit or escape clause for unraveling the deal. This cost many months and many dollars in mediation.

The devil is in the details. To sell your business, you've got to orchestrate a cast of characters, which will feel like you're directing a battle scene in a big-budget Hollywood film. The field will be littered with lawyers, accountants, industry consultants, bankers, and buyers, and you will be out front with your sword raised, leading the charge. You've got schedules and critical paths that look like a NASA launch. You need to manage leaks and information better than a White House press secretary—and you don't always have the luxury of saying "No comment."

It is your deal, the biggest deal of your life, so you are at the center. The buck stops with you. By now, you've lined up a great team of advisers, and they will deal with many of the details, but you need to have an overview of the process so you can understand what's ahead and what can go wrong. This chapter discusses the process of the sale. This includes site visits, presentations, offer letters, letters of intent (or LOIs), working the buyers, disclosure and diligence, customer calls, supplier calls, and management visits. We also examine key documents for the deal, and consider your ongoing involvement in the business as well as what you need to say, and when, to employees and customers.

When you are tearing your hair out sweating these many details, remember that the pain is temporary; the profit is permanent. Deal with all the little devils effectively, and there will be a little slice of heaven on the other side.

A FEW IMPORTANT CONSIDERATIONS

Since you're a diligent reader of this book, before you have begun selling discussions with your buyer, you have done all the careful groundwork:

1. You have groomed a strong management team or successor who can take over when you step back.

2. You have at least three years of audited financials from a respected firm.

3. You have diligently consulted your tax advisers, wealth management professionals, and legal counsel to make sure you avoid any minefields.

4. You have long since considered the gifting laws to ensure a tax-efficient exchange of ownership (as discussed in Chapter 9).

Before diving into the details, consider a few general observations about putting together a deal:

• *Don't get greedy.* Remember, you started with nothing, and if you push for more than you deserve, you may end up with nothing (or less than nothing given the costs of setting up the deal). It's easy to get carried away in the deal process and push too hard. While you want the best deal, don't forget that the buyer could choose to walk if the deal is no longer attractive.

• *Be patient, something will go wrong.* There are many issues the buyer will be examining during the due diligence process. (Appendix A-7 contains a fairly thorough checklist of due diligence issues, so you can see where you might need to pay attention and what the many different areas are where a problem might occur.) With the range of issues under consideration and the fact that a living, working business has so much complexity, there are many ways for something to go wrong. In completing more than fifty deals, I've often thought I've seen them all, and yet each new deal comes up with something new. There will be many surprises during the diligence process. Few of them will be pleasant. More unexpected troubles come out of the woodwork than relatives at a millionaire's funeral.

For example, in one deal for a $275 million company, we found that there was a single European investor who had bought only $160,000 in preferred stock more than six years earlier, but had a "change-of-control" provision in the contract. No one in the firm knew of this obligation until the lawyers turned over the rock, and there it was. When the issue arose, we didn't even know exactly where this investor lived.

After hiring a private investigation firm, we tracked him down in

Switzerland and had to fly over to see him. We told him we had excellent news, that we were cleaning up a few little financial matters and that we could pay for his shares with a $10,000 premium. In this case, the proposal worked, but we were sweating bullets to the end. It pays to look for "change-of-control" agreements, ownership of intellectual property, and other loose ends before they come up in the buyer's due diligence. If you do know about them, get them on the table. Remember the mantra: All will be disclosed.

- *Handle bad news head-on.* If you find out bad news on your own, you need to share it as quickly as possible. If you try to sweep something under the rug, it will end up being a bigger problem later. Get the bad news on the table early and deal with it as quickly and cleanly as possible. If there is a complaint that comes up during the diligence process, don't become defensive. Take it calmly, and put together a strategy to deal with it.

For example, what if a member of your management team had been convicted of a felony? That might not seem like something you'd go out of your way to share with a prospective buyer. But in one deal I worked on, the sellers did just that. They revealed a prior felony conviction of a manager to buyers fairly early in the process. It didn't derail the deal. In fact, instead of being a ding to their trust, this revelation helped to establish open communications and allowed them to deal with it openly. If the owner hadn't put it on the table and it came out in later diligence, it could very well have been a deal breaker.

- *Pay attention in the early stages.* Many key documents start out as one-page agreements that are nonbinding, later expand to more detailed documents that are more binding, and finally end up as legal treatises that are irrefutable law. That three-page letter of intent that you thought you could "adjust" later has now been enshrined in stone and is about as easy to change as the Ten Commandments. That is why it is almost always a mistake to put off crucial issues of the deal until later.

What should you as owner be looking for when all these documents come sailing into your hands? The main issue is to make sure that all the agreements will work from a business perspective. Don't get tied up in the minutiae of the legal issues. Instead, focus on their strategic implications. Will they really achieve the overall goals you have for the sale and the business after the sale? These are the issues that as a manager you can see most easily but are either outside the knowledge or outside the scope of the review of lawyers and other partners.

Even after reading this book, you may be one of the least knowledgeable people at the table about doing a deal of this type. But rather than focusing on your lack of knowledge about the deal process, apply the specific knowledge you have about your business and industry and your own goals. Trust your own gut and don't let the experts bully you. Remember, it is your business and your deal. Make sure everything you agree to passes your own personal smell test. The experts, even the best of them, will walk away to other deals. You will continue to live with the outcome of this one.

FULL DISCLOSURE

You've taken care of the big picture. But many owners are still unprepared for the many niggling details involved in selling a business successfully. In the process of conducting due diligence, the buyer or buyers will have a lot of people crawling all over your firm as if their careers and fortunes depend upon it (they often do). You can be guaranteed that there will be teams of experts looking for any skeletons in the closets. If you are not Jeffrey Dahmer, you may not have anything serious to worry about. But the search will still be disruptive, and about as uncomfortable as a trip to the dentist or a proctology exam. You will have to assemble documents and answer lots of tough questions. And you have to give this your full attention, because any of these details could sink the deal.

What is usually most shocking and uncomfortable about the due diligence process for owners is its "forensic nature." Teams of three or four accountants go over work papers. Lawyers go through all agreements. The buyer calls ten references and then asks those ten for less favorable references. The buyer does personal credit checks and background checks on management.

This analysis can even go right into the private lives of managers. Companies routinely hire consultants to do criminal investigations of managers (with their knowledge, of course). This investigation shows outstanding credit card balances and any felony or misdemeanor criminal charges. It also confirms job history, which should match with the resumes that were submitted earlier in the process. There are no secrets. Got a manager with a drinking or gambling problem? It could come out in this process. If there is any dirt in your firm, it could be out on the front page faster than celebrity gossip in a supermarket tabloid. There will also be site visits to company offices and plants and customer background checks.

In addition to general areas of diligence, there are some areas that are specific to a particular industry. A steel manufacturer will have to sweat environmental issues. A retailer will need to specify when leases expire. In an IT services firm, professional turnover will be the central concern.

THE SALE PROCESS

How do you get the sale done? Now that you've identified the universe of potential buyers, as discussed in Chapter 7, the next step is to pick out *the* buyer for your sale. An investment banker, if you've retained one, will get the business in front of buyers, and manage the prescreening. This will typically result in a pool of up to fifty prospective buyers (depending on the business and market). During the sale process, this field is narrowed down to a small number of very interested buyers, so that you have at least two (and, better yet, three or four) in the final horse race. At each stage of the process, the field is narrowed, as illustrated in Figure 8-1. (All the numbers and times are ballparks, but they give you a sense of what the typical process will look like.)

The process might start 90 days out from closing when you or your investment banker put out a teaser to let potential buyers know that the business is up for sale. This could go to about seventy buy-

FIGURE 8-1. NARROWING THE FIELD.

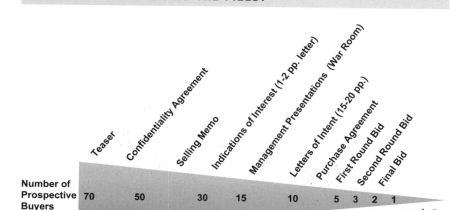

ers, twenty-five strategic and forty-five financial ones. Of these, about fifty might return a signed confidentiality agreement, which allows them to review basic information about the company as well as the *selling memo* you've developed with your advisers. This selling memo should be simple and punchy. Your advisers will help, but you should be the one to write this because you probably feel the most passion for the business.

About 60 days out, you'll receive *indications of interest* from maybe thirty potential buyers. These letters, typically about one to two pages, outline their broad interest as well as a price range that they'd consider fair for the business. These price ranges tend to be a bit inflated, but they give you a sense of the ballpark.

Of these thirty, maybe fifteen will be invited to come to the company for *presentations* by management ten days later. At the same time, you'll set up your offsite *war room* (discussed below) with all the key documents for the sale. You can also put together your own draft of the *purchase agreement.* While buyers will certainly revise this, by drafting it first, you get to frame the key issues and define the starting point. It will be your wish list.

Potential buyers and their advisers will be combing over documents in the war room and requesting information as they begin the process of putting together their *letters of intent*. These are more detailed letters, maybe 15 to 20 pages, describing their offer. While not binding, they will form the basis for the later *purchase agreement*, so they should be considered very carefully. You might receive ten letters back, and then invite five of these buyers to participate in the first round of bidding. By the second round of bidding, you will have narrowed the field to three, and then there might be one final bid from the two strongest buyers. All the time, the investment banker will be making the rounds, urging buyers to "sharpen their pencils."

The number of buyers you attract may not be this high. It depends on your industry and when you go to market. Don't be discouraged. Remember that while you might like to have four or five buyers participate in the first bid, you only need two to have a horse race, and one motivated buyer to make a good sale. There may be important reasons not to hold an auction, such as protecting employees or the integrity of the business, making a smooth transition, or ensuring your own continuing role within the business. For these or other reasons, you might choose to accept a fair price without surveying the whole market. But if you end up with several interested and qualified buyers, an auction could be the best way to make the choice.

Preparing the War Room

The "war room" (or "data room," for those who prefer less militaristic images) is the focal point for the buying process. It is usually set up in an off-site hotel or office building to avoid alarming staff and customers. Into this room go copies of every relevant document needed to review the deal. More documents are pulled in by the barrelful during the process. These include primary customer contracts, primary supply contracts, leases, lawsuits, articles of incorporation, insurance documents, 401K plans, all audits for the last four years, primary management reports, employment contracts, and recent industry analyses. This room becomes the center of the deal, with auditors, lawyers, investment partners, and others buzzing like bees around a hive.

It is important to manage access to the war room carefully so that key documents do not walk out. Buyers and their advisers will often ask to make copies of certain documents. This is sometimes OK. Your law firm will typically assign a low-level clerk to monitor the traffic and requests. The clerk will know which documents can be copied and which should never leave the room.

What will buyers be looking for in this process? They will be concerned with many issues during the due diligence process, including:

- *Legal.* Are there legal issues that could create problems later? Lawyers will be scanning supply contracts and real estate, environmental, and other agreements. They also will be developing and refining the key documents for the deal.

- *Accounting.* Are numbers what you say they are? Accountants for the buyer will be picking over the numbers to look for problems. Your accountants will also be busy. What audits will be needed and on what timeline?

- *Management Team.* As noted above, extensive background checks and references on the management team are par for the course if they are going to continue to run the business after the deal. And they'll look at any golden parachute agreements or other arrangements. Make sure they are ready.

- *Insurance/Benefits.* The buyer may hire a third-party insurance review firm to look at pension plans, 401K, workers' compensation reserves, D&O insurance, and other issues that might create risks. Are there insurance risks that could create problems later, or are there opportunities to improve the insurance costs? All the large insurers, such as AON and Marsh & McLennan, have groups that specifically analyze transactional insurance risks.

These are just a few of the issues that will be scrutinized in the diligence process. The more you can anticipate and prepare to answer these questions—looking at your business like a buyer—the better you will be prepared to give clear and compelling answers.

Sometimes the march of technology can be extremely helpful to getting your deal done. One important recent advance is the "Digital or Virtual War Room," where all of the documents important to the deal are scanned onto a disk and sent out to prospective buyers or posted to a secure Internet site. This is a terrific development because it eliminates all of the back-and-forth to the copier and a fair amount of travel. Now the documents come to you, when you want them. This is technology at its best. The only downside is that it is a little harder to segregate very sensitive documents, but that can be handled in separate files.

AGREEMENTS WITH THE BUYER

Your relationship with the buyer begins innocently enough with a *Letter of Intent*. It is usually a fairly simple agreement but forms the foundation for the deal. The process then moves on to a more formal *Purchase Agreement*. While detailed samples of major agreements with the buyer appear in Appendix A, here we discuss some of the major issues that need to be addressed in these agreements, including consideration, role of the owner after the sale, confidentiality and nonsolicitation agreements, and the representations and warranties you make to the buyer.

Consideration

Obviously, in all these early documents, price is the fundamental issue. But another important issue to address is the *consideration* (meaning how payments will be broken out between cash, notes, earn-outs, or equity). For example, there might be a provision for the owner to take 20 to 30 percent of the deal back in a debt instrument of some type, which can be advantageous for financing and boost the credibility of the new company. We've discussed some of these options already, including the positives and negatives of seller's notes and earn-outs.

Specifying Your Role

The agreements also typically specify the owner's role after the sale, as well as include noncompete clauses to protect the buyer. As owner, you might have a formal position in the newly acquired business, for a period of time, or have a paid consulting contract to ensure a smooth transition. These contracts are often made in consideration of lower payments at the time of the transfer, reducing the initial cost to the buyer and signaling a smooth transition to customers. This also gives the owner an ongoing, if mostly symbolic, financial interest in the company. Instead of paying $750,000 cash up front, the buyer pays $250,000 per annum to you to consult with the company for the next three years. In the covenant-not-to-compete, the buyer typically pays a certain amount each year as an inducement for you not to compete. These approaches can be viable ways to distribute purchase price over time rather than paying it up front, but be sure to have your accountants review any such agreements.

Confidentiality and Nonsolicitation Agreements

Before showing your financials and other documents, have the buyer sign a confidentiality agreement. (For a sample, see Appendix A-2.) Usually these agreements are routine. Once the deal is terminated, all the material must be returned or destroyed. The information needs to be kept in confidence for a specified period, usually a year and sometimes longer. The agreements usually also require the potential buyer not to solicit employees from the company during the period covered. (People have become very cavalier about these documents, but my advice is: Don't be. These are serious and meaningful agreements and should be treated as such.)

How long should the "tail" be on these agreements? Usually a year is plenty. With the pace of change in business today, most information is pretty useless within a year. If you are selling a public company, you'll also want to ask for a *standstill agreement*, which means that the potential buyer can't buy stock in the company during negotiations. You might need an even shorter tail on this agreement, maybe three to six months.

The language on nonsolicitation of employees should not be too broad. It should clearly read that the potential buyer should not actively "solicit" or recruit current employees. If, however, employees quit, the buyer typically should have the right to hire them. This is particularly important in a strategic sale where buyers in a similar business will have extensive contact with your top management during the development of the deal.

Remember that the confidentiality agreement, like all agreements, is negotiable. As with all negotiations, you need to clearly identify up front any points that are important to you, and be prepared to give a little on points that are less important. Let the other side feel good about winning a few points.

Pay attention to what happens during discussions of these "minor" agreements. The negotiations related to this simple agreement can tell you worlds about how the big deal is going to go. These discussions show you whether this buyer is realistic and whether there will be a deal. You will have to work out very tricky issues over the next few months, so don't just look at the numbers. Look for signs that the buyer will be easy to work with. Pay attention to body language and signals. It may still be easy to get out at this point or go with another buyer.

Representations and Warranties

Among the primary issues covered in both the letter of intent and the final purchase agreement are your *representations and warranties* about the business. As seller, you represent that the assets are in good quality and that the financials are accurate. You also represent that you control the assets, that you have the right and ability to transfer them to the buyer, that you have done nothing out of the ordinary to affect the assets or liabilities, that you have no specific litigation outstanding other than specifically noted, and that there are no material changes on the horizon other than those written out in closing schedules appended to the final purchase agreement.

On the other side, buyers represent that they have all the authorizations and capital necessary to close the transaction. Unless buyers have the money for the deal in their pocket, capital commitments normally come together only at the end of a deal. At this point, however, you need to see that they are lined up. Buyers almost always have financial outs until very near closing, or at least until the time of the signed purchase agreement. Keep this in mind during the process, because if the buyer doesn't come up with the money, you could be back to square one. Don't burn any bridges before you know that you have reached the other side.

The selling documents also specify how financial disputes related to the company and the deal are to be handled in the future, after closing. This is where, even if you have a good lawyer, you need to pay attention as a manager, because many of these thresholds and time frames vary by industry and business. For example, many documents will have a dollar threshold for taking action against the seller or a time limit on seller responsibility. In general, there is a "basket" of stuff that is too small to bother with. You don't want the buyer coming back to argue over nickels and dimes after the deal. On a $100 million deal, you might set up a $250,000 basket, below which the buyer group agrees to assume incremental costs. As owner, you may know that this is either too low or too high, so you might need to change the threshold. If you have a good argument for doing so, this should be possible.

Representations also have a lifespan, so specifying survival is very important. In some deals, the owner may make representations for one year, beyond which the buyer can't call to pursue any misrepresentations and monetary damages. Several representations, such as those relating to environmental issues and tax issues, which can haunt you for many years to come and are hard to evaluate, stand in perpetuity or for a ten-year period. The buyer may know that, because of your business cycles, problems might not surface until 18 months after the transfer. In that case, the buyer will typically push to extend the representations and warranties to at least 24 months. These are just a few of the cases in which strategic issues may affect the shape of the deal. For every document that comes by, carefully consider the strategic implications.

Despite the rumors of a paperless society, deals continue to generate more paper than ever. By the end of most deals, there will be files two feet thick and a massive leather-bound book of legal documents that looks like it could have been written by Leo Tolstoy. (Some of the documents actually read like Russian.) Samples of some of the less detailed versions of these documents appear in Appendix A.

KEEPING THE BUSINESS RUNNING

While all this is going on, you can't lose sight of your day-to-day business. You need to continue to communicate carefully with managers, employees, and customers as the deal progresses. But the timing of this communication can make or break the deal, so proceed with caution. Mishandling communications can create uncertainty among employees and defections by managers, and damage relationships with key customers, all of which can have a detrimental impact on the business or even undermine the deal. Aside from the death of its founder, probably the hardest transition to make in the life of a business is the sale of the company.

As we discussed in Chapter 1, Barbara Meade and Carla Cohen of Politics & Prose found out how important communication was when they brought in a new partner who was expected to take over their independent bookstore. In their case, communication with employees was more important than ever, because the employees acted as owners of their sections of the stores. They were experts in fiction, historical works, or children's books, with long relationships with customers. There were no secrets. Employees were treated like family. But when the owners started preparing for the sale of the business, all that changed.

While informing employees too soon can create unnecessary turmoil, lack of openness can sometimes cause more problems. As discussed in Chapter 1, the new partner at Politics & Prose ended up leaving the business, at significant cost to the firm. How much transparency should there be in the process?

Go to Managers First

The best thing to do in my judgment is to tell your senior-most people first, as soon as you are fairly sure you wish to sell the business and even before you have started looking for buyers or lining up members of the team. They need to be on board and know what is going on. Unless the business is a one-person show, you have to consider top managers as part of the team that will be involved in selling the business with you. But don't sit down with managers until you know the answers to two key questions:

1. What's in it for them?
2. Can they compete to buy the company?

On the first question, I am a big proponent, as noted earlier, of offering a sale or "stay" bonus for your senior managers. You will need them on your team to get a sale done and will want them to be as enthusiastic as possible. Carve off a percentage of the proceeds in a dollar amount that is meaningful to each key player and tell them they will get it on sale. This will keep them engaged and motivated, as well as compensate them for all the extra hassle involved in having potential buyers poking around the business. It will also encourage them to stick around if they decide that your exit from the business is a sign that they should get their own resumes out. Departures of key personnel can be damaging to a deal. So a stay bonus may be some of the best money you can spend.

As to whether you want to give managers a shot at buying the company in the process, that is not an easy call. It can make sense to allow it, but realize that in a certain sense they will then become a competitor in the bidding. This can lead to conflicts with outside buyers. If you believe the sale is likely to go to a strategic buyer, there is little point in having managers distracted with mounting their own bid. If it is likely to go to a private equity firm, your managers will be included in the process in any case, and you can encourage them to bid. Private equity firms usually will include them in the deal as the next tier of leadership to keep them motivated after the sale.

What to Tell Other Employees

How much you tell other employees and customers depends very much on the nature of your culture and your business. If you decide to have complete transparency, be prepared for the fact that employees may react to every hiccup in the process (and there will be many) and may have strong opinions about potential buyers. This can make the process more difficult, and employees could sabotage your plans. Think about the downsides of disclosure. What would happen if employees know about a potential sale and it falls through? What would happen to the business if the deal process drags on for months and months? Will employees be able to cope with a long period of uncertainty?

This is why owners often choose to treat deals as covert operations until they are able to announce them to employees, customers, suppliers, and the world. Unless the company has publicly put itself up on the auction block, an announcement that a deal is in the works will just unsettle the organization. Employees will either go into a holding pattern, waiting to see what happens, or they will preemptively jump ship. Customers will worry about signing contracts or will put off purchases to see what happens. It is best not to disclose what is in the works until the deal is firmly agreed upon and you can clearly see the finish line for completing it.

A deal is pretty easy to keep quiet when it is just a few small discussions over lunch or dinner. But once the plan starts to unfold, it takes a little more ingenuity. Managers use the following approaches:

• *Craft a cover story.* Any employee with a pulse will know *something* is up when all these suits show up in the business at once. The e-mails and the rumors will fly. You can't ignore them, but you can explain them. Management usually creates a cover story. As noted earlier, the most common story is that the company is working on getting some new financing, a fresh infusion of capital to drive growth.

Customers and suppliers also may get nervous about dealing with the company. In particular, when the buyer does customer reference checks, it is likely to arouse suspicion. These customer calls are usually done by an outside consultant under the guise of a customer satisfaction survey. While this is useful information to buyers—who, after all, are interested in knowing how customers feel about the company—it just doesn't explain to customers *why* the company is suddenly interested in customer satisfaction. Even with the cover story, customers might be suspicious about such moves. Does the firm have customer problems? Is something else afoot? That is why these external reference checks should be done as close as possible to the consummation of the deal.

• *Set up the war room.* To keep the diligence process a secret, you need to contain it. As discussed above, companies usually set up a war room at a hotel, an offsite office, or a hidden conference room, where potential buyers can go over company information without raising eyebrows.

• *Invite in a few insiders.* In addition to top managers, a small group of insiders from the finance department will need to be involved in pulling together the necessary information to sell the business. While all the troops may not know the details of the operation, you will need a few insiders who are not partners in the deal. Usually these added insiders sign nondisclosure agreements, and so they know that if they talk about the deal, they are history. (On one management buyout, a tight-lipped finance person spent so many late nights at the office that his wife suspected him of having an affair. Because of his nondisclosure agreement, he couldn't allay her fears until after the deal was concluded.)

• *Save sensitive information for last.* As in any situation in which the company is disclosing very sensitive information, save the most sensitive stuff for last. As noted above, the customer calls should be held until late in the process because they arouse suspicion. Don't reveal strategic pricing information until everything else is in place.

• *Be prepared for the leak.* Despite your best efforts, it's still possible that there will be a leak and that employees and customers will learn about the deal. All you can do about this is to make plans to address leaks as they occur. Most important, be prepared for your employee communications by writing an internal memo *before* the news breaks. Also be prepared with fact sheets on the deal and key talking points, so your employees, customers, and suppliers understand the rationale for the transaction and its inherent selling points. In the best of all worlds, you won't need these documents until *you* are ready to break the news. But if there is a leak, you will be able to move quickly and coherently. Many missteps are made because of hastily assembled communications or long delays that create anxiety and uncertainty among employees and customers.

Talking to Customers

When do you talk to customers? Customers will always be skittish about change. The traditional answer is to wait till you know you have a deal with the buyer. Then you can arrange a face-to-face meeting with key customers to introduce the buyer and provide the comfort, continuity, and confidence in the financial strength of the business. You'll also be able to tell customers about key managers who will continue with the business and your own role in the months or years after the sale.

If you do have concerns about a large customer reacting badly to a sale, you may want to go to them in advance to solicit their buy-in. This can be tricky. You have to think through how you will respond if they say: "We hate that idea!" It's all a judgment call, but in general it is best to go to them as late as possible, when the deal is done. As with managers, make sure you can tell them what is good for them in the sale. They'll be a lot happier if the situation has some upside.

Also, as a side note, be aware that once your competitors get wind of the sale, they will do all they can to use the sale of the company against you (another reason to restrict news to a small group of insiders). They will be the first to spread the rumor that the sale is a sign that "the company is falling apart." They will spread various tales about how the company will be way overleveraged after the deal, that service will suffer and, what's more, that the sky is falling. If they can, they will present the sale as a fire sale and a sign of desperation, and the new owners as jackals. Do not be surprised when this happens. It is just competitive nature. But be prepared. And remember: Loose lips sink ships.

Most of the time, the signing of the purchase agreement is the point at which the company needs to communicate to customers, suppliers, employees, and the world. Even though the bank agreements will not be finalized at that time, there are rarely problems in translating credit agreements into final covenants. (If you anticipate problems here, you might want to wait until the wires have actually changed hands to make the announcement, but this would give employees and customers a few more weeks of nervous anticipation.) By the time the purchase agreement is nailed down, almost everyone knows something is up, and what they imagine may be pretty bleak.

Companies that are not concerned about this kind of turmoil inside and outside the organization sometimes choose to announce that a division of the company is up for sale before they have any agreement or even buyers. The announcement itself is sometimes used to flush out potential buyers and get a bidding war started. But it is a risky strategy, given the potential reactions of customers, employees, and competitors, which may not be easy to anticipate.

DOWN TO THE WIRE

If you've navigated this process, you should be sitting across the table from the buyer, with lawyers, bankers, and other advisers assembled around you. As you sign the last document, you are ready to celebrate. Now, all you have to do is wait for the wire. The wire! Suddenly your bank account is going to be hit with the largest tsunami to ever wash over it. Are you ready to deal with this kind of wealth? And, you are soon going to be out of a job—if you are not already by the time the ink is dried. Now that you've successfully completed the biggest deal of your life, is your work over? Hardly! You still have to figure out what to do with your money—and your life. The following two chapters examine the challenges of postsale wealth management and life management. You've worked hard to get to this point. Do the work now to make sure you enjoy it.

MAKE THE MOST OF YOUR MONEY

Investing Wisely and Avoiding the Tax Man

INVESTING WISELY

What can we learn about managing wealth from the cases presented in Chapter 1?

Iconix: Leo Mullen and Helene Patterson worked with investment advisers from Friedman Billings Ramsey & Co (FBR) to plan and execute a strategy for wealth preservation.

For this chapter we are indebted to the input of several outstanding domain experts. First, we thank the terrific team from Goldman Sachs's Private Wealth Management Group, led by Scott Belveal, along with Steve Torbeck and Cristina Hug. We also very much appreciate the expert insights of Molly James of Hogan and Hartson LLP, and Michael Kennedy of PricewaterhouseCoopers. If there is useful advice on these pages, it is their doing. While we are grateful for their assistance, any mistakes are entirely our own. And, as noted below, these insights are not to be construed as formal investment advice. They are merely intended to point the way for discussions with experienced investment and tax advisers. Even so, they can identify opportunities to save you millions of dollars.

A Disclaimer: This chapter deals not only with managing your wealth postsale, but also with some very important concepts related to family wealth transfer and tax planning in advance of the sale. It is sad to say, but the understatement of the century is that "the tax code is complicated." I take that back. The tax law is

> **Homeland Designs** and **Politics & Prose:** Since the deals have not been completed, they are waiting for "substantial liquidity" to happen.

You've sold your business! You deserve congratulations, but your work is not yet over. The first challenge you have is that you now have more money than you've ever had in your life. This is a good challenge to have, but a challenge nonetheless. The minute you sell your business, you now have a new job, managing that huge pile of cash. While you may have experience with wealth management at some level, the sale of a business will ratchet it up a few notches. This chapter examines wealth management and tax implications of a sale, drawing upon the expert advice of consultants from Goldman Sachs, PricewaterhouseCoopers, and Hogan & Hartson. It will show you how to manage your money before the sale, during the transaction, and after the sale—to maximize your returns and minimize your headaches.

As with any financial matters, a little advance planning can have an impact—from the thousands that might be at stake in timing your wiring instructions to the millions that might be at stake in transferring wealth to children or a foundation. There are two very important concepts, addressed below, which can save your overall estate, and that of your heirs, millions of dollars in federal taxes. We also discuss strategies for selecting an investment adviser and insights on designing your portfolio.

JOIN SAM'S CLUB: GIVE AWAY THE BUSINESS BEFORE THE SALE

Why are Sam Walton's heirs so rich? The *Forbes 400* list sometimes looks like a Walton family reunion. Five Walton heirs are among the

---

"impossible, unruly, incoherent, senseless, really devoid of logic, and a ridiculous waste of time." I'll spare you my views on the federal government, and leave that for my next book. Suffice it to say that our tax code is massively complex and changing weekly. From the time this sentence is written until you read this book, the code will have changed many times. (This book deals with savings only in federal taxes. As each state has different tax laws, the opportunity to analyze and pay state taxes is left to you and your expert advisers.)

My point here is that on tax issues, just as on legal issues, you must consult an expert to get *correct and timely advice*. I am not a tax expert and am not herewith providing you with tax or investment advice. I am, top ten wealthiest Americans. Is it because Sam flew his own plane and drove a beat-up pickup truck? Is it because he and his executives stayed only in budget motels? Good genes?

Well, first of all, Sam built a massive company. Second, however, he was smart, generous, and *forward-thinking* in "gifting" valuable, low-basis stock in Wal-Mart to his heirs. When Wal-Mart was still a relatively small company, worth a million or so dollars, Sam gave percentages away to his children. One percent of a million-dollar Wal-Mart a few decades ago is worth many billions today. This value was transferred outside of gift and estate taxes because it was given at a low value.

Many owners don't think about investment and tax issues until after the sale. This is a big mistake, but a common one. You are so caught up in the work of setting up the sale, finding a buyer, and keeping the business running, it is not until someone asks you for wiring instructions that it dawns on you that you need to manage this fortune that has suddenly arrived at your doorstep. I urge you to think about this early and often. It could help save you and your heirs money and will certainly offer a smoother road to retirement.

The gifting laws are a terrific value creator and should be used diligently by any successful person whose goal is not to give his money away to the federal government. (I suspect this includes all of us!) Transfer gifting allows an individual to give value (in stock or cash) to individuals *without paying an estate tax.* Of course, there are limitations. As of this writing in 2006, an individual donor has a lifelong maximum ability to gift $1 million of value to heirs or others ($2 million total for a married couple) exempt from gift tax. In addition to this lifetime exemption, donors can make tax-free gifts of $12,000 *per individual per year* (or $24,000 per couple), called the "gift tax annual exclusion," so starting early can greatly increase tax-free wealth transfers.

At death, each individual's estate is exempt from death tax up to

---

however, providing you with important concepts and general principles, which are valid as of this writing and can potentially save your estate millions of dollars.

    Like a Grand Canyon river guidebook, I can point out the hazards and clear passages to help you avoid capsizing. You'll know what to expect and enjoy the journey more. But this is no substitute for an experienced guide to take you through the rapids. Do not try to do this on your own.

a total of $2 million. (The maximum is going up to $3.5 million in 2009 before dropping back to $1 million, adjusted for inflation, in 2011.) This total at death includes any use of the gift-tax exception during the lives of donors. So, if an individual with a properly structured estate plan who has given away the full $1 million tax-free during his lifetime can give away an additional $1 million at death, without paying death tax. In addition, depending on the number of people given annual exclusion gifts, and the number of years these gifts are made, total lifetime gifts can far exceed $1 million.

What might this mean in real dollars? Using today's tax rates, consider the following simplified example: Say your company is worth $2 million and you would like to transfer some value to a son or daughter. You and your wife could gift $100,000 of value, or 5 percent of the company, to your heir, tax-free, in the five years preceding the sale. Now, suppose over time, the company grows to be worth $20 million and is sold for cash. At this time, the heir's interest is worth $1 million pretax. At the time of the sale, the heir must pay a capital gains tax (today at 15 percent) on the $900,000 gain, or $135,000. The heir then ends up with a total of $865,000. Nice work if you can get it. (This assumes, of course, that the tax basis of the annual gift at the time of the gift is $100,000, as property has the same basis in the hands of the recipient as in the hands of the donor. This can get quite complicated and should be discussed with a competent adviser.)

Had the business owner waited until after the sale to transfer the same 5 percent interest in the company, without any "gift" component, you or your estate would have paid a much higher price—a federal estate tax of 45 percent rather than the 15 percent capital gains tax. Instead of paying $135,000, as in the above scenario, the estate and gift tax would now be $450,000. The heir would be left with just $550,000 instead of $865,000. This is a loss of $315,000 just because the owner didn't look ahead! Due to poor gift planning, the Feds were given over three hundred grand. (We are all patriotic, but seriously!)

The difference here is roughly 30 percent, or the difference between the capital gains and estate tax rates. Thus, the careful gift program saves 30 percent overall. By gifting smartly, Sam Walton literally saved his heirs *billions* of dollars of federal taxes and then created billions of dollars of value for his overall estate. Way to go, Sam! Call it the 30 percent gift bonus, and use it wisely. It is one of the few places where the tax code is working for you.

In fact, the patriarch may even transfer more than 50 percent of the ownership to children and other family members. Should the company be concerned about the kids going wild once they have a controlling interest? The trick is to transfer shares without transferring control. With experienced legal advice, this is often done by creating voting shares and nonvoting shares, and then keeping the "voting" shares in the owner's hands as long as possible. This approach also can be used when the owner wants to give equity in the business to family members while avoiding their meddling. The money moves first, and the vote moves to the kids last. An additional benefit to the use of nonvoting interest is that it lowers the value of the interest for gift tax purposes so that more of the business can be gifted within the gift exemption limits.

Can you do the same thing with managers? Sorry, but if you give money to managers in this way (even those within the family), the IRS will see it as compensation and tax it accordingly.

By the way, gifting also works in transferring stock into trusts to benefit your heirs. And your spouse (but not you) may control these trusts after the transfer. On all matters like this, of course, consult your tax and legal experts.

Establishing a Dynasty

Since the direct gifts to children and other family members, free of estate taxes, are limited to $1 million in a lifetime, with a larger death tax exemption, larger gifts take more ingenuity. Obviously, giving early, as Sam Walton did, can help, because the value of the business will only grow after the sale. A dynasty trust, or generation-skipping trust, is one tool to send wealth to generations beyond your own children while avoiding taxes. The *generation-skipping tax* in essence levies a tax for each generation, meaning that a gift from a grandmother to granddaughter is taxed twice, even if the grand-child's parents never touch the funds. A dynasty trust avoids the generation-skipping tax, which significantly reduces the tax burden.

It is never too early to think about such mechanisms. "Right when you set up the business, it might be a good idea to set up something like this," said Molly James of Hogan & Hartson. Trans-ferring the money early creates an "estate freeze," holding the value for transfer tax purposes and allowing all appreciation to pass gift- and tax-free.

How Do You Determine the Value?

We have covered valuation in Chapter 6, but offer a brief word here about valuation for gifting purposes. In general, if you value a pri-vate business before it goes up for sale, the value will be lower, and perhaps significantly so. But once you have an actual agreement with the buyer, that will set the value. There are many considerations, such as size, profitability, and the inherent liquidity (or lack thereof) in the stock. For example, what is a small piece of a private company worth? Not necessarily a lot, particularly if there is no market. The bottom line, though, is that you need to have a professional business appraiser or valuation firm—such as Marshall Stephens, Standard & Poors, or Houlihan Lokey—to determine the value for the purpose of the gift transfer. (We list a few in Appendix B-2.)

There are many firms that can value your business, such as re-gional investment banks or small-company specialists. The primary advice is to pick a well-known name. While it may be a bit more expensive at the time, the brand name will truly stand up better should there be any IRS scrutiny in the future. The valuation needs to be supported by appropriate analysis and be consistent with a rough market value of the company at the time of transfer. It is well worth the time and cost to have a professional valuation. When gifted, closely held stock can be valued at a 20 to 30 percent dis-count to the valuation level due the difficulty of transferring minority interests. There is a lot of case law on this, but again, seek the advice of a professional.

GIVING WISELY TO CHARITY: IF YOU WANT TO HELP THE TREE SLOTHS, DON'T DAWDLE

Headline to business seller: If you are going to transfer some business value to a charitable foundation, *do it in the same tax year in which your company is sold*. We heard the story recently of a business owner who sold his company near the end of the year. After the sale, he suddenly realized he wanted to set up a charitable foundation and spent the holiday season doing it just under the wire to meet the December 31 deadline. There are better ways to spend your holidays. Many business owners look forward to the luxury of making long, slow decisions about their philanthropic gifts. Well, take your time deciding how to give the money away—but get it into a foundation as soon as possible. This will make the whole transition much smoother—and could save you millions.

Why is it important to get the proceeds into a foundation in the same calendar year? This is again due to our friendly tax code—and it can involve tens of millions of dollars. This all relates to your ability to use tax planning. People don't always focus on it (they should!), but tax deductions *are not useful if you cannot use them*. This may seem obvious. But since time can only move in one direction, it is a mistake that many people make. And it is impossible to correct after the fact.

Here's the issue. For most business owners, their biggest income year will be the year in which they sell their business. After a sale, annual income may go way down, thus dramatically reducing taxes, and the ability to use tax deductions. Suppose you are selling your company for $10 million. Usually nearly all of this amount is treated as capital gains. So, without careful planning, you will pay 15 percent, or $1.5 million, in gains taxes. Suppose you would like to reduce your taxes and prepare to do good by establishing your own charitable foundation. You decide, for example, that you would like to give $3 million to set up a fund for a U.S.–based charity to support research on endangered three-toed tree sloths. (After all, it is your money, and you have the right.)

You might think that this charitable gift to your new foundation is fully tax-deductible, thereby saving you $450,000 (15 percent) in taxes. Well, it is not fully deductible. There are limitations. The limit (as of this writing) is that you can deduct a maximum of 30 percent of your adjusted gross income for cash gifts and 20 percent for stock gifts in any one year. So the time to make a gift like this is in a year in which you have a lot of income. That would be the year you sell your business—not the following year, when your income may fall to next to nothing.

For example, suppose you sell your business for $10 million in November and want to give away $2 million to your new Sloth Foundation. If the gift is made before December 31, you have $10 million in income that year, so with a limit of 30 percent for cash gifts, you can deduct up to $3 million. Thus the $2 million gift to the foundation might be fully deductible, resulting in a capital gains tax savings of $450,000.

But suppose you have become so engrossed in tromping through the Amazon to study tree sloths (enjoying your newfound wealth and freedom) that you just don't get around to setting up the foundation until January 1. No big deal, right? Big deal. If you had income of $1 million in the new year, you would only be able to deduct 30 percent, or $300,000. The capital gains tax savings on this is a mere $45,000. (Pay attention to the way the decimal point slides here.) You have missed the window and lost out on more than $400,000 in deductions. You can carry forward the unused deduction for the next four years, but in each year it is adjusted to the same percentage of income limitations. Think of how many little three-toed tree sloths you might have saved with that money! No wonder *sloth* is one of the Seven Deadly Sins! Make sure you avoid it in your own planning!

The exact percentage limitations differ based on whether your donation is to an owner-advised fund or to our own family-managed foundation, and may move around with our "whack-a-mole" tax laws, but you need to remember only one incredibly important point from these few pages: Establish your foundation and get the money into it in the same tax year as you sell your business. You will always be much better off. Better yet, start the foundation much earlier, and then you just have to make a transfer at the time of the sale. Even if you plan to do something like saving sloths, there is no reason to be foolish about it.

Have Your Charity and Income, Too

Transferring private stock into a *Charitable Remainder Trust* is a great vehicle for donating to a cause you care about while still retaining income from the asset. It can benefit the charity of your choice after your death, while still ensuring you a steady income while you are alive. This also has significant tax advantages, because it spreads out the tax impact of the sale. For example, if an owner sells a business and sets up a $20 million charitable trust, the money goes into the trust, which is a tax-exempt entity. The owner is paid out an annual annuity stream, so instead of taking a hit on the full amount in the first year, the tax burden is limited to the income distributed. The annuity you receive is treated as ordinary income to the extent of the trust's ordinary income and capital gains to the extent the trust has earned capital gains. In other words, it will be treated as ordinary income as long as the trust earns more than the annuity distributed, so basically you are deferring your capital gains when you use this trust. At the termination of the trust, the remainder then goes to the charity. This way, the business seller can ensure the necessary income from the trust while avoiding paying taxes on funds that would go to charity in the end. Also, the current value of the charitable remainder interest is a tax deduction for you.

For example, suppose an owner transfers a C corporation (this does not work for many partnerships or for any S corporation) valued at $50 million to a charitable remainder trust before a sale has been negotiated, and the owner receives an 11.5 percent annuity. If, based on the owner's age and IRS assumed rates at the time, the value of the remainder going to the charity is 10 percent, there would be an immediate charitable deduction of $5 million. When the business is later sold for $100 million, the trust would not have to pay capital gains tax. "It is a tax deferral mechanism for the seller," says Molly James of Hogan & Hartson. In addition, the owner could receive 11.5 percent of the $100 million, or over $10 million a year, given the trust payments to the owner of a percentage of the trust assets every year.

This type of trust needs to be set up before the sale is negotiated. It can be all lined up, and the owner can pull the trigger just before beginning to look for a buyer.

If the owner waits until after the $100 million sale, there may be a larger charitable deduction, but the owner will pay capital gains on the full $100 million amount. If the business tanks after the gift to the trust, as long as the original valuation was solid, the charitable deduction will still stand. Of course, you have to really want to give the money to charity, because these are not revocable.

A similar *Grantor Retained Annuity Trust* (GRAT) could be used to transfer the remainder to family members after paying an annuity to the holder for a set number of years (usually two). A GRAT can be used with any type of business interest, not just a C corporation. It has no serious tax advantage but can allow an owner to transfer most of the increase in the value of the business after the transaction. For example, if the owner transferred the business worth $50 million and then had an IPO or sale within a year that doubled the value to $100 million, the owner would receive back over two years $50 million plus about a 5 percent return (based on IRS assumed rates), and the entire remainder could pass to children or trusts for them completely gift (and death) tax-free.

There are many options, and this discussion is just designed to give you a lay of the land. You should explore options in more detail with an adviser to choose the best one for your particular situation.

START TODAY

What is the common moral of all these tales? You cannot start early enough in planning for after the sale. As can be seen from the power of compounding over time, the gifting of stock is most powerful when undertaken early in a company's history. It might take you years to give your relatives a substantial part of the business a little at a time. Planning your charitable giving also can save you piles of cash. This requires much foresight and planning.

This is yet another reason why any smart business owner must do two things, both of which are hammered home in this book: One, begin planning for your transition early, and two, have experienced domain experts to advise you at every step along the way. You might think that you need to have the cash in hand before sitting down with a wealth management specialist, and so you might first look to your current investment adviser for advice. This could be a mistake if they don't have the detailed knowledge to deal with the big-league investments you now have to make. Also, wealth management specialists, such as those at Goldman Sachs, Hogan & Hartson, or PricewaterhouseCoopers, are happy to meet with you *well before* the sale. This can give you the time to assess the field and find someone you'd be comfortable trusting with your life's earnings.

"We often begin a dialogue with an owner well before the sale of the company," said Scott Belveal of Goldman Sachs's Private Wealth Management group. "It is better for both sides to build this rapport rather than wait for the day of the wire." As you are thinking about selling, you need to meet with your whole team—wealth management, tax, legal, and investment bankers. Don't put this off even if it seems you don't have time for it.

How do you select the right adviser? Follow the general advice on selecting members of your team that we discussed in Chapter 5. In particular, look for an adviser who has experience working with entrepreneurs and people in your same net worth category. The entrepreneur's view is different from that of the person with inherited wealth, and you need an adviser who understands these differences.

Our friends at Goldman Sachs were kind enough to offer some advice on the questions that business owners should ask in selecting the right adviser. Among these are:

1. Who are the people on my team? Who is going to be the point person in dealing with issues every day? Is it a customer service representative or someone with an advanced degree or other experience in these areas?

2. How many clients do they have? Are the clients similar to you in background and net worth?

3. How convenient is the team? Are their account statements clear and easily accessible? (One word on convenience. Many owners actually prefer to work with an adviser who is out of town. They would rather not run into the person who knows all the details of their wealth at a Little League game or a backyard barbecue. Advisers will fly out to meet with you.)

4. How often does the team meet with you?

5. Can you visit? While advisers will meet you in your office, most of them are happy for you to come to their headquarters and "walk the factory floor." (If they aren't, this is probably a sign that you should run the other way.) You really should make these visits if at all possible. There is no substitute for going there and meeting the team that will be managing your money and the different parts of your investment portfolio. This will give you a very good sense of the strengths and weaknesses of the company and whether it will be a good fit.

A Word About Stock

This advance planning is even more essential if you are receiving stock as part of the proceeds in the sale. There are many reasons for this. First, from a tax planning perspective, taxes on stock can be deferred until sold. You need to make appropriate plans. But much more important, by taking stock in a sale, you are nearly always taking a moderate to risky security in the process. There may be an upside, and you will probably tend to focus on this, but there is also a downside.

You need to understand the risks of stock in advance, because they may affect your actual payout from the sale. You also need to make sure you understand all the issues if the buyer asks you to "lock up" your position, which means you cannot sell it for a period of time. *Lock-ups* are to be avoided at all costs. Not only do they inhibit your ability to sell the stock, but they hurt your ability to *hedge* your position. There are a broad range of techniques to limit your risk on your stock position.

Even without lock-ups, stock may be much less liquid than you think. The SEC watches where it goes, and there may be restrictions on what you do with the stock after the sale. Even after you are out of the business, you may be treated as an insider. This means you may fall under restrictions on insider trading or employee stock sale windows. This often comes as a surprise to sellers, who might feel that the whole point of the exercise was to become an *outsider*.

Trading volume can also affect your ability to cash out. If you receive 2 million shares of a $10 stock that is only trading ten shares a day, you are going to hold those shares for a long time or sell them at a substantial discount. If you can't sell your shares, this substantially reduces your ability to hedge, so you may still find most of your net worth is tied up in a business that you *no longer control*. You are *not* out of the old business—you are in deeper than ever.

On the other hand, if you receive shares in a Fortune 500 company trading 2 million shares a day, you can cash out of 1 million shares pretty quickly. So look carefully at the liquidity of the shares you receive and the restrictions that might apply to you. If you find yourself holding $20 million in very restricted shares that you can't sell and can't hedge, your $20 million payout may be worth more like $5 million.

Nearly all stocks are risky. For example, a private investment firm sold a company (a key holding) to Lernout & Hauspie Speech Products in the Netherlands for $600 million in stock. They thought they had done a great deal. However, a few months after closing, Lernout's huge accounting fraud was disclosed, and the firm lost everything, including their franchise. It is shocking, but they had not hedged their position. If you are taking stock in a sale, you must be very careful to integrate all of your investment and tax advisers into the process long before you close *so you can protect yourself.* You certainly wouldn't put all your eggs in one basket if you were creating a portfolio from scratch, but you could inadvertently end up with too much of your net worth in a single investment as a result of a business sale.

MONEY MANAGERS

As soon as you close your sale, you will note that you have many new friends. Lost cousins quickly emerge, professing their devotion, and investment managers will be approaching you on every street corner. High-end money management is a huge universe. There are literally hundreds of managers. All of the most prominent investment banks have large private wealth management groups, as do commercial banks. And there are hundreds of large and small independent managers. All will have compelling pitches. How do you choose among them? Before I tell you my biases, let me advise you on a few bare essentials:

• *Shop the best.* If you are receiving more than $2 to $3 million in your sale, all of the very best firms will want your business. And the top firms are there for a reason. They have the best people, with huge access to a wide range of alternatives, and deep experience. You should contact at least three and perhaps five or six managers. They all will give you extensive presentations with recommendations. There are three reasons to shop extensively. First, you need to find people whom you trust and with whom you have positive chemistry. Second, by shopping, you will get lots and lots of interesting ideas, all presented to you *for free.* (Like the investment banking freebie, this is the last freebie you will get, so enjoy it while it lasts!) Third, it will put you on the best footing to negotiate price. Like the bake-off for your investment bankers, you want investment advisers to compete for your business. They will not cut price dramatically, because they have plenty of demand for their services, but they will improve some terms if they want you.

• *Diversify your assets.* You've worked so hard to build your company and to sell it. Do not blow it by being foolish with your diversification. In addition to the perils of receiving stock, as discussed above, many sellers create very homogeneous investments simply by sticking to their area of expertise. In a simple example, in the last technology boom, the seller of a Silicon Valley tech firm decided to

MAKE THE MOST OF YOUR MONEY | 175

handle his own investments. Thinking he knew technology well and that he should "invest in what you know" (after all, isn't this what Warren Buffett always advises?), he poured his proceeds into other technology stocks. This meant, of course, that he was now totally underdiversified, and he saw his net worth crushed when the whole technology sector tanked. By creating a less correlated portfolio, he could have done much better. (He also didn't handle the wire well, which cost him money from the start.) No matter how brilliant you believe you may be, you should put your assets into a well diversified portfolio.

What Do the Pros Cost?

Private wealth managers perform a wide range of functions. They work with you to assess your personal risk profile, so they can balance a portfolio that suits you. They provide experienced counsel and a broad range of financial advice. They often provide you with access to specialized money managers you could not access on your own. They trade stocks for you; they will provide you loans against your portfolio as needed. Most can even provide credit cards, checking, and ATM cards. And the good ones provide the most important product, peace of mind. This last benefit should be your goal (along with good results!).

The costs of these services vary greatly, depending upon how much money you are turning over and the type of products they are providing. The annual charge is normally a percentage against your total account balance. A rough range of charges can be from 0.5 percent to 2 percent per year. If you are extremely conservative and want total protection of your principal in a bond fund, you may be able to negotiate an annual charge of 0.4 percent (or 40 basis points, as the Street guys like to say). If you have a $10 million balanced portfolio (half in bonds, a third in stocks, and a few sexy products like hedge funds or private equity), you should be thinking about 1 percent to 1.5 percent per annum. So, all in, to create value for you, these folks need to earn more than their fee in returns. I believe they can and often do. If they did not, they would not be in business.

A Sample Portfolio

What does a good, balanced portfolio look like? To give you some idea, our friends at Goldman Sachs have provided us with a snapshot of a typical balanced portfolio, shown in Figure 9-1. Diversification can often provide higher levels of return for similar levels of risk. For example, while the return for the hypothetical portfolio illustrated in the figure might be 6.43 percent, a similar investment in a portfolio equally divided between U.S. equity and investment-grade municipal bonds would be just 5.76 percent *with the same level of volatility.*

A well-diversified portfolio offers a broad range of products, including bonds, equities, and riskier products such as hedge funds, constructed in a balanced manner. This may not fit your risk profile or needs for current yield, but it is a good starting point. If you were

FIGURE 9-1. SAMPLE DIVERSIFIED PORTFOLIO.

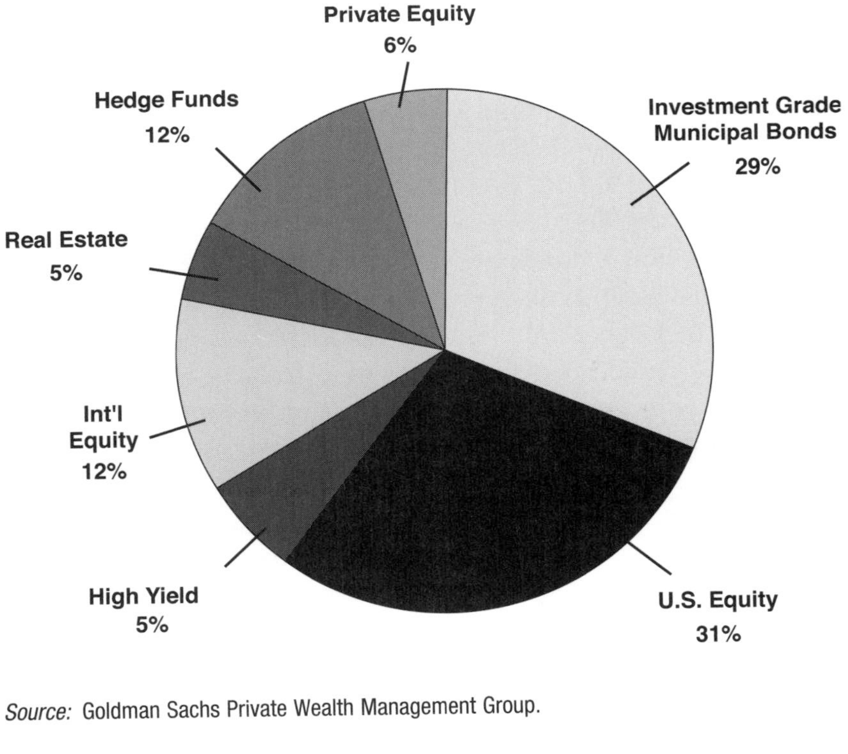

Source: Goldman Sachs Private Wealth Management Group.

to put $10 million into this allocation mix, your typical annual fee would be approximately 1 percent. And you could sleep easy.

INVESTMENT STRATEGY: NO BARS AND RESTAURANTS!

While your investment strategy is something that you'll want to discuss directly with your advisers, a few general comments are worth making here. The most important thing is to be clear about your goals. Then you can design the best portfolio to achieve them. While you may have taken risks in building your business, you may want to be much more conservative in your investments. If you haven't spent a lot of time investing, you might start off slow and get a feel for different asset classes. Take your time. Just because you have been successful in building a business doesn't mean that anything you touch will turn to gold.

Once you come into your money, you will suddenly find yourself with many new friends with great investment ideas. Many of them are crazy. You will have college buddies asking you to dump money into their restaurants and bars or retail malls. Remember that no serious investors are going to consider doing something like this. If you want to make a gift to your friends and family for this type of activity, go ahead. It is your money. But don't look at it as an investment, or you will be disappointed.

There are many sad tales of people who have invested in friends' great schemes, only to lose all the money they worked so hard to build. Entrepreneurs are used to taking risks and are sometimes reckless with their money because they feel bulletproof. Don't become a venture capital firm for your friends. If the ideas have real potential, why isn't anyone else investing in them?

This is no time to roll the dice with nontraditional approaches. It would be very easy to squander your hard-earned funds on risky investments. Like Odysseus in the old Greek tale, if you are going to listen to these "siren songs," you need to strap yourself to the mast and ensure that the sailors around you have plugs in their ears. Otherwise you could end up lured onto the rocks.

If you really enjoy investing on your own, or throwing some

money into a new start-up of a young entrepreneur who reminds you of yourself at that age, you've earned it. Many investors have self-directed funds—to invest in start-ups or engage in exotic currency or options strategies. But it is important to put some "guardrails" on them. Limit yourself to 5 to 10 percent of your proceeds. Take the rest and give it to the pros. Then you can go to the end of this leash but not off the cliff.

Should you use multiple institutions to handle your investments? Some sellers decide to divide up their investments among several different investment advisers. They think this will provide a sort of institutional diversification, offering protection against a Drexel Burnham–like meltdown. I do not believe this is necessary, but if it helps you sleep easier, then do what makes you comfortable. This way, you get to see how different folks handle the investments, keeping the advisers on their toes. Also, be aware that there are hidden risks to this approach. One negative is that you are a less important client to two or three institutions rather than a very important client at one. Your pricing will probably be worse.

The most important concern, however, is that your diversification across firms may be an illusion. Since none of these investments are coordinated, they could in fact be more correlated across the different portfolios than you might think. "There is no centralized quarterback, so no one determines whether there are correlations between asset classes," Belveal says. "The investor may sleep well at night thinking that he's diversified his investment, but it may be highly correlated. He may own triple positions across the board." In contrast, an adviser who can see the whole picture can ensure the right diversification overall to meet the needs of the investor's risk profile.

Risk is obviously not the only important consideration for your investment strategy. In addition to minimizing risk, your strategy will also reflect your other personal goals, such as providing for family and heirs, minimizing estate taxes, providing for charity, and minimizing income taxes. These different goals suggest different wealth management strategies, as Figure 9-2 illustrates. Go back to your goals for the sale, as discussed in Chapter 2, and make sure your wealth management strategy is aligned with these goals.

FIGURE 9-2. WHAT CONCERNS YOU MOST?

Your long-term objectives determine which strategies will be appropriate for your needs.

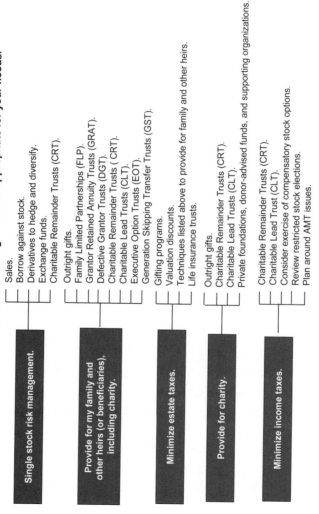

Single stock risk management.
- Sales.
- Borrow against stock.
- Derivatives to hedge and diversify.
- Exchange funds.
- Charitable Remainder Trusts (CRT).

Provide for my family and other heirs (or beneficiaries), including charity.
- Outright gifts.
- Family Limited Partnerships (FLP).
- Grantor Retained Annuity Trusts (GRAT).
- Defective Grantor Trusts (DGT).
- Charitable Remainder Trusts (CRT).
- Charitable Lead Trusts (CLT).
- Executive Option Trusts (EOT).
- Generation Skipping Transfer Trusts (GST).

Minimize estate taxes.
- Gifting programs.
- Valuation discounts.
- Techniques listed above to provide for family and other heirs.
- Life insurance trusts.

Provide for charity.
- Outright gifts.
- Charitable Remainder Trusts (CRT).
- Charitable Lead Trusts (CLT).
- Private foundations, donor-advised funds, and supporting organizations.

Minimize income taxes.
- Charitable Remainder Trusts (CRT).
- Charitable Lead Trust (CLT).
- Consider exercise of compensatory stock options.
- Review restricted stock elections.
- Plan around AMT issues.

Note that Goldman Sachs & Co. does not provide tax and/or legal advice to its clients, and all investors are strongly urged to consult with their own advisers regarding any potential investment or strategy. This material is intended for educational purposes only. While it is based on information believed to be reliable, no representation or warranty is given as to its accuracy or completeness, and it should not be relied upon as such.

Source: Goldman Sachs & Co.

Sweat the Details

While planning can help make sure the big picture issues, such as gifting and giving, are in place, planning also can help address the smaller details that can add up to significant sums. For example, a relatively small detail such as timing the wiring of the payment from the buyer can make a big difference. Wiring time is always a lovely day, never to be forgotten, when your incoming wire comes smashing into your bank account. Defying all logic in our always-on, high-tech age, it normally takes *four to five hours* for your wire to hit home. (Can someone please tell me what an electronic system is doing with that digital signal for all that time?) Normally, you might not give much thought to a delay of four or five hours or even a weekend, after you've waited your lifetime for this. But when you are talking about tens of millions of dollars, funny things happen. Hours and days translate very quickly into real money.

Here's a helpful hint from Goldman Sachs: Do your best *not* to have the wire arrive on Friday afternoon. If it does, it likely will take until Monday to hit your account. This means that the money will be suspended in cyberspace over the weekend, losing two interest-bearing days. "You should ensure that the buyer is sending the wire first thing in the morning so you can put it to work overnight," says Belveal. "You'd be surprised what a couple of basis points will mean on a $50 million wire overnight. It could be thousands of dollars in lost interest. This means a lot, particularly because most business owners made their money the old-fashioned way. They have worked very hard and don't want to give it away."

Make sure that the minute the money arrives it can be deployed immediately into interest-bearing instruments. Also pay attention to the different types of transfers, such as wire stock distributions, fed funds wires, or clearinghouse wires. They all have their particular nuances. You need someone who knows about the differences and can choose the best mechanism for your transfer.

As this example illustrates, the stakes for all decisions are much higher with numbers of this size. You need to sweat all the details, and have advisers who know where to look, because these details can potentially cost you or make you a lot of money.

Keep Your Plan Tuned-Up

Once you have an estate plan in place, it will be useful to revisit it with your advisers up to the time of the sale, and then at least every three to five years afterward. Some of the issues to look at during these tune-ups are new tax legislation that might affect your estate, changes in family situation (marriage, divorce, death of a spouse or beneficiary), and changes in financial situation (increase in net worth, shift in portfolio). If any of these changes are significant between regular tune-ups, this might be a reason for a special session with your advisers.

OFF TO THE JUNGLES

If you have planned in advance, when the wiring day arrives, the money should flow into predetermined investments and gifts. Your family is taken care of through advance gifting. Your funds are deployed in a strategic asset management model that reflects your own personal risk profile. You can pack up and go into the Amazon with a clear and easy conscience. (Or, if you feel that you've already spent your life in the *jungles*, you might try something a little more tame and relaxing). You have worked hard for what you have. And you've done the planning to keep it and grow your wealth.

As you ride off into the sunset, I am sure you can't help thinking: What will I do for an encore? You've sold your business and done it successfully. That is an accomplishment every bit as important as building the enterprise in the first place. You've spent a good part of your life tied to the business. Now you have converted your sweat and blood into a much more liquid set of assets. You are free and clear, with money in the bank. What next? That important question is the focus of the next chapter.

AND NOW, FOR YOUR NEXT ACT . . .

You're a Millionaire, Now What?

LIFE AFTER

What can we learn about life after the deal from the cases presented in Chapter 1?

Homeland Designs: Bill Chambers hired a professional manager so that he would be able to devote more attention to growth. However, he is still very much involved in his business.

Iconix: After a brief period of decompression, and then going stir-crazy, Leo Mullen reimmersed himself in starting a new business. His wife, Helene Patterson, became involved in volunteer work at a hospital.

Politics and Prose: The owners of Politics & Prose are still at the helm of their business and very much involved in the daily details of running their bookstore.

As part of the sale of his print and digital strategy business, Leo Mullen agreed to stay on to help run the business, which was a roll-up of five different companies. Integration was a problem. The new leadership left the organization rudderless in a very stormy environment. There were firings and bloodletting. Mullen ended up in the hospital with ulcers. He found himself watching the business he had worked so hard to build and sell self-destruct.

"I was richer than I had any right to be. I had pulled off this incredible piece of alchemy, and yet I was so profoundly unhappy," he said. "I had all of the responsibilities I had before but no authority to make the kind of decisions we needed to make. I was scared to death for all the employees who trusted me." Given that he had given employees a fifth of the business, some used their money to retire. One became a goat farmer. But many stayed on and invested their money back into the new company, watching in horror as it crashed and burned.

In December of 2000, a year after the sale, Mullen walked into the new CEO's office and asked to be allowed to leave. His contract required him to stay another two years. Mullen argued, however, that there was nothing he could do about the free fall, and at least the company would save the burden of his salary. He told the new CEO that there was nothing left to do here. "I said, 'You need to fire me.' The business had evaporated. We were doing triage. Then I was fired."

When he walked out of the office for the last time just before Christmas, it was a relief to know it was finally over. He had pulled off an outrageously successful deal. He was a multimillionaire. Of course, no one escapes from something like this without some heartache and pain. But he comforted himself with the thought that, given the retrenchment in the industry, some of the turmoil would have happened with or without his deal. But now he was out, and was a very wealthy man.

Then it hit him: Now what?

NOW WHAT?

Mullen worked out at the gym like a maniac for six weeks, pouring all his superabundant energy into exercise. He had a stack of books that he had never found time to read, and now he drove through them, and dug back into his old philosophy books from his undergraduate years. "Now, I realized what [my wife] Helene was feeling when she left the company," he said. "I had defined myself as CEO for so long. All of a sudden, I'm just another guy on the street." He had a noncompete clause for three years, so going back into the same business was out of the question, even if the market had been more attractive.

There were a lot of hours in the day. An early riser, he would wake, work out, read three newspapers, and look through his e-mail. Then, he'd look at the clock. It was only quarter to nine. He started to learn to play golf and renovated his house. He noticed with horror a decline in his mental acuity and awareness of current events.

Whiteboards in the Living Room

One day, when his wife came home, she noticed that he had taken down all the paintings in the living room. He had hung giant whiteboards in their place. On one of the boards was an idea for a new business. On another, he was calculating a system for identifying the best fit for a college for his daughter, based on SATs and GPAs. They looked around at the whiteboards on the living room walls. Then they looked at each other. They knew they had to do something. They held a family council, and the consensus was absolute: They needed to find a way to get dad out of the house. In other words, he was fired from his home.

After buying out his noncompete clause, Mullen went out and started a new business, consulting with companies to optimize the experiences that customers have when interacting with online systems. Where he had looked at the challenge from the corporate side with Iconix, he was now looking from the other direction. He built a small organization with twenty-two people. Having a pair of active partners offered more flexibility and a little less intense pace. He certainly now had the wherewithal to take it easy, but he chose to pour his heart into his new business. "My wife says I must be crazy, leaving for work at 6 or 6:30 in the morning and getting home around 7:30 or 8 in the evening. But I'm having fun. That has been my internal guidance system."

He invited his wife to join the new business, but she declined. She has, instead, put her time and care into community service, volunteering at the oncology center at a children's hospital and serving on their board. She also runs the family and keeps track of their investments—still on the legal pads she used to use as CFO of Invisions.

If Mullen were to exit the new business, his goals for the sale would be a little different. "When and if the time comes to exit this new business—in part because of the security we now have—I'll be much more determined to preserve the human values," Mullen said. "That would trump economic value to me." But he is in no hurry. His two partners, who each own 30 percent of the business, create a strong opportunity for an internal sale.

EXPLORING THE OPTIONS FOR AFTER

Once you are completely out on the street, your true work begins. You've put your heart and soul into this business for decades. Now what? A few CEOs make the transition to a life of yachting or golf, but most find themselves left with a hole that all the cash in the world cannot fill. There are many options, including:

- Starting a new enterprise, or working with younger partners to launch a new venture.

- Using your expertise on a corporate board or working with a private equity firm.

- Going back to school to earn the master's or doctoral degree you've put off.

- Serving as a mentor to other business owners or executives.

- Serving on a nonprofit board (although this can sometimes be a surprisingly frustrating experience).

- Setting up a family foundation and, as Andrew Carnegie advised, spending the last part of your life distributing the wealth that you've created in the first part. This can be a very rewarding channel for the passion that you had poured into the business.

The key is to think ahead and prepare for this change. As with the sale itself, be clear about your goals, and be prepared for the emotions that will hit you after you sell your business. Beyond very practical matters of financial planning, examined in the preceding chapter, there are many much softer, but vital issues, to consider.

You need to be clear about what you are doing next. This will often be unfamiliar territory because you are used to waking up with your business demanding attention or some new fire to put out. In this chapter, we will examine a process for "life transition solutions," part coaching and part strategic planning, which can help owners do serious preparation for their postsale life.

First, Give Yourself Some Space

The first action you need to take is—to do nothing. You need to resist the urge to jump into something new and create some space for yourself. This is my admonishment to you, my beloved entrepreneur. After your deal is done, please take three months off and do nothing but decompress. Avoid the temptation to set up the whiteboards in the living room. Do nothing! (In your own way, of course.) Read a frivolous book. Read *Don't Sweat the Small Stuff,* but don't sweat it if you don't finish it! Go to a comedy club! Take a nap in the middle of the day. Drink champagne before lunch in bed. (This worked well for Churchill!) It may drive you absolutely bonkers to have so much free time, but force yourself to do it. Your long-term happiness and health depend upon it.

This will probably be the hardest work that you have ever done. After working nonstop every day, this vast open expanse will about as refreshing as being dumped into the middle of the ocean. You'll immediately start wondering how long you can last out here. You'll start looking for the sharks. You'll be worrying about drowning. But if you relax into it, you will begin to see the sun shining and appreciate the experience. You'll engage in a little scuba diving or explore some forgotten reefs. This is where you are most likely to discover your next act.

And then, after decompression, do me a favor. Look into your heart and find your *passions* in life. If it is cars, great. Art, great. Tulip collecting, great. Building another business, great. But find your passion and live your dream. I genuinely believe that most people, as Thoreau said, lead lives of quiet desperation. Do not let that be you. Go to the Everest Base Camp. Make your list of the top twenty things you must do in your life and *do them*. Then make a list of another twenty. Live your life and go for it. You've earned it!

Take a few days and go to a resort without phones, fax, or e-mail (and don't even take your BlackBerry). Spend some time alone, and then develop your personal goals for one year, five years, and ten years. It will have a surprising impact on the way you live your life.

LIFE TRANSITION SOLUTIONS

Most people expect to be challenged by the negative events of their lives—illness, divorce, loss of loved ones. But they are blindsided by the impact of a positive event such as selling a business. The sale is often at a time when the owners are going through predictable mid-life transitions, during which every aspect of their lives comes into question. About 80 percent of the men studied by Daniel J. Levinson, author of *The Seasons of Man's Life,* experienced a midlife transition. They realized they needed to change their direction and rethink the meaning of their lives. Being cut loose from the business at this moment just adds to the angst.

Among the common questions our friends at The Global Consulting Partnership hear from owners selling their businesses are:

- "How am I going to add value to the world now?"
- "How am I going to continue to grow, not to mention lead?"
- "How am I going to remain motivated and passionate?"
- "How am I going to continue to live a disciplined, responsible, and accountable life?"

A Personal Retreat

After the period of decompression for a few months, after you've cleared out some of the adrenaline of running your business, you can begin to take a more focused look at your life. The Global Consulting Partnership has developed a process for creating what they call "Life Transition Solutions." It illustrates one possible path for thinking about what happens after the sale of a business.

This process begins with a personal retreat. Executives are used to planning retreats to work out the next stages of growth for their business. Apply the same principles to your personal life. It is the same process, just a different focal point. Go to a beautiful offsite location that takes you completely away from your ordinary life. Shut off the phone and the BlackBerry. Then begin to plan for the future in a directed way. The retreat allows time for regrouping, conducting a life inventory, and refining or resetting your focus, direction, and personal mission. As TGCP's Mark Brenner notes, "A personal *retreat* is the most effective way to lay the groundwork for a life *advance*."

There are many ways to approach such a retreat. One framework for thinking through some of the key issues is the life transitions solutions created by TGCP to help executives develop a plan for living by design. There are no rules for how you approach this process, however. Even if you don't use such formal tools, they suggest some of the key areas you will need to consider in developing your own plan:

• *Create an in-depth life inventory.* You have been successful, but what are the experiences and skills that have driven that success? You need to take a careful inventory of your strengths and talents. These will form the building blocks for your next act.

• *Make use of psychometric inventories.* In assessing strengths and weaknesses, professionals such as those at TGCP can use various psychological tests to assess your work style, interpersonal style, thinking style, influencing style, and motivational style. This will give you insights into the types of business contexts or organizational contexts that will be the best fit for you. Then you can develop plans that are in line with your motivations.

• *Value your "Me Portfolio."* Like your investment portfolio, your personal portfolio has certain assets. Where can this personal capital be deployed to achieve the most bang for the buck? What is the portfolio of activities that is the best investment for you?

• *Develop personal vision, mission, and core values.* As with a business, personal vision, mission, and values provide a foundation for how you want to operate in this world. Life is about more than business or making money. It is up to you to define what this purpose is. It provides a compass and touchstone for future decisions. If the idea of a vision and mission statement turns you off—you may have sat through too many meetings working on corporate mission statements— just work on coming up with a sense of your own value and what you want to remembered for. One strategy for doing this is to write your own obituary.

There is a famous story about Alfred Nobel, whose obituary was accidentally published when his brother died. He saw that he was going to be remembered as the inventor of dynamite, one of the most destructive forces known to mankind. When he read the obituary, it was an eye-opener that this was to be his legacy. He then set up the Nobel Prizes, including one for peace, which were established at his death in 1896. He rewrote his history. We all write our own stories about what our lives stand for. This is an opportunity to think about what you want your legacy to be.

• *Create a wish list audit.* The next step is to define the key goals for health, intellectual development, financial success, social gratification, and other areas. While your thinking about the business has typically been convergent, this work is divergent, brainstorming about possibilities in each area and stepping back to see a whole range of possibilities.

• *Explore future scenarios.* Just as a business might look at different scenarios for the future, you can consider different personal futures. This requires looking at the changes in the world and the opportunities they create. It encourages you to look beyond a linear projection of the past. You are then able to imagine yourself in diverse possible futures. What will it take to succeed in each future? Which ones feel like the best fit? Which of these possible worlds do you truly want to live in?

• *Create a roadmap.* The goal of this work is to develop a strategic plan for your life, similar to the strategic plan for the business that might come out of a company planning retreat. This is an action plan. It is, of course, a living document that will change over time.

GUIDELINES FOR A SUCCESSFUL TRANSITION

What are the keys to making a successful transition to life after the sale? While thinking about postsale transition long before it arrives and giving yourself space to think immediately after the sale are the biggest factor, there are also other elements that can help increase your likelihood of making a smooth and successful transition:

• *Find a change partner.* To make your plans stick, you ideally should find a change partner. This could be an old friend, a spouse, or someone who is going through a similar transition. This person can help you stay true to your direction and goals and provide support in the transition. This will ensure that you keep your plans and goals alive and don't lose sight of your direction.

• *Rediscover your dreams.* Many times this process takes you back to the beginning. After the sale, owners often rediscover passions from childhood that were set aside in the press of building a business, making money, and raising a family. Now, there is a chance to rediscover the buried interests and passions of your youth. What is it that animates you? Some business owners return to painting, studying history, writing, or other activities that they were fired up about when they were young but have long since forgotten.

• *Trust the process.* These hidden interests may not be immediately apparent. They will only be discovered if you give yourself time and space to do so. Don't give up. Keep at it. Don't be self-conscious about spending so much time thinking about yourself.

Avoid the pressures that will be all around you to jump immediately into something new. This will often be much more appealing and easier in the short term than spending time thinking about what you want to do. But it might take you in the wrong direction. If you get in touch with your own passions, you will be surprised at what emerges. Don't worry about getting it perfect out of the box. Start somewhere and keep experimenting until you find what works.

• *Talk to your spouse.* One business owner in his fifties sold his firm and expected to travel the world with his wife. He figured that they didn't need the money, so she would just quit her job. But she was committed to her successful career and had no intention of leaving it all behind to tour the globe. He had never thought to ask her. This derailed his plans and created unnecessary tension in their relationship.

If your plans call for you to spend much more time at home than in the past, you also need to begin discussions about this with your spouse. Many times, the idyllic view of life of a second honeymoon at home turns out to be a far cry from the truth. Both spouses are not used to spending so much time in one another's space, and it doesn't work at all. These are all issues you need to discuss with your spouse before, during, and after the sale. It will be a constant negotiation. When you determine your own ideal direction for after the sale, you'll typically need to discuss and adjust these plans based on input from your spouse.

A MATTER OF SURVIVAL

As we have noted, the postsale life you will develop will be completely idiosyncratic. There are no simple recipes. There are no easy guidelines. There are no ten steps to a successful life after selling your business. That is the beauty of it. You get to design your own life. This is the greatest opportunity that you have ever been presented with. Take advantage of it. Get in touch with what fires you up and live out your dreams. You've done this to a certain extent in building your business. But there is more to you than an economic actor. This is a chance to explore the many diverse other aspects of your personality that can contribute to your own life, your family, and the world.

Every plan that emerges will be unique to the distinctive interests of the person creating it. For example, one owner who sold his business to a large firm stayed on for a few years before retiring at 57 with about $15 to $20 million in net worth from the sale of the business. He continues to serve on some corporate boards and began traveling extensively with his wife. In the course of the traveling, he began investing in resort real estate and flipping it for a profit, discovering a passion for this work. He also serves on the boards of several nonprofit organizations and is active in his community. He has cobbled together a portfolio of activities that fit his particular interests and aptitudes. There may not be a single focus of activity and interest but rather a balanced set of activities that add up to a satisfying life solution.

Another retired executive serves on several corporate boards. He also spends much of his time painting, a passion he rediscovered from his youth. He supports the local arts and engages in various volunteer activities. The best solution is often a balance between personal, professional, and community activities.

Although this work on postsale transition may seem soft and mushy after the hard issues you've dealt with in your business, it is vital to do it. If the idea of having a more productive life after selling your business is not enough motivation, consider that this could be a matter of survival. People who have a sense of vision and purpose are more likely to live longer. If you don't have something to tie you to the earth, your mortality risk could be quite high. You could open yourself up to illness or premature death.

This is one reason why many business owners in their eighties are still at the helm. They are realistically frightened that if they give up the business it might mean the end of them. They have nothing else. Who they are is so tied up in the business that without this purpose, what would life be? This is one reason why they put off selling. But there is a better route. You can find new passions.

This is why it is so important to define this broader purpose before the sale, or at least immediately afterward. Find out what animates you, and go after it. Create a new positive dream even as you sell the product of your old one. Then you will not only be moving *away* from your old business, but moving *toward* something. Remember, this is what you worked so hard for. Now it is within your grasp. It is up to you to seize it.

CONCLUSION: THE POWER OF ENTREPRENEURS

Entrepreneurs who build companies are the backbone of American business. They create the most jobs. They provide livelihoods to families throughout the country. They satisfy legions of customers. To do this, entrepreneurs take great personal risk and make enormous personal sacrifices. They work eighty-hour weeks, jump on airplanes on Sundays, and spend days away from their own families. They personally guarantee bank lines. When things go bad, they lose their houses. When things go well, they make many millions of dollars. But this success is hard-fought, hard-earned. Like raising a child, it takes years of sweat and blood.

I always laugh when people begrudge an entrepreneur's pay, or big houses, or fast boats. They simply do not understand the truly enormous pressure and stress that comes with building a business. "The Buck Stops Here" is not an idle slogan. It is a way of life that can add a lot of gray to a man's or woman's scalp and can even cost marriages. Bottom line: It ain't easy folks, to build a business. It is not for the faint of heart.

And after all of that building, owners have every right to get every dollar out of the business that they have built up through years of hard work.

We hope this book will help you to do this, and create a successful life on the other side. You have every right to enjoy your new-found wealth and time. You have worked hard to get to where you are. You have worked hard to sell your business successfully. Now you deserve to build the life that you have always wanted. Go out and get it!

GET IT IN WRITING

Documents for the Deal

APPENDIX A PROVIDES SAMPLES of the various documents and checklists you might encounter in a deal, including a letter of intent, a confidentiality agreement, and a due diligence checklist. By reviewing some of these basic agreements, you avoid being surprised at the time of the deal. The following samples are included:

APPENDIX A-1. LETTER OF INTENT WITH BUYER

Note: This sample LOI reflects a $100 million transaction but can be adjusted to meet any transaction size.

Investor
1515 Big Hitter Lane
Cash Flow, Wisconsin

CONFIDENTIAL

Target
Street
City, State, Zip

Target Parent CEO
Street
City, State, Zip

Dear Ladies & Gentlemen:

This letter of agreement (the "Letter") sets forth the general terms pursuant to which Investor (the "Purchaser") is prepared to purchase all of the outstanding capital stock of Target and any majority-owned subsidiaries of Target (collectively, "Company") from the Target Parent Co. ("Seller") (the "Transaction").

1. **Form of Transaction.** Subject to the terms of this Letter, Purchaser will purchase 100% of the Capital Stock of Company for the Purchase Price (as described in paragraph 2). As a result, Company will become a wholly owned subsidiary of Purchaser. For purposes of this Letter, "Capital Stock" includes all of the Company's common stock, preferred stock (if any), and any other securities (whether contingent or not) that are convertible into common stock or preferred stock. Purchaser will use its best efforts to structure the Transaction in the most tax-advantageous manner possible, which

does not result in a tax or other economic detriment to Seller or Purchaser.

2. **Purchase Price.** The purchase price ("Purchase Price") shall be the sum of the following:

(1) $95 million in cash.
(2) $5 million in the form of a performance-based promissory notes (the "Notes"). The Notes are described in detail in Section 3 of this Letter.
(3) Common stock in Purchaser equal to 9.2% of Purchaser's common stock that is currently outstanding (after giving effect to unexercised options in Purchaser).

Purchaser will work with Seller to provide X% of the Purchase Price to the Company's key employees, as identified by Seller. (It is anticipated that the entire $95 million cash amount go to Seller, that the Notes be payable to the Company's key employees, and that the common stock in Purchaser be divided in the same 80%/20% proportion among Seller and Company's key employees.)

3. **Notes.** The Notes shall have the following features:

A. **Priority.** The Notes shall be:

- senior in liquidation only to the amounts that Purchaser owes to its parent company, Target Parent Co. ("Parent") (except for indebtedness described below in this Section 3).
- junior to Purchaser's indebtedness to _____ and _____ in the amount of $X, which arose prior to Purchaser's acquisition of its interest in _____. (Of this amount, _____ assigned $X to Parent.)
- junior to any acquisition debt that may be incurred in connection with the Transactions contemplated by this Letter.

B. **Performance Feature.** The Notes shall be payable in three equal installments: 12, 24 and 36 months after the closing of the Transactions contemplated by this Letter, provided, however, that no amounts shall be due and payable under those Notes whose original holder is not employed by Company or one of its affiliates as of the scheduled payment date.

4. **Sources and Uses.** In summary, cash sources and cash uses of funds are as follows:

Cash Uses (millions)		Cash Sources (millions)	
Purchase Price		Senior Bank Debt	50.000
Cash	95.000	Performance Equity	3.000
Note	5.000	Cash Equity	50.000
Transaction Exp's	3.000		
	103.000		103.000

5. **Purchaser's Due Diligence Review.**

(a) Purchaser's due diligence review ("Purchaser's Due Diligence Review") will consist of a general review of the business and prospects of the Company, including an investigation of Company's historical financial statements, its products and competitive position, and the sustainability of its originations, revenue, and cash flow, as well as customary legal, regulatory, tax, accounting, and investment structure due diligence. As part of Purchaser's Due Diligence Review, Purchaser will evaluate Company's future business prospects, will review its direct marketing and advertising processes, will assess the Company's ability to securitize its products, and will review loan files and underwriting procedures. Concurrent with Purchaser's Due Diligence Review, parties providing financing and their respective agents and representatives may also conduct due diligence reviews. Purchaser's Due Diligence Review will begin on the date upon which Purchaser and its agents, representatives, and financing sources are granted access to the Company's books, records, portfolio tapes, facilities, key personnel, officers, directors, independent accountants, and legal counsel in accordance with Section 9 below.

The Seller agrees that such access will be granted promptly to the Purchaser, its agents, representatives, and financing sources following execution of this Letter. The Purchaser will complete due diligence within 30 days thereafter.

(b) Seller's due diligence review ("Seller's Due Diligence Review") will consist of a general review of the business and prospects of the Purchaser, including an investigation of Purchaser's historical financial statements, its products, and its competitive position. Seller's Due Diligence Review will begin on the date upon which Seller and its agents and representatives are granted access to the Purchaser's key personnel, key officers, directors, independent accountants, and legal counsel. The Purchaser agrees that such access will be granted promptly to the Seller and its agents and representatives, following execution of this Letter. The Seller will complete due diligence on the earlier of (1) the date on which Purchaser completes its diligence, or (2) 30 days after execution of this Letter.

6. **Definitive Purchase Agreement.** The Purchaser will prepare and deliver to the Seller within 10 days of the conclusion of Purchaser's Due Diligence Review a definitive Purchase Agreement (the "Purchase Agreement"). The Purchase Agreement will contain terms and conditions customary in transactions of this type (including standard representations, warranties, covenants, and indemnifications), or which are reasonably necessary as a result of the Due Diligence Review. Representations regarding the Company will, for most items, survive closing for three years, and for other items, including without limitation environmental, taxes, ERISA, and title, the survival shall be for longer periods (and in some cases indefinite).

7. **Closing Conditions.** Purchaser's obligation to consummate the Transactions contemplated by this Letter is subject to, among other things, the following conditions:

i. completion of, and Purchaser's satisfaction, in its sole discretion, with the results of Purchaser's Due Diligence Review;

    ii. negotiation and execution of a Purchase Agreement and all other necessary Transaction-related documentation mutually satisfactory to the parties thereto;

   iii. receipt of third-party financing on terms and conditions satisfactory to the Purchaser;

   iv. negotiation and execution of employment agreements with _____ and other selected executives of the Company, identified by Purchaser during its due diligence, which agreements will contain noncompete/nonsolicit/confidentiality provisions. A *draft* employment agreement for _____ is attached hereto as Exhibit A;

    v. absence of a material adverse change in the financial condition, results of operations, business, assets, properties or prospects of Company since December 31, 20_____;

   vi. compliance of the Transactions contemplated hereby with all laws and regulations applicable thereto, including (a) obtaining all necessary governmental and third-party approvals and consents (including consent by all applicable state licensing authorities), and making all necessary filings with regulatory authorities (including Hart-Scott-Rodino filings and approvals), and (b) the expiration of all waiting periods during which objections to the Transaction contemplated hereby can be raised; and

  vii. compliance by the Seller with its obligations hereunder.

The obligation of Seller to consummate the Transactions contemplated hereunder is subject to, among other things, the following conditions:

    i. completion of, and Seller's reasonable satisfaction with, the results of Seller's Due Diligence Review (provided, however, Seller shall only be able to terminate this Letter based on this paragraph if Seller's Due Diligence Review reveals items that would reasonably cause Seller to believe that the Purchaser will lack the financial resources to repay the Note);

ii. negotiation and execution of a Purchase Agreement and all other necessary Transaction-related documentation mutually satisfactory to the parties thereto;

iii. compliance of the Transactions contemplated hereby with all laws and regulations applicable thereto, including (a) obtaining all necessary governmental and third-party approvals and consents (including consent by all applicable state licensing authorities), and making all necessary filings with regulatory authorities (including Hart-Scott-Rodino filings and approvals), and (b) the expiration of all waiting periods during which objections to the Transaction contemplated hereby can be raised; and

iv. compliance by the Purchaser with its obligations hereunder.

8. **Schedule.** Purchaser, Seller, and Company agree to use their reasonable efforts to adhere to the following schedule of events leading up to the closing (assuming acceptance of this Letter by September 5, 20__):

September 15, 20__: Hart-Scott-Rodino filing will be prepared and filed, if necessary.

October 6, 20__: Purchaser's Due Diligence Review will be completed.

October 16, 20__: Purchaser will deliver a first draft of the Purchase Agreement to Seller.

October 29, 20__: Purchase Agreement will be executed, and closing will occur as soon as practicable thereafter.

9. **Cooperation.** Upon the Seller's acknowledgement of and agreement with the terms and conditions set forth in this Letter, the

Seller will permit the Purchaser and its agents, representatives, and financing sources (including attorneys, accountants, and any financing sources, and their agents and representatives) access to the Company's books, records, portfolio tapes, facilities, key personnel, officers, directors, independent accountants, and legal counsel in connection with Purchaser's Due Diligence Review.

10. **Exclusivity.**

A. **Cessation of Other Acquirer Activity.** Company and Seller agree that from the date of their acknowledgment of and agreement with the terms and conditions set forth in this Letter through the closing of the Transactions contemplated by this Letter, or the earlier termination of this Letter, neither Company nor any of its record and beneficial shareholders, officers, directors, affiliates, agents, or representatives will, directly or indirectly:

    i. submit, solicit, initiate, encourage, or discuss with third parties any proposal or offer from any person relating to any (a) reorganization, dissolution, or recapitalization of Company, (b) merger or consolidation involving Company, (c) sale of the stock of Company, (d) sale of any assets of Company outside the ordinary course of business or in connection with whole loan sales or securitizations unless consented to in advance by Purchaser, or (e) similar transaction or business combinations involving Company or its business or assets including, without limitation, any debt or equity financing thereof, or

    ii. furnish any information with respect to, assist or participate in, or facilitate in any other manner any effort or attempt by any person to do or seek the foregoing.

B. **Notification.** Company and Seller will, and will cause Company's officers, directors, affiliates, agents and representatives to, terminate all discussions with any third party regarding the foregoing and will notify Purchaser of the fact of receipt of any proposals or offers.

C. **Representation and Indemnification.** Company's and Seller's acknowledgment of and agreement with the terms and conditions set forth in this Letter also constitutes a representation and warranty that neither Company, Seller, nor any of Company's record and beneficial shareholders, officers, directors, affiliates, agents, or representatives have entered into any executory agreements or accepted any commitments concerning any of the foregoing transactions. Company and Seller hereby agree to indemnify and hold harmless Purchaser and each director, officer, investor, employee, and agent thereof (each, an "Indemnified Person") from and against any and all losses, claims, damages, liabilities (or actions or proceedings commenced or threatened in respect thereof), and expenses that arise out of, result from, or in any way relate to the breach of the foregoing representation and warranty. The obligations of Company and Seller under this paragraph will survive any termination of this Letter and will be effective regardless of whether a definitive agreement is executed.

11. **Conduct of the Business.** Upon acceptance of this Letter and until the earlier of closing of the Transactions contemplated by this Letter or the termination of this Letter, Company agrees to preserve substantially intact its business operations and assets and to conduct its operations in the ordinary course of business consistent with past operations. Without limiting the generality of the foregoing, Company shall not, without the prior written consent of Purchaser, (i) make any material capital expenditures, (ii) make or pay any dividends or distributions of any kind, (iii) enter into any material contracts, commitments, or arrangements (except in the ordinary course of business), (iv) change any compensation plans or pay any bonuses, (v) change any underwriting guidelines, or (vi) launch materially new products.

12. **Management.** It is anticipated that Company will be a stand-alone subsidiary of _____. _____ will re-

main President of the Company for three years, pursuant to an employment agreement, a draft of which is attached to this letter.

13. **Reimbursement of Fees and Expenses.** If the Transaction is not consummated by reason of a breach by the Seller or Company of any obligations under this Letter, the Seller and the Company hereby agree that Seller and the Company will jointly and severally reimburse the Purchaser and its affiliates for their out-of-pocket costs and expenses, including legal and other professional fees and expenses, incurred in connection with Purchaser's Due Diligence Review, the preparation, review, negotiation, execution, and delivery of this Letter, the definitive agreements and other documents relating to the Transaction, and the financing of the Transaction. If the Transaction is consummated, Seller and Purchaser will each bear their own expenses (and Seller will bear Company's expenses). No party to this Transaction has any liability to brokers in connection with this Transaction, or to which any other party to this Letter could become obligated. No employees of the Company will receive any payment, bonus, or other extraordinary compensation as a result of this Transaction.

14. **Termination.** Purchaser's offer hereunder will expire at 12:00 noon, Wisconsin Time, on September 5, 20__ ("Expiration"), unless the Seller and Company agree to the terms and conditions of this Letter by signing and returning to the Purchaser the enclosed counterpart of this Letter and the Purchaser receives such signed counterpart prior to that time. The Purchaser may terminate this Letter at any time if: (i) any information is disclosed to or discovered by the Purchaser or its representatives, after the conclusion of the Purchaser's Due Diligence Review which the Purchaser believes in good faith may be materially adverse to the Transaction or to the financial condition, results of operations, business, assets, properties, or prospects of the Company, or (ii) the Purchaser believes in good faith that one or more of the conditions to closing set forth herein will not be fulfilled. The Seller shall be permitted to terminate this Letter at any time after 60 days from the date hereof

in the event that the Purchase Agreement is not executed on or before that time. Notwithstanding the foregoing, (i) this Letter shall not be terminated if the closing is delayed solely due to delays in obtaining regulatory approval, (ii) the Reimbursement of Fees and Expenses section shall not terminate even if this Letter is terminated, and (iii) the obligations under subparagraph "C" of the Exclusivity section of this Letter shall not terminate even if this Letter is terminated.

15. **Binding Effect.** Subject to the conditions set forth herein, the obligations of each of the parties under this letter shall be binding at the time this letter is executed; provided, however, that the parties acknowledge that not all terms to be reflected in the Purchase Agreement and related documents have been discussed and agree to negotiate in good faith to finalize these agreements setting forth such additional terms.

16. **Announcements.** All press releases and other announcements relating to the Transaction shall be subject to prior approval by Purchaser, Company, and Seller.

17. **Counterparts.** This Letter may be executed in one or more counterparts.

18. **Governing Law.** The Transaction shall be governed by the laws (which shall mean all laws other than conflict of laws) of the State of Delaware.

Please sign and date this Letter no later than the time of Expiration (as set forth in the "Termination" Section, above) in the spaces provided below to confirm our mutual understandings and agreements as set forth in this Letter and return a signed copy to the undersigned. By signing this Letter, you are representing that you have authority to consummate this Transaction and that you are the sole shareholder of the Company (and that no other shareholders exist whose approval could be necessary to consummate this Transaction).

PURCHASER

By: _____
Investor and Management

ACKNOWLEDGED AND AGREED TO
AS OF SEPTEMBER _____, 20__

_____

Selling CEO
COMPANY

By: _____
Selling CEO

APPENDIX A-2. CONFIDENTIALITY AGREEMENT

[Date]
[Name/address]

Dear   :

As an inducement to [Company Name] (the "Company") to furnish us with information regarding the Company and its business in order to enable us to evaluate our interest in acquiring the stock assets of the Company (the "Evaluation") and in consideration of the Company's disclosure thereof to us, we enter into this confidentiality agreement (this "Agreement") and hereby agree as follows:

As used herein, "Confidential Information" means all data, reports, interpretations, forecasts, and records, to the extent they contain information concerning the Company that is not available to the general public and that the Company will provide to us in the course of our discussions with the Company. However, the term "Confidential Information" does not include information which (i) is or becomes available to the public other than as a result of a disclosure by us or our representative, (ii) was available to us prior to its disclosure to us by the Company or its representatives, (iii) becomes available to us from a source other than the Company or its representatives, provided that such source is not known by us either to be bound by a confidentiality agreement with the Company or its representatives or to otherwise be prohibited from transmitting the information to us by a contractual, legal, or fiduciary obligation, or (iv) is independently developed by us.

All Confidential Information will be held and treated by us and our Representatives (as defined below) in confidence and will not be disclosed by us or our Representatives except (i) in connection with the Evaluation, (ii) as may be required by law or deemed advisable by our attorneys in connection with any legal or governmental proceeding, or (iii) with the prior consent of the Company. Our "Representatives" means any of our agents, directors, officers, representatives, advisers (including, without limitation, our attorneys, accountants, bankers, and consultants), affiliates, and employees that actually receive written Confidential Information from us.

We undertake not to use any of the Confidential Information delivered to us for any purpose other than the Evaluation.

Except with the other party's written consent or if required by law, neither we nor you nor our respective representatives will disclose (i) that the Evaluation has occurred or is occurring, (ii) that we are negotiating for the acquisition of the stock or assets of the Company, or (iii) any of the potential terms or conditions of such acquisition. [**Add for a public company**: The Company acknowledges and agrees that we may be compelled by securities laws requirements to disclose the information referred to in the preceding sentence and, and in such case, the Company agrees that such disclosure may be made and will not constitute a breach of this Agreement.]

This Agreement shall be governed by and construed in accordance with the laws of the State of _____ without regard to the conflicts of law provisions thereof. No amendment to this Agreement shall be binding upon any party hereto unless in writing and signed by both parties hereto. Any provision of this Agreement that is illegal, invalid, prohibited, or unenforceable shall be ineffective to the extent of such illegality, invalidity, prohibition, or unenforceability without invalidating or impairing the remaining provisions hereof. This Agreement does not bind the parties to enter into any other contract or agreement. This Agreement represents the entire understanding between the parties with respect to the subject matter hereof and supersedes all prior oral and written communications, agreements, and understandings relating thereto. This Agreement may be executed in counterparts, and copies of original signatures sent by facsimile shall be binding evidence of this Agreement's execution.

The undersigned's obligations and the obligations of our Representatives under this Agreement shall terminate upon the earlier to occur of (i) Investor's consummation of an acquisition of, or other business transaction relating to, all or part of the Company's assets or stock or (ii) one year from the date hereof.

To the extent that the Investor or its affiliates provide to the Company any information regarding the Investor that is not available to the general public, the Company agrees that it (and its respective agents, directors, officers, representatives, advisers, affiliates, and employees) will treat all such confidential information with the same level of confidentiality afforded the Company hereunder and will not use such confidential information for any purpose other than in connection with the Evaluation.

[**Add where feasible**: The Company and its shareholders agree that from the date hereof until the first to occur of (i) the termination by the Investor of its due diligence regarding the Company without a decision to proceed to negotiate a definitive purchase agreement, or (ii) the sixtieth day following the completion by the Company of its responses to the Investor's requests for due diligence information, neither the Company nor its shareholders shall entertain, initiate, or continue discussion of any offer to sell, or solicit or continue to solicit any proposals regarding the sale of, all or any part of the stock or assets of the Company with any party other than the Investor; provided, however, that this period shall be extended for so long as the parties hereto are continuing to negotiate in good faith.]

If the foregoing reflects our agreement, kindly sign and return a copy of this Agreement to us.

Very truly yours,

Investor
By: Its General Partner

By: _____
       [Name]
       [Title]

Agreed to as of the date set forth above:

[Name of Company]

By: _____   [Note: add signature for each shareholder
    An Authorized Officer   if including the exclusivity clause]

APPENDIX A-3. INVESTMENT BANK ENGAGEMENT LETTER

The engagement letter with your investment banker is a reasonably important document. It is not as critical as your purchase and sale agreement with your buyer, which is utterly critical and requires extensive diligence and negotiation, but it is important. It lays out the terms under which the banker will be representing you in your sale or financing.

Sadly, due to massive overlawyering, Sarbanes-Oxley, and the the ever-evil word processor, these documents have gotten quite long. They can be much shorter than the one below (perhaps two to three pages, with some luck) but I thought the most comprehensive example would be helpful. I have added annotations (in italics) to comment on important provisions.

[June 30, 2006]

STRICTLY CONFIDENTIAL

[Name of Client]
[Street Address]
[City, State, Zip Code]

Attention: [Name]
             [Title]

Dear Sirs:

This letter (the "Agreement") constitutes the agreement between COMPANY NAME (the "Company") and INVESTMENT BANKER NAME ("IB") that IB will serve as the exclusive financial adviser of the Company with respect to: any sale or similar transaction involving the assets or capital stock of the Company; any merger or consolidation involving the Company; or any recapitalization or reorganization of the Company (hereinafter collectively referred to as a "Transaction"). The terms of this Agreement are as follows.

A. **Services.** At the Company's request, IB shall provide the following services:

1. Analyze the business, properties, and operations of the Company;

2. Prepare a Confidential Information Memorandum for distribution and presentation to potential purchasers, which shall

be reviewed for accuracy and completeness, and approved in writing, by the Company;

3. Assist in identifying and screening prospective purchasers and prepare a list of such purchasers;

4. Assist in soliciting and evaluating proposals from prospective purchasers, structuring a transaction and negotiating a definitive agreement for the Transaction; and

5. Assist in making presentations regarding any proposed Transaction to the Board of Directors of the Company.

Obviously this preparation of your "Selling Memorandum," the "book" that represents your company, is important. Ask to see examples of some other "books," and make sure they have a good writer on your team. The IB is normally quite good at distilling the primary selling points, or "Key Investment Considerations."

B. **Fees and Expenses.** In connection with the services described above, the Company shall pay to IB the following compensation:

1. *Advisory Fee.* A nonrefundable cash fee of $[_____] for financial advisory services (the "Advisory Fee") shall be due upon execution of this Agreement. This fee shall be credited against the Transaction Fee payable pursuant to Paragraph B.2. below if and when such fee is paid;

The "Advisory Fee" is also often called a "Retainer Fee." Like most elements, it is negotiable. It exists to cover the IB's out-of-pocket expenses and is not supposed to be a ton of money—$30,000 to $50,000 is typical. Get it as low as you can.

2. *Transaction Fee.* If during the term of this engagement or after termination of this engagement as set forth in Paragraph D below, a Transaction is consummated, the Company shall pay IB, at the time of the closing (the "Closing") of the Transaction, in immediately available funds, a transaction fee (the "Transaction Fee") equal to the sum of:

1. ____% of the Aggregate Consideration up to $__ million; plus
2. ____% of the amount of the Aggregate Consideration over $__ million.

This is obviously where the rubber hits the road. As mentioned in the book, the Transaction Fee is a percentage of the total purchase price. Depending upon the size of the deal, it can range from as low as 1% to as high as 3 -4 % for very small deals. As is referenced above, sometimes there is a higher percentage on the first dollars like the famous "Lehman Formula" for small deals, which is 5% of the first million, 4% of the second, 3% of the third, 2% of the fourth, and 1% of the fifth million and all dollars beyond. Many firms also have a flat dollar minimum fee, such as $250,000 regardless of outcome. IBs don't come cheap of course, but a good one can add dramatic value. As per the book, think about an incentive fee as well if the banker knocks it out of the park. It gives them something to shoot for.

For purposes of this Agreement, "Aggregate Consideration" shall mean the total amount paid or payable, directly or indirectly, to, or for the benefit of, the Company (including any subsidiary thereof) and/or its security holders of (i) cash; and (ii) equity or debt securities or other equity interests (valued at the higher of the fair market value thereof on the date of Closing or announcement), including equity retained by the Company's shareholders; plus (iii) the face amount of any debt of the Company that is (A) in a sale of assets, assumed or repaid by the purchaser at Closing, or (B) in any other Transaction, assumed or repaid at Closing or remaining on the Company's balance sheet after Closing; (iv) in an asset sale, the fair value of assets remaining on the Company's balance sheet after Closing; and (v) the amount of any other form of consideration paid to the Company or to any shareholder, owner, or partner of the Company, including pursuant to noncompete, employment, or consulting agreements outside the normal course of business of the Company, any consideration held in escrow, and future payments that are contingent upon the performance of the Company or any successor to the Company. When such future payments are determinable at Closing, that portion of the fee will be paid at Closing based upon the present value of such payments, discounted at the prevailing rate on Treasury securities having a maturity most closely approximating the period over which such payments are expected to be made. When such future payments are contingent upon the Company's future performance and not determinable at Closing, that portion of the fee will be paid at the time of receipt by the Company or its shareholders, bondholders, or other security holders.

The "definition" of total consideration obviously has the kitchen sink and the kitchen (and the house!) but is fairly traditional. It avoids any future debates.

3. *Expenses.* In addition to any fees payable to IB hereunder and regardless of whether a Transaction is consummated, the Company hereby agrees, from time to time upon request, to reimburse IB for all reasonable travel and other Transaction-related expenses, including production, communication, research and reference materials, and postage and shipping, that are incurred in connection with IB's role hereunder or otherwise arising out of or in connection with any actual or potential Transaction, including reasonable fees and expenses of IB's counsel. To the extent that officers or employees of IB or its Affiliates assist in, or provide testimony (whether at trial or in deposition) for or documents in connection with, any action, suit, or proceeding related to, or arising from, IB's engagement hereunder, the Company shall pay IB its customary charges for the services of such officers and employees then in effect.

The Expense reimbursement is traditional. Just make sure you are kept apprised. This should not be a big number. Ask them to tell you at every $10,000 clipping level. And make sure they are not flying first class or staying in fancy hotels on your nickel.

C. **Coordination.** To coordinate IB's efforts on behalf of the Company during the period of IB's engagement hereunder, neither the Company nor its management will initiate or solicit any discussions looking toward or contemplating any Transaction except through IB. In the event the Company or its directors or management receives an unsolicited inquiry concerning any such Transaction, IB shall be informed promptly so that it can assess such inquiry and assist the Company in any resulting negotiations. If IB receives such an inquiry, it will promptly inform the Company.

D. **Termination of Engagement.** IB's engagement hereunder may be terminated by any party hereto at any time, with or without cause, upon ten days' prior written notice. In the event of any termination of this engagement, IB shall be entitled to the entire Advisory Fee provided for in Paragraph B.1. Further, IB shall be entitled to the full amount of the Transaction Fee provided for in Paragraph B.2 in the event that, at any time within two years after IB's engagement terminates, a Transaction is consummated (or an agreement is reached with respect thereto, which is subsequently consummated) with any party (i) identified orally or in writing as a prospective purchaser by IB during IB's engagement hereunder; or (ii) with whom the Company had any discussions regarding a potential Transaction during IB's engagement hereunder, whether or not such discussion was initiated by IB; or (iii) who proposed or to whom the Company proposed a Transaction during IB's engagement hereunder. Notwithstanding any such termination, the provisions of Paragraphs B and D and E through K hereof shall survive and shall be binding upon any successors or assigns of the Company.

This paragraph describes what is called a "tail." It is an important notion. It may seem offensive but it is fair. If the IB does a lot of work on your behalf and you pull the deal, they should still be paid if in a reasonable amount of time there is a transaction, even if they are no longer involved. This can be negotiated. The shortest tail you will get is 12 months and 24 is the longest; 18 is also usually acceptable.

E. **Reliance Upon and Accuracy of Information.** The Company understands, acknowledges, and agrees that IB may rely entirely upon publicly available information and information provided by the Company and the Company's officers, directors, shareholders, accountants, counsel, and other agents and advisers without independent verification of the accuracy and completeness of such information. If any information provided to IB becomes inaccurate, incomplete, or misleading in any material respect during IB's engagement hereunder, the Company shall so advise IB. The Company will continuously advise IB with respect to any material developments or matters that occur or come to the Company's attention during the term of IB's engagement hereunder.

F. **Confidentiality.** In the event of consummation of any Transaction, IB shall have the right to disclose its participation in such transaction, including, without limitation, the placement of "tombstone" advertisements in financial and other newspapers and journals, provided that IB shall submit a copy of any such advertisements to the Company for its approval, which approval shall not be unreasonably withheld.

Except as required by law or pursuant to order of a court of competent jurisdiction, no written or oral advice provided by IB pursuant to this Agreement shall be disclosed, in whole or in part, to any third party, or circulated or referred to publicly, without the prior written consent of IB. The fact of IB's engagement hereunder may be disclosed to prospective purchasers, but the Company may not publicly announce or advertise IB's engagement without the prior written consent of IB.

IB agrees to keep confidential all material nonpublic information provided to it by the Company, except as required by law or as contemplated by the terms of this Agreement. Notwithstanding anything to the contrary herein, IB may disclose nonpublic information to its affiliates, agents, and advisers whenever IB determines that such disclosure is necessary to provide the services contemplated hereunder.

G. **Indemnity.** IB and the Company agree to the provisions with respect to indemnification by the Company of IB and certain other parties as set forth on Annex A attached hereto.

It's a sad fact of today's business environment that the "CYA" provisions (a technical term meaning Cover Your Ass) are so long that they now go in an addendum. This basically means that no matter what happens, you cannot sue the IB. Of course you can try to take action if their work is awful (Ron Perelman just won a $750 million judgment against Morgan Stanley for poor mergers advice), but success is unlikely. And, by the way, you will not have much luck in trying to negotiate these provisions. The very best thing you can do, as in nearly all business matters, is to hire quality people of high repute (and limited or no history of litigation) to work with you.

H. **Limitation of Engagement to the Company.** The Company acknowledges that IB has been retained only by the Company, and that the Company's engagement of IB is not deemed to be on behalf of, and is not intended to confer rights upon, any shareholder, owner, or partner of the Company or any other person not a party hereto as against IB or any of its controlling persons, affiliates, directors, officers, employees, or agents. Unless otherwise expressly agreed to in writing by IB, no one other than the Company is authorized to rely upon this engagement or any other statements or conduct of IB, and no one other than the Company is intended to be a beneficiary of this Agreement. The Company acknowledges that any advice or recommendations, written or oral, given by IB to the Company in connection with IB's engagement are intended solely for the benefit and use of the Company's management and directors in considering a possible Transaction, and any such recommendations or advice shall not confer any rights or remedies upon any other person or be used or relied upon for any other purpose.

I. **Limitation of IB's Liability to Company.** IB and the Company further agree that neither IB nor any of its controlling persons, affiliates, directors, officers, employees, or agents shall have any liability to the Company, its security holders, or creditors, or any person asserting claims on behalf of or in the right of the Company (whether direct or indirect, in contract, tort, for an act of negligence or otherwise) for any losses, fees, damages, liabilities, costs, expenses, or equitable relief arising out of or relating to this Agreement or the services to be rendered hereunder, except to the extent that it is finally determined (by a court of competent jurisdiction and after exhausting all appeals or in an arbitration conducted in accordance with this Agreement) that such losses, fees, damages, liabilities, costs, expenses, or equitable relief resulted solely from the gross negligence or willful misconduct of IB.

J. **Governing Law.** The Company acknowledges that this Agreement has been negotiated, executed, and delivered in Charlotte, North Carolina, and that this Agreement shall be interpreted, and the rights and liabilities determined, in accordance with the laws of the State of North Carolina.

K. **Arbitration of Disputes.** Except as provided below, any claim or controversy arising out of or relating to this Agreement, or the breach thereof, shall be settled by arbitration in accordance with the Commercial Arbitration Rules of the American Arbitration Association, and judgment on the award rendered by the arbitrator(s) may be entered in any court having jurisdiction thereof. The arbitration of any such claim or controversy shall take place in Charlotte, North Carolina. In the event that IB is named as a party in a lawsuit arising out of or related to its engagement or to a Transaction and the Company is not named as a party in that lawsuit, IB has the right but not the obligation to file a third-party claim against the Company or to otherwise join the Company in that lawsuit in accordance with applicable law. If IB does not exercise that right, any dispute over a claim for indemnity or contribution by IB arising out of the lawsuit in which the Company was not named as a party shall be settled by arbitration as contemplated herein.

L. **Affiliate; Broker/Dealer.** For the purposes of this Agreement, "Affiliate" shall mean any entity directly or indirectly controlling, controlled by, or under common control with such entity. Furthermore, IB Partners is the trade name for IB Partners LLC and its subsidiaries and affiliates, which include EVP Securities LLC, a North Carolina limited liability company, a registered broker-dealer and NASD member firm that provides investment banking, private placement, merger, acquisition, divestiture services, and merchant banking services.

M. **Miscellaneous.** This Agreement shall not be modified or amended except in writing signed by IB and the Company. This Agreement shall not be assigned without the prior written consent of IB and the Company. This Agreement constitutes the entire agreement of IB and the Company with respect to the subject matter hereof and supersedes all prior agreements. If any provision of this Agreement is determined to be invalid or unenforceable in any respect, such determination will not affect such provision in any other respect, and the remainder of the Agreement shall remain in full force and effect. In connection with the services it renders pursuant to this Agreement, IB shall not be required to obtain any additional licenses, consent to service of process, or otherwise make any further material filing under any applicable state or federal statutes or regulations. This Agreement may be executed in counterparts, each of which shall be deemed an original but all of which together shall constitute one and the same instrument.

In acknowledgment that the foregoing correctly sets forth the understanding reached by IB and the Company, please sign in the space provided below, whereupon this letter shall constitute a binding Agreement as of the date indicated above.

Sincerely,

IB PARTNERS LLC

By: _____

Name: _____

Title: _____ Partner _____

Accepted and Agreed:

COMPANY NAME

By: _____

Name: _____

Title: _____

Date: _____

Investment Banking Engagement Letter: ANNEX A

In connection with IB's engagement to advise and to assist the Company pursuant to the Agreement dated [_____] to which this Annex A is attached, the Company agrees to indemnify and to hold harmless IB and each of its officers, directors, employees, affiliates, associated companies, agents, counsel and other advisors, and each other person or entity who controls any of them (hereinafter collectively referred to as an "Indemnified Party"), to the full extent allowed by law or equity, from and against any and all judgments, losses, claims (whether or not valid), damages, costs, fees, expenses, or liabilities, joint or several, to which an Indemnified Party may become subject, related to or arising out of IB's engagement or performance under the Agreement, the transactions contemplated thereby, the services rendered by IB under the Agreement, or any actual or threatened claim, litigation, investigation, proceeding, or action in any court or before any regulatory, administrative, or other body relating to any of the foregoing (hereinafter referred to collectively as a "Claim"), and shall, upon request, reimburse an Indemnified Party for all legal and other costs, fees, and expenses as they are incurred in connection with investigating, preparing, or defending a Claim; provided, however, that no such indemnification shall be required to be paid to an Indemnified Party with respect to a Claim that is finally determined by a court of competent jurisdiction (after exhaustion of all appeals) or in an arbitration conducted in accordance with this Agreement to have resulted solely from the gross negligence or willful misconduct of such Indemnified Party.

In the event that the foregoing indemnity is unavailable or insufficient for any reason (other than by reason of the terms hereof), then the Company shall contribute to any amounts paid or payable by an Indemnified Party in such proportion as appropriately reflects the relative benefits to such Indemnified Party and to the Company in connection with the matters to which the Claim relates. If such allocation is judicially determined to be impermissible, then the Company shall contribute in such proportion as appropriately reflects the relative benefits and relative fault of the Company and such Indemnified Party, as well as any other equitable considerations. The aggregate liability of IB and any other Indemnified Party for contribution pursuant to this paragraph in connection with all Claims shall not exceed the amount of fees actually received by IB under the Agreement.

All amounts due to an Indemnified Party hereunder shall be payable by the Company promptly upon request by such Indemnified Party. In addition, the Company agrees to pay all costs and expenses (including attorneys' fees) incurred by any Indemnified Party to enforce the terms of this Annex A.

Upon receipt by an Indemnified Party of actual notice of a Claim as to which indemnification may be sought hereunder, such Indemnified Party shall promptly notify the Company of the nature and basis of the Claim. In addition, an Indemnified Party shall promptly notify the Company after any action is commenced against the Indemnified Party (by way of service with a summons or other legal process) and shall transmit a copy to the business address of the Company. In any event, failure to notify the Company shall not relieve the Company from any liability which the Company may have on account of this indemnity or otherwise, except to the extent that the Company is actually prejudiced thereby. The Company may, and shall, if requested by any Indemnified Party, assume the defense of any Claim against such Indemnified Party in respect of which indemnity may be sought hereunder, including, without limitation, the employment of counsel reasonably satisfactory to such Indemnified Party and the payment of the fees and expenses of such counsel and necessary experts, in which event, except as provided below, the Company shall not be liable for the fees and expenses of any other counsel retained by such Indemnified Party in connection with such litigation or proceeding. In any such litigation or proceeding the defense of which the Company shall have assumed, any Indemnified Party shall have the right to participate and to retain its own counsel, but the fees and expenses of such counsel shall be at the expense of such Indemnified Party unless (i) the Company and such Indemnified Party have agreed in writing to the retention of such counsel; or (ii) the named parties to any such litigation or proceeding (including any impleaded parties) include the Company and such Indemnified Party and representation of both parties by the same counsel would, in the opinion of counsel to such Indemnified Party, be inappropriate due to actual or potential conflicts of interests between the Company and such Indemnified Party.

The Company shall not be liable for any settlement of any litigation or proceeding effected without its written consent; however; if settlement occurs with such consent or if there is a final judgment against the Indemnified Party, then the Company agrees to indemnify, pursuant to the terms hereof, against any loss or liability by reason of such settlement or judgment. The Company shall not settle any Claim, action, or proceeding where indemnity may be sought hereunder, whether or not any Indemnified Party is an actual or potential party to such Claim, without IB's written consent, which consent will not be unreasonably withheld.

The provisions of this Annex A shall be in addition to any liability which the Company may otherwise have to IB; shall not be limited by any rights that IB or any other Indemnified Party may otherwise have; shall remain in full force and effect regardless of any termination of IB's engagement; and shall be binding upon any successors or assigns of IB and the Company. Capitalized terms used herein which are not otherwise defined herein shall have the meanings set forth in the Agreement.

APPENDIX A-4. EXECUTIVE REFERENCE CHECKLIST

1. Integrity of Executive
2. Deal-savvy? Disciplined in pricing? Due diligence discipline/experience?
3. Financing knowledge; ability to handle lenders
4. Vision
   a. Does it make sense/hold water; synergies realistic, revenue growth realistic?
   b. Has he done it before, is he a strong leader?
5. Operating Skills
   a. Understand how to keep and motivate people? Detail-oriented?
   b. Focus on expense/margins? Financial savvy?
   c. What level of salesmanship, charisma, and intelligence does he have?
   d. Ability to manage budget/expense?
   e. Quality of the team; have managers followed him in the past?
   f. Does he keep promises? How often have results varied from operating plans?
6. Investor Relations
   a. Ability to work with VCs; open to input?
   b. Understands and reports to board?
   c. Would be good in front of public analysts?
7. Strengths and Weaknesses

8. Would you put money behind him/this effort? What would you worry about as an investor?

9. What is his profile in the industry and credibility?

10. What are his industry contacts and relationships with potential targets? (If doing a roll-up)

11. Who else would be good to talk to about this executive?

APPENDIX A-5. WORKING GROUP LIST

WORKING GROUP LIST

COMPANY/ CONTACT	OFFICE	HOME/OTHER
MANAGEMENT TEAM Company Address	Phone: (123) 456-7890 Fax: (123) 456-7890 Email@mail.com	Home Address Phone: (123) 456-7890 Fax: (123) 456-7890 Pager: (800)888-8888
CEO	Phone: (123) 456-7890 Fax: (123) 456-7890 Email@mail.com	Home Address Phone: (123) 456-7890 Fax: (123) 456-7890 Pager: (800)888-8888
Chairman	Phone: (123) 456-7890 Fax: (123) 456-7890 Email@mail.com	Home Address Phone: (123) 456-7890 Fax: (123) 456-7890 Pager: (800)888-8888
President	Phone: (123) 456-7890 Fax: (123) 456-7890 Email@mail.com	Home Address Phone: (123) 456-7890 Fax: (123) 456-7890 Pager: (800)888-8888
CFO	Phone: (123) 456-7890 Fax: (123) 456-7890 Email@mail.com	Home Address Phone: (123) 456-7890 Fax: (123) 456-7890 Pager: (800)888-8888

BUYER'S LAW FIRM
Address

Partner	Phone: (123) 456-7890	Home Address
	Fax: (123) 456-7890	
	Email@mail.com	Phone: (123) 456-7890
		Fax: (123) 456-7890
		Pager: (800)888-8888

Associate	Phone: (123) 456-7890	Home Address
	Fax: (123) 456-7890	
	Email@mail.com	Phone: (123) 456-7890
		Fax: (123) 456-7890
		Pager: (800)888-8888

BUYER'S ACCOUNTING FIRM
Address

Partner	Phone: (123) 456-7890	Home Address
	Fax: (123) 456-7890	
	Email@mail.com	Phone: (123) 456-7890
		Fax: (123) 456-7890
		Pager: (800)888-8888

Associate	Phone: (123) 456-7890	Home Address
	Fax: (123) 456-7890	Phone: (123) 456-7890
	Email@mail.com	Fax: (123) 456-7890
		Pager: (800)888-8888

INVESTOR GROUP
Address

Partner	Phone: (123) 456-7890	Home Address
	Fax: (123) 456-7890	
	Email@mail.com	Phone: (123) 456-7890
		Fax: (123) 456-7890
		Pager: (800)888-8888

Associate	Phone: (123) 456-7890	Home Address
	Fax: (123) 456-7890	
	Email@mail.com	Phone: (123) 456-7890
		Fax: (123) 456-7890
		Pager: (800)888-8888

Associate	Phone: (123) 456-7890	Home Address
	Fax: (123) 456-7890	
	Email@mail.com	Phone: (123) 456-7890
		Fax: (123) 456-7890
		Pager: (800)888-8888

SELLER'S LAW FIRM
Address

Partner   Phone: (123) 456-7890   Home Address
                                Fax: (123) 456-7890
                                Email@mail.com   Phone: (123) 456-7890
                                                              Fax: (123) 456-7890
                                                              Pager: (800)888-8888

Associate   Phone: (123) 456-7890   Home Address
                                Fax: (123) 456-7890
                                Email@mail.com   Phone: (123) 456-7890
                                                              Fax: (123) 456-7890
                                                              Pager: (800)888-8888

SELLER'S ACCOUNTING FIRM
Address

Partner   Phone: (123) 456-7890   Home Address
                                Fax: (123) 456-7890
                                Email@mail.com   Phone: (123) 456-7890
                                                              Fax: (123) 456-7890
                                                              Pager: (800)888-8888

Associate   Phone: (123) 456-7890   Home Address
                                Fax: (123) 456-7890
                                Email@mail.com   Phone: (123) 456-7890
                                                              Fax: (123) 456-7890
                                                              Pager: (800)888-8888

BANK 1
Address

Managing Director   Phone: (123) 456-7890   Home Address
                                Fax: (123) 456-7890
                                Email@mail.com   Phone: (123) 456-7890
                                                              Fax: (123) 456-7890
                                                              Pager: (800)888-8888

Associate   Phone: (123) 456-7890   Home Address
                                Fax: (123) 456-7890
                                Email@mail.com   Phone: (123) 456-7890
                                                              Fax: (123) 456-7890
                                                              Pager: (800)888-8888

BANK 2

| Managing Director | Phone: (123) 456-7890
Fax: (123) 456-7890
Email@mail.com | Home Address

Phone: (123) 456-7890
Fax: (123) 456-7890
Pager: (800)888-8888 |
| Associate | Phone: (123) 456-7890
Fax: (123) 456-7890
Email@mail.com | Home Address

Phone: (123) 456-7890
Fax: (123) 456-7890
Pager: (800)888-8888 |

INVESTMENT BANK

Managing Director	Phone: (123) 456-7890 Fax: (123) 456-7890 Email@mail.com	Home Address Phone: (123) 456-7890 Fax: (123) 456-7890 Pager: (800)888-8888
Principal	Phone: (123) 456-7890 Fax: (123) 456-7890 Email@mail.com	Home Address Phone: (123) 456-7890 Fax: (123) 456-7890 Pager: (800)888-8888
Associate	Phone: (123) 456-7890 Fax: (123) 456-7890 Email@mail.com	Home Address Phone: (123) 456-7890 Fax: (123) 456-7890 Pager: (800)888-8888

APPENDIX A-6. TIME AND RESPONSIBILITY SCHEDULE

IG = Investor Group

TARGET = Target Company

ABC = Insurance Company

F	Detailed Financial Statements by Month (FY '05 & '06 YTD)	TARGET, IG
F	Management Letters (or any qualitative text)	TARGET, IG
F	Depreciation Schedules and Spending (FY '03, '04, '05 & '06 YTD)	TARGET, IG

F	Audited Financial Statements (FY '04, '05 & '06 six months), when available	TARGET, IG
F	2006–2008 projections	TARGET, IG
F	Tax Returns, (FY '03, '04 & '05)	TARGET, IG
F	Analysis of Accounts Receivable and other balance sheet items	TARGET, IG
F	Schedule of bill rates by branch, business line, and/or region	TARGET, IG
D	Customer Contracts (current and historical contracts;) please include amendments, if any	TARGET
D	Other Material Contracts (including license & employment agreements)	TARGET
D	Insurance Policies	ABC
D	Lease Summaries; please note capital or operating	TARGET
D	Patents, Trademarks, Service Marks, Copyrights, or Intellectual Property	TARGET
D	Description of any current or less than 3-year-old suits/ disputes	TARGET
D	Description of any Pending or Threatened Litigation	TARGET
D	Any Agreements with Bankers, Brokers, Finders, or Consultants	TARGET
D	Fully Diluted Share Ownership Table	TARGET
G	Board of Directors packages and minutes, last 24 months	TARGET
G	Customer Comments/Audit/Quality Feedback	TARGET, ISP
G	Publicity/Articles	TARGET
G	Detailed Systems Description & Review	TARGET
G	Interviews with staffing industry research analysts	TARGET
G	Interviews with eSolutions industry research analysts	TARGET
HR	Employee Handbook	TARGET
HR	Policies & Procedures Manual	TARGET
HR	Newsletters, etc.	TARGET
HR	Payroll; please indicate title and department or other head count proxy (by business line, function, region)	TARGET
HR	Stock Option Plan, if any	TARGET
HR	Pension Plan/Deferred Comp Plan, if any	TARGET
HR	Detailed Organizational Charts	TARGET

HR	Results of Recent Inspections (OSHA, EEOC, etc.)	TARGET
HR	Workers' Compensation Ratings	TARGET
HR	Hiring & Employment & Turnover by division, "level," team, etc. ('03, '04, '05 & '06 YTD)	TARGET
HR	Detail of current benefit plans and costs per employee (include wage and benefit rates)	TARGET
HR	Recruiting process and employee retention	TARGET
M	Schedule of management carry distribution, planned executive compensation packages, planned employee stock option plan, existing employment agreements	TARGET
M	Legal structure of business	TARGET
M	Business descriptions of XYZ acquisitions with status of transaction	TARGET
M	LOIs for XYZ acquisitions, transaction structure detail	TARGET
M	Financial statements and projections for XYZ acquisitions	TARGET

Codes:
F: Financial Information
D: Documents
G: General
HR: Human Resources/Organization
M: Management

APPENDIX A-7. DUE DILIGENCE CHECKLIST

Table of Contents

• Industry Review
• Company's Position in the Industry

• Products
• Demand and Customer Analysis
• Marketing
• Distribution

- Production
- Litigation

Accounting Issues 3
- Accounting Responsibility and Function
- Profitability
- Asset Management
- Capital Structure
- Cash Flow
- Taxes
- Dividend Policy and Restrictions

Management & Personnel 4
- Management
- Board of Directors
- Shareholders
- Industrial Relations

Document Checklist 5
- List of Participants
- Financials
- Product Lines
- Industry Publications
- Legal Documents

INDUSTRY AND COMPANY OVERVIEW

Industry Classification
1. Client definition/Form 10-K
2. Business section of prospectuses
3. Trade association publications/data
4. Manufacturing process or principal areas of value added
5. Production—Sales cycle
6. Customer profile
7. SIC code
8. Security analysts' reports

Growth Trends and Prospects; Size and Profitability of Other Firms in Each Industry Segment

1. Industry's Performance and Trends
   a. Industry's historical performance
      i. rate of increase in sales and earnings
      ii. market share growth, primary and secondary demand
      iii. consistency among companies
      iv. compare the industry's performance with that of other industries
      v. compare the Company's performance with that of its industry
      vi. determine the cause of any company variations
      vii. financial market acceptance, including credit ratings
   b. Stability of companies within industry
      i. turnover of competitors
      ii. volatility of earnings and access to financial markets
      iii. credit ratings changes
      iv. mergers, acquisitions, and consolidations
      v. bankruptcies and reorganizations
   c. Trends within industry and potential impact upon the Company's future operations. Examples of such trends include:
      i. scarcity of raw materials
      ii. new regulations
      iii. shift in product mix or demand
      iv. increase or erosion in profit margins
      v. increased competition or demand from abroad
2. Structure of Competition in the Industry
   a. Industry structure
   b. Identity of principal competitors and share of market
      i. the Company's market share and position within the industry
      ii. elements of competition
         (a) price
         (b) quality and features

        (c) delivery or service

        (d) engineering

        (e) advertising

     iii. shifts of competitive structure within the industry

        (a) market share changes

        (b) price reductions

        (c) extended credit terms

        (d) producing and holding merchandise

  c. Susceptibility to changes in economic environment

     i. Product substitution or alternatives potential

     ii. Cost/Price relationships

     iii. Predominant suppliers

     iv. Likelihood of forward or backward integration

3. Industry Business Characteristics

  a. Research and development

     i. dependence on R & D and technology

     ii. product or process successes by others

     iii. the Company's success compared to competitors

     iv. importance of patents and cases of infringement

     v. rate of R&D expenditures compared to norm

     vi. potential obsolescence due to:

        (a) new equipment or processes

        (b) technology

        (c) products

  b. Marketing and distribution

     i. method of distribution and control of these channels

     ii. advertising or promotional expenditures

     iii. margin structure throughout the distribution chain

  c. Manufacturing process

  d. Labor relations

     i. organization status

     ii. strike history

     iii. wage and benefit trends

     iv. availability and skill level

  e. Seasonality or cyclicality of industry

Company's Relative Position Within the Industry

1. Relative sales and earnings levels and growth rates
2. Market shares and positions
3. Company strengths and weaknesses vis-à-vis relevant competitive factors in the industry
4. Company's geographic coverage and customer type
   a. Analyze stability
   b. Demographic trends
5. Reputation and product recognition

PRODUCTS

Major Individual Products and Product Lines

1. Sales—unit and dollar volume
   a. Five-year historical and current interim figures
   b. Projections
      i.   Management
      ii. Independent industry analysts
   c. Product catalogue and price list
2. Quality and feature comparisons
3. Pricing
   a. Seasonality or cyclicality
   b. History of discounting and price reductions
   c. Ability to pass along cost increases
   d. Preferred customer discounts
4. Product life cycle
   a. pending obsolescence due to:
      i.   new equipment or processes
      ii. new products
      iii. underlying demand or demographic shift
5. Seasonality or cyclicality of product demand
6. Substitutes and complementary products

Product Development

1. Resources and requirements as compared to the industry
2. Historical and projected R & D expenditures

3. Feasible studies on marketing and production—is the technology marketable?
4. Patents
   a. licensing agreements
   b. actual or potential cases of infringement

Earnings

1. Profit contribution by product line
   a. Five-year historical and current interim figures
   b. Projections
      i. management
      ii. independent industry analysts
2. Stability and consistency of earnings
3. Earnings growth
   a. Acquisitions
   b. Internal growth

DEMAND AND CUSTOMER ANALYSIS

List of Major Customers
1. Industry position of customers
2. Dollar size of sales
3. Customer turnover and loyalty
4. Domestic vs. international breakdown

Purchase Decision
1. Price
2. Quality/features
3. Engineering
4. Customer decision process
5. Are the Company's name and trademark well known?

MARKETING

Marketing Focus (Advertising, Packaging, Delivery, Etc.)
1. Advertising
   a. Expenditure relative to industry

  b. Importance to marketing strategy
 2. Design and packaging
 3. Discounting
 4. Trade shows
 5. Customer contact method
 6. Marketing expense

Marketing Staff
 1. List and evaluate
 2. Structure of incentive system
 3. Branch offices, warehouses, service facilities, etc.

DISTRIBUTION

Channels
 1. In-house capability
  a. transportation
  b. order processing
 2. Retail operations
  a. layout
  b. number of locations and their geographic distribution
 3. Dependence on outside channels
  a. flexibility of distribution channel
  b. margins along distribution chain

PRODUCTION

Description of the Processes
 1. Nature of manufacturing processes
  a. Batch or line process
  b. Labor- or capital-intensive
  c. Wage structure and demands
   i. unionization and history of labor relations
   ii. recent or pending strike activity
  d. Abundance, age, and educational level of workforce
  e. Licensed or patented?

2. Inventory control
   a. Breakdown by finished goods, work in process, and raw materials
   b. Warehousing
3. Flow of materials and plant efficiency (and compared to industry)
4. Quality control
5. Maintenance procedure and expense
6. Hazards and insurance
7. Internal vs. outside services for various production stages

Raw Materials and Other Inputs

1. Cost
   a. Trends and variability
      i.   Extent of substitutability
      ii. Ability to pass through cost increases
2. Competition for and control of supply
   a. Same industry vs. outside
   b. Major suppliers
      i.   contracts
      ii. financial condition of suppliers, particularly foreign
      iii. dependability
   c. Purchasing arrangements
3. Subcontractors for parts or subassemblies?

Facilities and Equipment

1. Condition and age
   a. Planned capital expenditures
   b. Capacity utilization
      i. historical
      ii. planned
   c. Facilities
      i.   owned vs. leased facilities
      ii. general use or specialized capacity
      iii. factors preventing capacity expansion
         (a) zoning

(b) production process

(c) access

2. Maintenance expense
   a. expected replacement near-term
   b. expected replacement long-term
3. Power, water, and waste disposal
   a. availability
   b. adequacy

LITIGATION

Material and Pending Litigation
1. Potential exposure
   a. consequences to operations
   b. consequences to financial condition
2. Insurance

ACCOUNTING RESPONSIBILITY AND FUNCTION

Quality and Size of Financial, Accounting, and Internal Audit Staff—Reporting System

Existence of Ongoing Records
1. Description
2. Equipment used to keep records
3. Accuracy of interim financials

Differences Between Book and Tax Records

Budgeting System
1. Integration of costing and financial records
2. Analysis of costing system
3. Replacement cost accounting

Frequency and Adequacy of Physical Counts

Variations in Company's Accounting Policies From Industry Norms
1. Revenue recognition
2. Inventory

3. Replacement cost accounting
4. Depreciation
5. Treatment of foreign exchange gains or losses

Credit Control Procedures

Accountants
1. Status of audits
2. Accountants' management letter
   a. Suggested improvements
   b. Formal reviews and changes during last five years

SEC or FAS Opinions or Payments

Insurance

PROFITABILITY

Cost Accounting
1. Major elements
2. Overhead history
3. Allocation

Sales
1. Returns and allowances
2. Recognition of income—sale or delivery
   a. Installment sales
   b. Affiliates
3. Intercompany sales and profits
4. Other sources of income—royalties, rents
5. Consolidation policies

Profitability Forecast
1. Factors most likely to affect estimates
2. Change in financing structure and effect on profits
3. Overhead or corporate expense

Other Sources of Income
1. Royalties
2. Rents

Treatment of Minority Interest

ASSET MANAGEMENT

Inventory
1. Inventory valuation and reserve structure
2. Breakdown work-in-progress, raw materials, and finished goods

Receivables
1. Aging schedule
2. Bad debt allowance

Prepaids
1. Identification
2. Valuation

Other Assets
1. Notes receivable
2. Intangible assets
   a. Identification
   b. Amortization

Fixed Assets
1. Book value
2. Replacement cost
3. Original cost and/or adjustments for purchase accounting
4. Potential write-offs
5. Depreciation
   a. Average life
   b. Type of depreciation
      i. Book vs. tax

    c. Accelerated to account for obsolescence

6. List of properties

Current Liabilities

1. Credit by major vendors
2. Discounts received or lost
3. Provisions for outstanding liabilities and contingencies

Other Liabilities

1. Penalties
2. Litigation
3. Additional taxes
4. Contingent
5. Pension funding items

CAPITAL STRUCTURE

Long-term Debt

1. Amount outstanding
2. Rates
3. Maturity—prepayment provisions and penalties
4. Debt ratings
5. Covenants
    a. Coverage—interest, fixed charges, assets
    b. Principal repayments
    c. Ratio requirements, etc.
6. Convertibility
7. Events of default

Short-term Debt—Lines of Credit

1. Interest expenses during start-up
2. Availability and draw-down
    a. current
    b. historical
    c. cost

Lease Obligations
1. Capital leases
2. Operating leases

Preferred or Hybrid Securities

Shareowners' Equity
1. Paid-in
2. Retained earnings
3. Treasury stock

CASH FLOW

Working Capital Requirement
1. Relationship among inventories, receivables, and payables
2. Minimum cash required to run business
3. Ability to convert nonproductive assets into cash for working capital

Capital Expenditures
1. Desired
2. Required

Depreciation and Amortization
1. Adequacy of estimated useful life of equipment being written off
2. Goodwill

TAXES

Tax Issues
1. Deferred Taxes: Revenue Recognition, Depreciation
2. Reserves for Prior Year's Taxes
3. States in which Returns Are Filed
4. Treatment and Availability of Investment Tax Credit
5. Availability of N.O.L.

6. Allocation
7. Foreign vs. Domestic

DIVIDEND POLICY AND RESTRICTIONS

Dividend Policy
Dividend Restrictions

MANAGEMENT

List Key Personnel—Salaries and Titles
1. Turnover and experience
2. Depth of management
3. Recruiting and training
4. Affiliations

Compensation
1. Wage scale, promotion and review
2. Employee contracts and service agreements
3. Incentive awards—stock options plans, earn-outs, etc.
4. Insurance (life and medical), autos, personal loans and vacations
5. Deferred

BOARD OF DIRECTORS

Board of Directors
1. Age and Service
2. Other Directorships and Affiliations
3. Meetings—Review Frequency and Substance
4. List of Committees and Assignments
5. Insider or Related-Party Transactions

SHAREHOLDERS

Security Issues
1. Rights of each class

   2. Stock options

   3. Stockholder agreements

Shareholders
1. Principal holders of various classes
2. Geographic distribution
3. Institutions
4. Unidentified

Securities Convertible into Common and Major Holders Thereof

INDUSTRIAL RELATIONS

Employees
1. Number of employees
2. Source of labor
3. Skilled vs. unskilled

Competition for Labor
1. Turnover
2. Ability to vary workforce

Unions
1. History of strikes
2. Next scheduled bargaining

Work Conditions
1. Accident frequency
2. Last OSHA review
3. Morale—grievances and suits
4. Wage scale and promotion review and policies

Compensation and Benefits
1. Compensation structure
   a. Frequency
   b. Overtime

    c. Profit sharing

    d. Vacations and holidays

    e. Guarantees and indemnities

2. Pension plan

    a. Level of benefits

    b. Extent of funding of accrued pension benefits

       i.   Unfunded past service liability

       ii. History of expenditures

    c. Last revision

    d. Transferability

    e. Effect on profitability

3. Life insurance and medical benefits

DOCUMENT CHECKLIST

List of Participants—business and home address, phone number, telecopy number

1. Client team

2. Investor team

3. Attorneys

4. Accountants

5. Lenders

6. Other involved parties

Financials

1. 10K—audited last five years

2. 10Q—unaudited stub period

3. Annual reports

4. Registration statements—any pending?

5. 8K—Reports on recent unscheduled material events or corporate changes

6. Five-year plan with assumptions

7. Historical budgets

8. Policy manual

9. Proxies

10. Accountant letters

11. Pension plans including latest actuarial evaluation
12. Filings unique to industry (bank call reports, insurance convention blanks, etc.)

Product Lines

1. Sales and earnings reports
2. Price lists
3. Market size and share estimates

Industry Publications

Legal Documents

1. Articles of incorporation and by-laws
2. Domicile of major operations—name and address of subsidiaries
3. Indenture agreements
4. Corporate history
   a. Name changes
   b. Ownership structure
   c. Acquisitions
5. Patents, trademarks and copyrights
6. Licensing agreements
   a. Distribution
   b. Technology
   c. Franchises
   d. Royalty agreements—basis, expiration, renewal and cancellation
7. Government contracts
8. Noncompete restrictions
9. Warranty and service agreements
10. Assets pledged or notes cosigned
11. Litigation or suits in progress or pending
12. Relationship with financial and business community
    a. Institutional lenders
    b. Investment bankers
    c. Analysts and broker presentations
13. Union contracts

RESOURCES

APPENDIX B CONTAINS lists of important resources you need in putting together your deal. These lists are not intended to be comprehensive and information may change, so more current information may be found on the website for this book.

Potential contacts in the following areas are included:

APPENDIX B-1. BUSINESS BROKERS

ACT Consultants, Inc.
1521 N. Jantzen, No. 426
Portland, OR 97217
Contact: K. Perry Campbell, PhD, CBI
Phone: 503-520-5050
Fax: 503-296-2452
pcampbell@actconsultants.com

Alliance Business Brokers, LLC
154 Broad Street, Suite 1526
Nashua, NH 03063
Contact: John F. Coto, CBI
Phone: 603-880-8200
Fax: 603-880-0631
johnc@allbizbrokers.com

Allied Business Group, LLC
1789 Kirby Parkway, Suite # 2
P. O. Box 38286
Memphis, TN 38183-0286
Contact: C. R. Blohm, CBI, CRS, GRI,
    LREB
Phone: 901-767-2354
Fax: 901-761-9244
cblohm@alliedbusinessbrokers.com

American Business Brokerage, Inc.
2831 Ringling Boulevard, F-121
Sarasota, FL 34237
Contact: Stacy L. Alario, CBI
Phone: 941-957-1414
Fax: 941-953-5394
ameribusbrkrfl@aol.com

Matthew Bass & Associates
420 Lexington Avenue, Suite 300
New York, NY 10170
Contact: Matthew H. Bass, CBI
Phone: 212-297-6153
Fax: 212-656-1811
matt@mattbass.com

Beacon Business Exchange
6750 E. 75th Street
Indianapolis, IN 46250
Contact: John M. Blayney
Phone: 317-594-5151
Fax: 317-594-5150
jblayney@beaconbiz.biz

Business Brokerage Press
1 Highland Road
Westford, MA 01886
Contact: Thomas L. West, CBI
Phone: 978-692-0323
Fax: 501-638-6803
tom@businessbrokeragepress.com

Business ValueXpress/Illinois Corp.
175 Olde Half Day Road, 100-17
Lincolnshire, IL 60069
Contact: Mike Adhikari,
    CBI,MBA,MSEE,MSM
Phone: 847-438-1657
Fax: 847-438-1835
madhikari@att.net

Business Ventures of Tampa Bay, Inc.
VR Business Brokers
4625 E Bay Dr, Suite 305
Clearwater, FL 33764-5738
Contact: Russ C. Bieber, CBI
Phone: 727-499-6500 Ext. *320
Fax: 727-536-3080
russbieber@businessinfo.com

The Capital Corporation
809 E. Main Street
Spartanburg, SC 29302
Phone: 864-542-2562
Fax: 864-542-1661
Contact: C. Dan Adams, CBI, M&AMI,
    CCIM
cdadams1@thecapitalcorp.com
***
or contact: Christy Thompson
cthompson@thecapitalcorp.com

Certified Business Advisors
23586 Calabasas Rd, Suite 105
Calabasas, CA 91302-1322
Contact: Matt Coletta, CBI
Phone: 818-999-9621
Fax: 818-999-1148
mattcoletta@aol.com

Certified Business Brokers
8002 Forest Breeze Lane
Spring, TX 77379
Contact: Marcia Bowron
Phone: 713-826-5783
Fax: 713-680-8300
marciab@houston.rr.com

Certified Business Brokers
10301 N.W. Freeway, Suite 200
Houston, TX 77092
Contact: Raymond R. Doba
Phone: 713-680-1200
Fax: 713-680-8300
rdoba@sbcglobal.net

Chase Business Services
1455 Lincoln Parkway, Suite 260
Atlanta, GA 30346
Contact: Bruce B. Kapteyn
Phone: 770-391-7242

Fax: 770-396-5333
bkapteyn@chaseatlanta.com

CompuFocus Resources
P.O. Box 47248
Atlanta, GA 30362
Contact: Jim Oxford, CBI
Phone: 770-938-2695
Fax: 770-822-6228
jimoxford@compufocus.com

CORE Business Advisors, Inc.
3700 Mansell Road, Suite 220
Alpharetta, GA 30022
Contact: Stephen E. Capizzi, CBI, CFP
Phone: 770-625-5050
Fax: 770-625-5051
Sec.coreadvisors@mindspring.com

Cornerstone Business Services, Inc.
200 S. Washington Street, Suite 205
Green Bay, WI 54162
Contact: Nancy Schott
Phone: 920-436-9890
Fax: 920-436-9894
nschott@cornerstone-business.com

Corporate Finance Associates
3067 Avellano Drive
Walnut Creek, CA 94598
Contact: Henry S. James, CBI, M&AMI
Phone: 925-934-3072
Fax: 925-934-3077
hankjames@cfaw.com

Corporate Finance Associates
2431 E. 51st. Street Suite 60
Tulsa, OK 74105
Contact: S. Lee Crawley, MBA, AVA
Phone: 918-743-1130
Fax: 918-743-1131
slc@cfaw.com

Corporate Investment International, Inc.
1999 W. Colonial Drive
Orlando, FL 32804
Contact: Richard E. Read, CBI, M&AMI,
CBC, CBB
Phone: 407-682-9600
Fax: 407-682-3676
rread@corporateinvestment.org

First Business Resources, Inc.
8117 Preston Road, Suite 300
Dallas, TX 75225
Contact: George E. Chamblee, III, CBI
Phone: 214-363-7774
Fax: 214-378-6899
gc@first-biz.com

Freedom Business Brokers
2102 Business Center Drive, Suite 130

Irvine, CA 92612
Contact: Brody Mape, CBI
Phone: 949-400-8743
Fax: 949-266-9435
brody@mapecommercial.com

Freedom Business Brokers
2102 Business Center Drive
Irvine, CA 92612
Contact: Gregg Tobin
Phone: 949-546-0903
Fax: 949-546-0904
gtobinocbroker@cox.net

The Geneva Companies
125 S. Wacker Drive, Suite #2100
Chicago, IL 60606
Contact: James Korreck
Phone: 312-364-4832
Fax: 312-364-4866
Jim_Korreck@genevaco.com

Hallmark Business Group
One Perimeter Park South, Suite 100 North
Birmingham, AL 35243
Contact: Daniel E. Hall, CBI, BCB, CMEA
Phone: 205-970-6059
Fax: 205-970-6224
DH@hmbg.biz

International Business Exchange Corp.
PO Box 15046
Austin, TX 78761
Contact: Jeff H. Hamilton, CBI
Phone: 512-310-2966
Fax: 512-310-8113
jhamilton@ibectx.com

Kensington Services
Regency Towers Center, 1415 W. 22nd
Street, Tower Floor
Oak Brook, IL 60523-2074
Contact: George A. Petrulis, CBI, M&AMI,
CM&A
Phone: 630-990-1500
Fax: 630-969-2234
georgep@kensingtonservices.com

MainSource Business Services Corp.
PO Box 802393
Santa Clarita, CA 91380
Contact: Robert O. Groag
Phone: 661-753-9400
Fax: 661-753-9462
rgroag@msourcecorp.com

New England Venture Resource Group Inc.
231 Sutton Street #2B
North Andover, MA 01845
Contact: Warren S. Burkholder, CBI, CBA,
ASA

Phone: 978-975-7600, ext. 14
Fax: 978-685-0637
warren@NEVRG.com

Spaulding Group
Corporate Center One At Intrn'l Plaza, 2202
   N. West Shore Blvd, Suite 200
Tampa, FL 33607
Contact: Bryan K. Spaulding, CBI, SBA,
   MEA
Phone: 813-926-9300
Fax: 813-926-9344
bspaulding@spauldinggroupinc.com

Sterling Bank
1250 W. Mockingbird Ln, #100
Dallas, TX 75247
Contact: Kenneth Byrd
Phone: 214-678-8102
Fax: 214-678-8133
ken.byrd@banksterling.com

Sunbelt Business Advisors Network, LLC
2000 Daniel Island Drive, Suite 446
Charleston, SC 29492
Contact: Edward T. Pendarvis, CBI
Phone: 843-853-4781, ext. 2411
Fax: 843-284-2419
etp@sunbeltnetwork.com

Sunbelt Businesss Brokers
9920 E. Harry, Suite 150
Wichita, KS 67207
Contact: Randy L. Browning, CBI, MBA,
   SBA, MEA
Phone: 316-684-9040
Fax: 316-684-5834
success@sunbeltnetwork.com

Sunbelt Business Brokers
3212 Rice Street
Little Canada, MN 55126
Contact: Daniel Arcand
Phone: 651-484-2677
Fax: 651-484-9658
darcand@sunbeltnetwork.com

Sunbelt Business Brokers
Westmoreland Building
5700 Cleveland Street, Suite 315
Virginia Beach, VA 23462
Contact: Robert K. Adams, PhD
Phone: 757-557-0006
Fax: 757-557-6387
bobadams@sunbeltnetwork.com

Sunbelt Business Brokers of Minnesota
1809 Plymouth Road, #221
Minneapolis, MN 55305
Contact: Robert Daudt, CBI
Phone: 952-545-6342
Fax: 952-545-6757
rdaudt@sunbeltnetwork.com

Sunbelt Business Brokers: Orange Coast
74 Shade Tree
Irvine, CA 92603
Contact: Jeanette Bailey
Phone: 949-679-1407
Fax: 949-679-1408
jeanette@sunbeltorangecoast.com

Sunbelt Business Brokers of Orange Coast
The Pacifica Building
111 Pacifica, Suite 250
Irvine, CA 92618
Contact: R. Stephen Thomson, CBI
Phone: 949-727-2412
Fax: 949-666-5823
steve@sunbeltorange.com

Sunbelt Business Brokers of Pittsburgh
4232 Northern Pike, Suite 102
Monroeville, PA 15146
Contact: David E. Ball, CBI
Phone: 412-380-0590
Fax: 412-380-0592
daveb@sunbeltnetwork.com

Sunbelt Business Brokers of Southern Cal
22700 Crenshaw Blvd, #115
Torrance, CA 90505
Contact: Roger Civalleri, MBA, CBI
Phone: 310-539-8300 x208
Fax: 310-539-8364
roger@bizsellbroker.com

Sunbelt Business Brokers of Texas
1660 S. Stemmons Freeway, Suite 260
Lewisville, TX 75067-6398
Contact: Kelly E. DeWitt, CBI, M&AMI,
   BCB
Phone: 972-219-6961 x11
Fax: 972-353-9580
kdewitt@bizsellnet.com

Sunbelt Corporate Advisors
4035 NW 43rd St
Gainesville, FL 32606-4598
Contact: Gilles Maillart, CBI
Phone: 352-380-0404
Fax: 352-376-6140
inc1051@bellsouth.net

Sunbelt MidSouth
3350 Players Club Parkway, Suite 130
Memphis, TN 38125
Contact: R. Edward Adams, CBI
Phone: 901-748-3111
Fax: 901-748-0339
memphis@sunbeltnetwork.com

Utah Business Consultants
10 Exchange Place, Suite 610
Salt Lake City, UT 84111-2743
Contact: Bradley G. Marlor
Phone: 801-534-0186

Fax: 801-534-0187
brad@ubcutah.com

Wells Fargo Investment
90 S. Cascade Avenue, 2nd Floor
Colorado Springs, CO 80903
Contact: Loren H. Burlage
Phone: 719-577-5575

Houlihan Lokey Howard & Zukin
1750 Tysons Boulevard, #650
McLean, VA 22102
Phone: 703.847.5225
Fax: 703.848.9667
www.hlhz.com

APPENDIX B-2. VALUATION FIRMS

Acadia Asset Advisors Inc.
1285 Avenue of the Americas, 35th Floor
New York, NY 10019
Phone: 212-554-4038
e-mail: info@AcadiaAdvisors.com

Duff & Phelps, LLC
Two Commerce Square, 25th Floor
2001 Market Street
Philadelphia, PA 19103
Contact: Timothy P. Golden CFA, ASA
Managing Director
timothy.golden@duffandphelps.com
Phone: 215-430-6010
Fax: 215-430-6103

Robert M. Haas & Associates, Inc.
261 Old York Road, Suite 820
Jenkintown, PA 19046
Phone: 215-887-6500
Contact: Robert M. Haas, Jr.
rhaasjr@rmha.com

Houlihan Lokey Howard & Zukin
3475 Piedmont Road, Suite 950
Atlanta, GA 30305
Phone: 404-495-7000

Fax: 404-495-9545
www.hlhz.com

Mentor Group, Inc.
1900 E. Tahquitz Canyon Way
Suite B-4
Palm Springs, CA 92262
Tel: 800-325-6411
Tel: 760-325-6411
Fax: 760-325-7260

Mercer Capital
5860 Ridgeway Center Parkway
Suite 400
Memphis, TN 38120
901-685-2120
Fax 901-685-2119
http://www.bizval.com/

Stout Risius Ross, Inc.
1600 Tysons Boulevard, 8th Floor
McLean, VA 22102
Contact: Scott D. Levine, Director
slevine@gosrr.com
Phone: 703-245-6612
Fax: 866-808-7621
www.srr.com

APPENDIX B-3. INVESTMENT BANKERS

A.G. Edwards & Sons, Inc.
1 N. Jefferson Avenue
St. Louis, MO 63101
Phone: 314-955-3000
Fax: 314-955-2890
www.agedwards.com

Acadia Capital Advisors
2144 S. 2000 E.
Salt Lake City, UT 10024
Phone: 212-787-1057
Fax: 212-787-2183

Adams Harkness & Hill Tech Ventures
99 High Street
Boston, MA 02110
Phone: 617-371-3900

Fax: 617-371-3798

Advest Inc.
90 State House Square
Hartford, CT 06103
Phone: 860-509-1000
Fax: 860-509-2131
www.advest.com

AgriCapital Corporation
1410 Broadway, Room 1802
New York, NY 10018
Phone: 212-944-9500
Fax: 212-944-9525
www.agricapital.com

Alexander Dunham Capital Group, Inc.
10850 Wilshire Boulevard, Suite 350

Los Angeles, CA 90024
Phone: 310-779-2712
Fax: 310-788-7774
www.alexanderdunham.com

Alexander Hutton, Inc.
999 Third Avenue, Suite 3700
Seattle, WA 98104
Phone: 206-341-9800
Fax: 206-341-9801
www.alexanderhutton.com

Alimansky Capital Group, Inc.
14 E. 44th Street, Suite 400
New York, NY 10117
Phone: 212-832-7300
Fax: 212-832-7338
www.alimansky.com

Allen & Co. LLC
711 Fifth Avenue
New York, NY 10022
Contact: Kim Wieland
Phone: 212-832-8000
Fax: 212-832-7057

Allen C. Ewing & Co.
50 N. Laura Street, Suite 3625
Jacksonville, FL 32202
Phone: 904-354-5573
Fax: 904-354-7033
www.allenewing.com

Allen Commercial Services
4513 Creedmoor Road, Suite 502
Raleigh, NC 27612
Phone: 919-781-1100
Fax: 919-781-1118
www.allencommercial.com

American Classic Financial Co.
15745 Roller Coaster Road
Colorado Springs, CO 89210
Phone: 719-488-9266
Fax: 719-488-9711

American Corporate Services
515 Madison Avenue
New York, NY 10022
Phone: 212-688-6600
Fax: 212-688-9710
www.acsdeals.com

American Express Tax & Business Services
Inc.
1 S. Wacker Drive, Suite 800
Chicago, IL 60606
Phone: 312-634-4752
Fax: 312-634-3410
www.americanexpress.com/tbs

American General Securities, Inc.
2727 Allen Parkway, Suite 290

P.O. Box 4556
Houston, TX 77201
Phone: 713-831-3806
Fax: 713-831-3366
www.agsecurities.com

Amerimark Capital Corporation
511 E. John Carpenter Freeway, Suite 220
Irving, TX 75062
Phone: 214-638-7878
Fax: 214-638-7612
www.amcapital.com

Amvest Financial Group, Inc.
P.O. Box 1590
Independence, MO 64055-0590
Phone: 816-461-3312
Fax: 816-461-4644
contact@amvest.com
www.amvest.com

Anderson & Strudwick, Inc.
707 E. Main Street, 20th Floor
Richmond, VA 23218
Phone: 804-643-2400
Fax: 804-648-3404
www.anderson-strudwick.com

Anthony Fowler & Co.
20 Walnut Street, Suite 320
Wellesley Hills, MA 02481
Phone: 781-237-4201
Fax: 781-237-7718

AreteCapital Group
2 Wall Street
Manchester, NH 03101
Phone: 603-625-0234
Fax: 603-625-0236
www.aretecapitalgroup.com

Argentum Group
60 Madison Avenue, Suite 701
New York, NY 10010
Phone: 212-949-6262
Fax: 212-949-8294
www.argentumgroup.com

Arnold S. Cohen Financial Consultants
110 E. 57th Street, Suite 6-C
New York, NY 10022
Phone: 212-753-1490
Fax: 212-753-2983

Arsht & Co.
45 Rockefeller Plaza, Suite 2520
New York, NY 10020
Phone: 212-397-1600
Fax: 212-397-1782

Arthur P. Gould & Co.
1 Wilshire Drive

Lake Success, NY 11020
Phone: 914-723-2560
www.gouldco.com

Askar Corporation
2 Applebee Square, Suite 350
Bloomington, MN 55425
Phone: 952-854-9463
Fax: 952-854-6813
askar@askar.com
www.askar.com

Aston Associates LLC
35 Mason Street, 4th Floor
Greenwich, CT 06830
Phone: 203-861-0850
Fax: 203-861-0840

Atalanta/Sosnoff Management Capital
101 Park Avenue, 6th Floor
New York, NY 10178
Phone: 212-867-5000
Fax: 212-922-1820
www.atalantasosnoff.com

Atlantic Capital Corporation
87 Cambridge Street
Burlington, MA 01803-4115
Phone: 781-272-0088
Fax: 781-272-4744
www.atlanticap.com

Avalon Group Ltd.
1375 Broadway
New York, NY 10018
Phone: 212-764-5610
Fax: 212-764-6013
www.avalongroupltd.com

B. C. Ziegler & Co.
215 N. Main Street
West Bend, WI 53095
Phone: 262-334-2882
Fax: 262-334-1790
www.ziegler.com

Babcock & Brown, Inc.
2 Harrison Street, 6th Floor
San Francisco, CA 94105
Phone: 415-512-1515
Fax: 415-267-1500
www.babcockbrown.com

Bachow & Associates, Inc.
3 Bala Plaza East
5th Floor, Suite 502
Bala Cynwyd, PA 19004
Phone 610-660-4900
Fax 610-660-4930
www.bachow.com

Banc of America Securities
9 W. 57th Street, 29th Floor

New York, NY 10019
Phone: 212-847-5855

Bangert Dawes Reade Davis & Thom, Inc.
605 Third Avenue, 15th Floor
New York, NY 10158
Phone: 212-573-6716
Fax: 212-573-6719

Bank America Corporate Banking
Bank of America Plaza
9 W. 57th Street, 26th Floor
New York, NY 10017
Phone: 212-847-6705

Barrington Associates
11755 Wilshire Boulevard, Suite 2200
Los Angeles, CA 90025
Phone: 310-479-3500
Fax: 310-477-4955
www.baib.com

Barrington Research Associates, Inc.
161 N. Clark Street, Suite 2950
Chicago, IL 60601
Phone: 312-634-6000
Fax: 312-634-6350
www.brai.com

BB&T Capital Markets
P.O. Box 1575
Richmond, VA 23218
Phone: 804-780-3230
Fax: 804-649-2615
www.bbandt.com/capitalmarkets

Beacon Hill Financial Corporation
19 Elm Street
Cohasset, MA 02025
Phone: 781-383-2300
Fax: 781-383-2330
www.beaconhillfinancial.com

Beaconsfield Financial Services, Inc.
101 W. Mall Plaza, Suite 204
Carnegie, PA 15106
Phone: 412-276-5600
Fax: 412-276-5070

Bear Stearns Merchant Banking
383 Madison Avenue
New York, NY 10179
Phone: 212-272-6607
Fax: 212-881-9510
www.bearstearns.com

Bechtel Financing Services, Inc.
50 California Street, Suite 2200
P.O. Box 193965
San Francisco, CA 94119
Phone: 415-768-6745
Fax: 415-951-0848

Beecken Petty O'Keefe & Co.
200 W. Madison Street, Suite 1910
Chicago, IL 60606
Phone: 630-435-0300
Fax: 630-435-0371
www.beeckenpetty.com

Benedetto Gartland & Co.
1330 Avenue of the Americas
New York, NY 10019
Phone: 212-424-9700
Fax: 212-262-8708
www.bgg.com

Benefit Capital Cos.
P.O. Box 542
3235 N. Pioneer Road
Logandale, NV 89021
Phone: 702-398-3222
Fax: 702-398-3700
rsandifer@benefitcapital.com
www.benefitcapital.com

Bengur Bryan & Co.
16 W. Madison Street
Baltimore, MD 21201
Phone: 443-573-3030
Fax: 443-573-3040
www.bengurbryan.com

Bentley Associates LP
101 Park Avenue, 22nd Floor
New York, NY 10178
Phone: 212-972-8700
Fax: 212-972-1820
www.bentleylp.com

Beringea
32330 W. 12 Mile Road
Farmington Hills, MI 48334
Phone: 248-489-9000
Fax: 248-489-8819
www.beringea.com

Berkeley International Capital Corporation
650 California Street, 28th Floor
San Francisco, CA 94108
Phone: 415-249-0450
Fax: 415-392-3929
www.berkeleyvc.com

Berkery Noyes & Co.
1 Liberty Plaza
165 Broadway, 13th Floor
New York, NY 10006
Phone: 212-668-3022
Fax: 212-747-9092
www.berkerynoyes.com

Bernard L. Madoff Investment Securities
885 Third Avenue, 18th Floor
New York, NY 10022

Phone: 212-230-2424
Fax: 212-486-8178
www.madoff.com

BIA Capital Strategies LLC
15120 Enterprise Court, Suite 100
Chantilly, VA 20151
Phone: 703-818-8115
Fax: 703-803-3299
www.biacapital.com

Bigelow Co. LLC
1 Harbour Place, Suite 575
Portsmouth, NH 03801
Phone: 603-433-5888
Fax: 603-433-4155

Blackman Kallick Bartelstein LLP
10 S. Riverside Plaza
Chicago, IL 60606
Phone: 312-980-2934
Fax: 312-756-3934
pmcnally@bkadvice.com
www.bkadvice.com

Blackstone Group
345 Park Avenue
New York, NY 10154
Phone: 212-583-5000
Fax: 212-583-5712
www.blackstone.com

Blount Parrish, Inc.
10 Court Square
Montgomery, AL 36104
Phone: 334-264-8410
Fax: 334-264-7608
www.blountparrish.com

Blum & Co.
11800 Sunrise Valley Drive, Suite 322
Reston, VA 20191
Phone: 703-860-3736
Fax: 703-715-8487
info@blumandco.com
www.blumandco.com

Blum Capital Partners
909 Montgomery Street, Suite 400
San Francisco, CA 94133
Phone: 415-434-1111
Fax: 415-434-3130
www.blumcapital.com

BMO Nesbitt Burns Equity Partners
1 First Canadian Place
Toronto, Ontario M5X 1H3
Canada
Phone: 312-461-3855
Fax: 312-765-8000
www.bmonesbittburns.com

Bodell Overcash Anderson & Co.
1 Fenton Building
P.O. Box 1237
Jamestown, NY 14701
Phone: 716-484-7141
Fax: 716-661-3357

Bond Timing Securities Corporation
420 Bedford Street, Suite 340
Lexington, MA 02420
Phone: 781-863-2545
Fax: 781-860-9050
www.btsmanagement.com

Botts & Co.
41-44 Great Queen Street
London WC2B 5AA
United Kingdom
Phone: 44-20-7841-1550
Fax: 44-20-7242-5160
www.bottscompany.com

Brandywine Asset Management, Inc.
381 Brinton Lake Road
Thornton, PA 19373
Phone: 610-361-1000
Fax: 610-361-1001
www.brandywine.com

Bristol Capital Management, Inc.
135 E. 57th Street, 15th Floor
New York, NY 10022
Phone: 212-593-3157
Fax: 212-593-3155
www.bristoldirect.com

Broadmark Capital LLC
2800 One Union Square
600 University Street
Seattle, WA 98101
Phone: 206-623-1200
Fax: 206-623-2213
broadmark@broadmark.com
www.broadmark.com

Broadview
520 Madison Avenue, 10th Floor
New York, NY 10017
Phone: 212-284-8100
Fax: 212-284-8101
www.broadview.com

Brookridge Funding Corporation
26 Mill Plain Road, Suite 3A
Danbury, CT 06811
Phone: 203-790-7301
Fax: 203-790-7326
www.brookridgefunding.com

Brooks Houghton & Co.
444 Madison Avenue, 25th Floor
New York, NY 10022

Phone: 212-753-1991
Fax: 212-753-7730
www.brookshoughton.com

Brookwood Associates, Inc.
5 Piedmont Center, Suite 205
Atlanta, GA 30305
Phone: 404-874-7433
Fax: 404-564-5101
www.brookwoodassociates.com

Brown Brothers Harriman & Co.
140 Broadway
New York, NY 10005
Phone: 212-493-8426
Fax: 212-493-7293
www.bbh.com

Brown Gibbons Lang & Co.
1111 Superior Avenue, Suite 900
Cleveland, OH 44114
Phone: 216-241-2800
Fax: 216-241-7417
www.bglco.com

Bruml Capital Corporation
1801 E. Ninth Street
Ohio Savings Plaza, Suite 720
Cleveland, OH 44114-3103
Phone: 216-771-6660
Fax: 216-771-6673
www.brumlcapital.com

Buis & Co.
301 Commerce Street, Suite 1450
Fort Worth, TX 76102
Phone: 817-877-3147
Fax: 817-877-1709

Burrill & Co.
1 Embarcadero Center, Suite 2700
San Francisco, CA 94111-3776
Phone: 415-591-5400
Fax: 415-591-5401
www.burrillandco.com

Bushkin Associates, Inc.
88 Caterson Terrace
Hartsdale, NY 10530
Phone: 914-761-3024
Fax: 914-761-3119
www.bushkin.com

C. E. Unterberg Towbin
350 Madison Avenue
New York, NY 10022
Phone: 212-572-8000
Fax: 212-888-8611
www.unterberg.com

C. G. Lopp & Co.
P.O. Box 7514, FDR Station

New York, NY 10017
Phone: 212-752-9300
Fax: 212-752-9300

C. L. King & Associates, Inc.
9 Elk Street
Albany, NY 12207
Phone: 518-431-3500
Fax: 518-431-3550

Calgary Enterprises, Inc.
4 Park Avenue, Suite 12G
New York, NY 10016
Phone: 212-683-0119
Fax: 212-683-3119
www.calgaryenterprises.com

Calvert Street Capital Partners
111 S. Calvert Street, Suite 1800
Baltimore, MD 21202
Phone: 443-573-3700
Fax: 443-573-3702
www.cscp.com

Canadian Corporate Funding
Suite 2140, Canadian Pacific Tower
P.O. Box 86, Toronto-Dominion Centre
Toronto, Ontario M5K 1G8
Canada
Phone: 416-977-1450
Fax: 416-977-4001
www.ccfl.com

Capital Alliance Corporation
2777 N. Stemmons Freeway, Suite 1220
Dallas, TX 75207
Phone: 214-638-8280
Fax: 214-638-8009
www.cadallas.com

Capital Dynamics
Bahnhofstrasse 22
Zug 6301
Switzerland
Phone: 41 41 7488444
Fax: 41 41 7488440
info@capdyn.com
www.capdyn.com

Capital Network Securities LLC
2700 Via Fortuna, Suite 450
Austin, TX 78746
Phone: 512-314-0711
www.cngroupllc.com

Cappello Capital Corporation
1299 Ocean Avenue, Suite 306
Santa Monica, CA 98101
Phone: 310-393-6632
Fax: 310-393-4838
www.cappellogroup.com

Capstan Partners
1201 Third Avenue, Suite 2790
Seattle, WA 98101
Phone: 206-626-0800
Fax: 206-623-1419

Carolina Barnes Capital, Inc.
37 Purchase Street, Suite 203
Rye, NY 10580
Phone: 914-925-0001
Fax: 914-925-9811
www.carolinabarnes.com

Carolina Financial Securities LLC
9 Park Place, Suite 201
Brevard, NC 28712
Phone: 828-883-4400
Fax: 828-883-4402
www.carofin.com

Carver Cross Securities Corporation
10 Rockefeller Plaza, Suite 1405
New York, NY 10020
Phone: 212-292-7800
Fax: 212-292-7805
www.carvercross.com

CBIZ Mergers & Acquisitions Group, Inc.
780 Johnson Ferry Road, 6th Floor
Atlanta, GA 30342
Phone: 404-257-2299
Fax: 404-497-9156
www.cbiz.com/magroup

Chaffe & Associates, Inc.
201 St. Charles Avenue, Suite 1410
New Orleans, LA 70170
Phone: 504-524-1801
Fax: 504-524-7194
www.chaffe-associates.com

Chapman Spira & Carson LLC
111 Broadway, 5th Floor
New York, NY 10006
Phone: 212-425-6100
Fax: 212-425-6229
www.chapmanspira.com

Chatsworth Securities LLC
95 E. Putnam Avenue
Greenwich, CT 06830
Phone: 203-629-2612
Fax: 203-629-5963
rd@chatsworthgroup.com
www.chatsworthgroup.com

Cherry Tree Investments, Inc.
301 Carlson Parkway, Suite 103
Minnetonka, MN 55305
Phone: 952-893-9012
Fax: 952-893-9036

info@cherrytree.com
www.cherrytree.com

Cheslock Bakker & Associates, Inc.
695 E. Main Street, Suite 103
Stamford, CT 06901
Phone: 203-969-0513
Fax: 203-969-0525
www.cba.com

Chestnut Partners, Inc.
1 Financial Center, 28th Floor
Boston, MA 02111
Phone: 617-832-8600
Fax: 617-832-8610
chestnut@chestnutp.com

CIBC World Markets
161 Bay Street, BCE Place
P.O. Box 500
Toronto, Ontario M5J 2S8
Canada
Phone: 416-594-7000
www.cibcwm.com

City Securities Corporation
30 S. Meridian Street, Suite 600
Indianapolis, IN 46204
Phone: 317-634-4400
Fax: 317-955-2518
bwelch@citysecurities.com
www.citysecurities.com

Cleary & Oxford Associates
603 King Street, Suite 200
Alexandria, VA 22314
Phone: 703-684-5868
Fax: 703-977-3215
www.clearyoxford.com

Cleary Gull, Inc.
100 E. Wisconsin Avenue, Suite 2400/2500
Milwaukee, WI 53202
Phone: 414-291-4500
Fax: 414-270-2209
www.clearygull.com

The Cohen Group
1200 19th Street NW
Suite 400
Washington, DC 20036
Phone: 202-689-7900
Fax: 202-689-7910
www.cohengroup.net

Colmen Capital Advisors, Inc.
487 Devon Park Drive, Suite 216
Wayne, PA 19087
Phone: 610-964-9020
Fax: 610-964-9024
www.colemancapital.com

Colmen Menard Co.
994 Old Eagle School Road, Suite 1000
Wayne, PA 19087
Phone: 484-367-0300
Fax: 484-367-0305
www.colmenmenard.com

Colonnade Advisors LLC
200 W. Adams, Suite 2005
Chicago, IL 60606
Phone: 312-425-8145
Fax: 312-425-8146
www.colonnade.net

Comann & Montague
1110 Mar West Street
Tiburon, CA 94920
Phone: 415-391-2400
Fax: 415-789-0283
www.investmentbank.com

Communications Equity Associates, Inc.
101 E. Kennedy Boulevard, Suite 3300
Tampa, FL 33602
Phone: 813-226-8844
Fax: 813-255-1513
www.ceaworldwide.com

Comstock Partners LLC
1875 Century Park E., Suite 300
Los Angeles, CA 90067
Phone: 310-278-6444
Fax: 310-861-5010
www.comstockpartners.com

Conning & Co.
City Place II
185 Asylum Street
Hartford, CT 06103
Phone: 860-527-1131
Fax: 860-520-1229
www.conning.com

Context Capital Group
51 E. 42nd Street, 7th Floor
New York, NY 10017
Phone: 212-867-1414
Fax: 212-202-6442
www.contextcapital.com

Corporate Growth Assistance Ltd.
1 Benvenuto Place, #420
Toronto, Ontario M4V 2L1
Canada
Phone: 416-222-7772
Fax: 416-222-6091

Corum Group Ltd.
10500 NE 8th Street, Suite 1500
Bellevue, WA 10500
Phone: 425-455-8281

Fax: 425-451-8951
www.corumgroup.com

Coview Capital, Inc.
780 Third Avenue, 31st Floor
New York, NY 10017
Phone: 212-750-0011
Fax: 212-750-7234
www.coviewcap.com

Credit Suisse First Boston
11 Madison Avenue
New York, NY 10010
Phone: 212-325-2000
Fax: 212-325-8279
www.csfb.com

Crestview Investment & Financial Group
431 Post Road E., Suite 1
Westport, CT 06880
Phone: 203-222-0333
Fax: 203-222-0000

Croft & Bender
4200 Northside Parkway NW
Building One, Suite 100
Atlanta, GA 30327
Phone: 404-841-3131
Fax: 404-841-3135
www.croft-bender.com

Cronus Partners, Inc.
101 Merritt 7
Norwalk, CT 06851
Phone: 203-855-8358
Fax: 203-286-1209
www.cronuspartners.com

Crosbie & Co.
150 King Street W., 15th Floor
P.O. Box 95
Toronto, Ontario M5H 1J9
Canada
Phone: 416-362-7726
Fax: 416-362-3447
www.crosbieco.com

Crown Capital Corporation
540 Maryville Centre Drive, Suite 120
St. Louis, MO 63141
Phone: 314-576-1201
Fax: 314-576-1525
www.crown-cap.com

D. F. Blumberg Associates, Inc.
1300 Virginia Drive, Suite 110
Fort Washington, PA 19034
Phone: 215-643-9060
Fax: 215-643-9066
www.dfba.com

Daniels & Associates
711 Fifth Avenue, Suite 405

New York, NY 10022
Phone: 212-935-5900
Fax: 212-863-4859
www.bdanielsonline.com

David Lerner Associates, Inc.
477 Jericho Turnpike
Syosset, NY 11791
Phone: 516-921-4200
Fax: 516-364-1673
www.davidlerner.com

David N. Deutsch & Co. LLC
150 E. 58th Street
New York, NY 10155
Phone: 212-980-7800
Fax: 212-980-2987
www.dndco.com

Decosimo Corporate Finance
1100 Tallan Building
2 Union Square
Chattanooga, TN 37402
Phone: 423-756-7100
www.decosimo.com

DeSilva & Phillips LLC
415 Park Avenue South
New York, NY 10016
Phone: 212-686-9700
Fax: 212-686-2172
www.mediabakers.com

Deutsche Bank
130 Liberty Street, 33rd Floor
New York, NY 10006
Phone: 212-250-5426
Fax: 212-250-8693
www.db.com

Dick Israel & Partners
8929 Wilshire Boulevard, #214
Beverly Hills, CA 90211
Phone: 310-208-1234
Fax: 310-657-4486

Dinan & Co. LLC
3550 N. Central Avenue, Suite 700
Phoenix, AZ 85012
Phone: 602-248-8700
Fax: 602-248-9100
info@dinancompany.com
www.dealassist.com

DN Partners LLC
77 W. Wacker Drive, Suite 4550
Chicago, IL 60601
Phone: 312-332-7960
Fax: 312-332-7979
www.dnpartners.com

Dominion Partners L.C.
4801 Cox Road, Suite 104

Glen Allen, VA 23060
Phone: 804-418-6269
Fax: 804-217-8199
cmoncure@dominionpartners.com
www.dominionpartners.com

Dominion Securities, Inc.
211 First Avenue SE
Cedar Rapids, IA 52401
Phone: 319-368-8010
Fax: 319-368-8011

Dougherty & Co.
90 S. Seventh Street, Suite 4400
Minneapolis, MN 55402
Phone: 612-376-6400
Fax: 612-376-7055
www.doughertymarkets.com

Downer & Co. LLC
211 Congress Street
Boston, MA 02110
Phone: 617-482-6200
Fax: 617-482-6201

Dresdner Kleinwort Wasserstein
75 Wall Street
New York, NY 10005
Phone: 212-429-2100
Fax: 212-429-2127

Dresner Investment Services, Inc.
29 S. LaSalle Street, Suite 310
Chicago, IL 60603
Phone: 312-726-3600
Fax: 312-726-7448

Driehaus Securities Corporation
25 E. Erie Street
Chicago, IL 60611
Phone: 312-587-3800
Fax: 312-932-3585
www.driehaus.com

Duff & Phelps LLC
311 S. Wacker Drive, Suite 4200
Chicago, IL 60606
Phone: 312-697-4600
Fax: 312-697-0115
www.duffllc.com

Edgeview Partners
301 S. College Street
Suite 3700
Charlotte, NC 28202
Phone: 704-602-3900
Fax: 704-602-3939
www.edgeviewpartners.com

ECDI Group, Inc.
302 N. Market Street, Suite 400
Dallas, TX 75202

Phone: 214-880-8640
Fax: 214-880-8646
www.ecdigroup.com

Edward Jones
12555 Manchester Road
St. Louis, MO 63131
Phone: 314-515-2000
Fax: 314-515-2820
www.edwardjones.com

EGL Holdings
3495 Piedmont Road
Ten Piedmont Center, Suite 412
Atlanta, GA 30305
Phone: 404-949-8300
Fax: 404-949-8311
www.eglholdings.com

Einhorn Associates, Inc.
2675 N. Mayfair Road, Suite 410
Milwaukee, WI 53226
Phone: 414-453-4488
Fax: 414-453-4831

England & Company, LLC
1775 Pennsylvania Avenue, NW
Suite 1150
Washington, DC 20006
Tel: 202-386-6500
Fax: 202-386-6599
Washington, DC
www.englandco.com

Equity Dynamics, Inc.
2116 Financial Center
Des Moines, IA 50309
Phone: 515-244-5746
Fax: 515-244-2346

Eurorient Capital
16133 Ventura Boulevard, #855
Encino, CA 91403
Phone: 818-990-5080 x 102
Fax: 818-990-5566
www.eurorient.com

Evarts Capital, Inc.
23220 Chagrin Boulevard, Suite 305
Cleveland, OH 44122
Phone: 216-831-1448
Fax: 216-831-9781
www.evartscapital.com

Explorer, Inc.
611 Commerce Street, Suite 2602
Nashville, TN 37203
Phone: 615-244-0148
Fax: 615-242-1407

Exvere, Inc.
1301 Fifth Avenue, Suite 3405

Seattle, WA 98101
Phone: 206-728-1800
Fax: 206-728-7611
www.exvere.com

Ferris Baker Watts, Inc.
100 Light Street
Baltimore, MD 21202
Phone: 800-436-2000
Fax: 410-468-2746
www.fbw.com

FHL Capital Corporation
600 20th Street N., Suite 350
Birmingham, AL 35201
Phone: 205-328-3098
Fax: 205-323-0001

Financial America Securities, Inc.
925 Euclid Avenue, Suite 1525
Cleveland, OH 44115
Phone: 216-781-5060
Fax: 216-781-5379

First Albany Corporation
677 Broadway
Albany, NY 12207
Phone: 518-447-8500
www.fac.com

First Analysis
1 S. Wacker Drive
Suite 3900, 39th Floor
Chicago, IL 60606
Phone: 312-258-1400
www.firstanalysis.com

First New England Advisors, Inc.
P.O. Box 79226
Belmont, MA 02479
Phone: 617-924-2300
Fax: 617-924-7707

FiServ Securities, Inc.
255 Fiserv Drive
P.O. Box 979
Brookfield, WI 53008
Phone: 262-879-5000
Fax: 262-879-5013
www.fiserv.com

Focus Capital Group
1 Hashikma Street
P.O. Box 72
Savyon 56530 Israel
Phone: 972 3 535 6667
Fax: 972 3 535 0708
www.focuscap.com

Fogel International
5110 N. 32nd Street, Suite 206
Phoenix, AZ 85018

Phone: 602-508-0728
Fax: 602-508-0729
www.fogelinternational.com

Forest Street Capital
125 Elm Street
New Canaan, CT 06840
Phone: 203-972-3100
Fax: 203-966-4197
www.foreststreet.com

Fortis Private Equity
P.O. Box 64284
St. Paul, MN 55164
Phone: 651-738-4000
Fax: 651-738-5579
www.fortisprivateequity.com

Frederick & Co.
1234 E. Juneau Avenue
Milwaukee, WI 53202
Phone: 414-271-1500
Fax: 414-271-1506
www.biomedicalrenaissance.com

Friedman Billings Ramsey & Co.
1001 19th Street North
Arlington, VA 22209
Contact: J. Rock Tonkel, Jr.
Phone: 703-312-9500
Fax: 703-312-9501
www.fbr.com

Fulcrum Securities LLC
2425 Green Street
San Francisco, CA 94123
Phone: 415-440-6744
Fax: 415-440-6788

G. A. Herrera & Co. LLC
600 Jefferson, Suite 1080
Houston, TX 77002
Phone: 713-978-6590
Fax: 713-978-6599
www.herrera-co.com

Gean Overseas, Inc.
4434 Covington Highway
Decatur, GA 30035
Phone: 404-284-1828
Fax: 404-284-3156
www.geanoverseas.com

Geneva Cos.
P.O. Box 19599
Irvine, CA 92623
Phone: 800-854-4643
Fax: 949-756-1779
www.genevaco.com

George K. Baum & Co.
4801 Main Street, Suite 500

Kansas City, MO 64112
Phone: 816-474-1100
Fax: 816-283-5325
www.gkbaum.com

Gerken Capital Associates
110 Tiburon Boulevard, Suite 5
Mill Valley, CA 94941
Phone: 415-383-1464
Fax: 415-383-1253
www.gerkencapital.com

Gilford Securities, Inc.
777 Third Avenue
New York, NY 10017
Phone: 212-888-6400
Fax: 212-826-9738
www.gilfordsecurities.com

Glenthorne Capital, Inc.
1525 Locust Street, Suite 1301
Philadelphia, PA 19102
Phone: 215-732-7315
Fax: 215-732-5053
www.glenthornecapital.com

Globus Growth Group, Inc.
44 W. 24th Street
New York, NY 10010
Phone: 212-243-1000
Fax: 212-645-0332

Goldman Sachs & Co.
85 Broad Street, 29th Floor
New York, NY 10004
Phone: 212-902-1000
Fax: 212-902-3925
www.gs.com

Goldsmith Agio Helms
225 S. Sixth Street, 46th Floor
Minneapolis, MN 55402
Phone: 612-339-0500
Fax: 612-339-0507
www.agio.com

Gradison & Co. Div. of McDonald & Co.
580 Walnut Street
Cincinnati, OH 45202
Phone: 513-579-5945
Fax: 513-579-5947
www.medinvest.com

GrandWest & Associates
2423 Pine Bend Drive, Suite 200
Houston, TX 77339
Phone: 281-358-4880
www.grand-west.com

Grant Thornton LLP
226 Causeway Street
Boston, MA 02114
Phone: 617-848-4890

Greenough & Co.
12 Leroy Street
New York, NY 10014
Phone: 212-727-0021
Fax: 212-924-2776

Gruppo Levey & Co.
104 W. 40th Street, 16th Floor
New York, NY 10018
Phone: 212-697-5753
Fax: 212-949-7294
www.glconline.com

Gulfstar Group, Inc.
700 Louisiana Street, Suite 3800
Houston, TX 77002
Phone: 713-300-2020
Fax: 713-300-2021
www.gulfstargroup.com

Guttman & Associates
1022 Frick Building
Pittsburgh, PA 15219
Phone: 412-281-1666
Fax: 412-281-8850
www.guttman.pfyf.com

H. C. Wainwright & Co.
250 Park Avenue, 5th Floor
New York, NY 10177
Phone: 212-856-5730
Fax: 212-856-5750
www.hcwainwright.com

Haas Financial Corporation
230 Park Avenue, Suite 1547
New York, NY 10169
Phone: 212-490-1510
Fax: 212-983-0493

Hakman & Co.
1 Bay Plaza
1350 Bayshore Highway, Suite 300
Burlingame, CA 94101
Phone: 650-348-1700
Fax: 650-348-6872
www.hakman.com

Hamilton Miller Investments LLC
5350 S. Roslyn Street, Suite 350
Greenwood Village, CO 80111
Phone: 303-768-8896 x 16
Fax: 303-768-9020
www.hamiltonmiller.com

Hammond Kennedy Whitney & Co.
230 Park Avenue, Suite 1616
New York, NY 10169
Phone: 212-867-1010
Fax: 212-867-1312
www.hkwinc.com

Hampshire Capital Corporation
P.O. Box 178
New Castle, NH 03854
Phone: 603-431-1415
Fax: 603-431-7755

Hanifen Imhoff, Inc.
1125 17th Street, Suite 1500
Denver, CO 80202
Phone: 303-296-2300
Fax: 303-291-5318
www.hanifen.com

Hannon Armstrong
1997 Annapolis Exchange Parkway, #520
Annapolis, MD 12401
Phone: 703-684-7776
Fax: 703-684-8922
www.hanarmco.com

Harris Nesbitt Gerard
3 Times Square
New York, NY 10036
Phone: 212-885-4000
Fax: 212-885-4139
www.harrisnesbitt.com

Harris Williams & Co.
1001 Haxall Point, 9th Floor
Richmond, VA 23219
Phone: 804-648-0072
Fax: 804-648-0073
www.harriswilliams.com

HCFP Brenner Securities LLC
888 Seventh Avenue, 17th Floor
New York, NY 10106
Phone: 212-707-0300
Fax: 212-707-0308

Health Business Partners
5784 Post Road, Suite 5
Warwick, RI 02818
Phone: 401-885-4670
Fax: 401-885-4686
www.healthbusiness.com

Health Care Ventures LLC
44 Nassau Street
Princeton, NJ 08542
Phone: 609-430-3900
Fax: 609-430-9525
www.hcven.com

Healthcare Communications Group
100 N. Sepulveda Boulevard, Suite 1825
El Segundo, CA 90245
Phone: 310-606-5700
Fax: 310-606-5705
www.healthcarecommgroup.com

Healthcare Markets Group
42 Meachen Road

Sudbury, MA 01776
Phone: 978-440-7041
Fax: 978-440-7043
www.healthcaremarkets.com

Heffernan & Co.
745 Fifth Avenue, 33rd Floor
New York, NY 10151
Phone: 212-371-6400
Fax: 212-371-7639

Heinemann & Co.
100 Broadway, 7th Floor
New York, NY 10005
Phone: 212-366-7668
Fax: 212-406-4035
www.heinemannco.com

Hibernia Southcoast Capital, Inc.
909 Poydras Street, Suite 1000
New Orleans, LA 70112
Phone: 504-528-9174
Fax: 504-523-1925
www.hibernia.com

Hilliard Lyons, Inc.
501 S. Fourth Street
Louisville, KY 40202
Phone: 502-588-8400
Fax: 502-585-8925
www.hilliard.com

Hindin-Owen Engelke, Inc.
639 S. Washington Street
Naperville, IL 60540-6643
Phone: 630-717-8679

Hooke Associates LLC
8000 Towers Crescent Drive, Suite 940
Vienna, VA 22182
Phone: 703-761-4591
Fax: 703-847-0911

Houlihan Lokey Howard & Zukin
1930 Century Park West
Los Angeles, CA 90067
Phone: 310-553-8871
Fax: 310-553-2173
www.hlhz.com

HT Capital Advisors LLC
437 Madison Avenue, 39th Floor
New York, NY 10022
Phone: 212-759-9080
Fax: 212-759-0299
www.htcapital.com

Hultquist Capital LLC
1 Embarcadero Center, Suite 1200
San Francisco, CA 94111
Phone: 415-477-0155
Fax: 415-477-0165

Hunter Wise Financial Group
2171 Campus Drive, Suite 200
Irvine, CA 92612
Phone: 949-852-1700
Fax: 949-852-1722
www.hunterwise.com

ING Barings
Park Avenue Plaza
1325 Avenue of the Americas
New York, NY 10019
Phone: 646-424-6000
www.ingbarings.com

Inter-Pacific Capital Corporation
21250 Hawthorne Boulevard, Suite 500
Torrance, CA 90503
Phone: 310-792-8698
Fax: 310-540-9872
www.interpacific.com

Invemed Associates, Inc.
375 Park Avenue
New York, NY 10152
Phone: 212-421-2500
Fax: 212-421-2523

Ironwood Capital Ltd.
200 Fisher Drive
Avon, CT 06001
Phone: 860-409-2100
Fax: 860-409-2120
www.ironwoodcap.com

J. H. Chapman Group Ltd.
9700 Higgins Road, Suite 630
Rosemont, IL 60018
Phone: 773-693-4800
Fax: 773-693-6255
www.jhchapman.com

J. P. Morgan Chase
1211 Avenue of the Americas, 42nd Floor
New York, NY 10036
Phone: 212-508-7631
Fax: 212-508-7640
www.jpmorganchase.com

J. W. Korth & Co.
32481 Middlebelt Road, Suite 400
Farmington Hills, MI 48334
Phone: 248-855-4500
Fax: 248-855-6681
www.shop4bonds.com

James A. Matzdorff & Co.
537 Newport Center Drive, Suite 144
Beverly Hills, CA 92660
Phone: 800-348-4212
www.loanbusiness.net

Janney Montgomery Scott LLC
1801 Market Street

Philadelphia, PA 19103
Phone: 215-665-6000
Fax: 215-665-6197
www.janneys.com

Jeffries & Co.
11100 Santa Monica Boulevard, 10th Floor
Los Angeles, CA 90025
Phone: 310-445-1199
Fax: 310-575-5165
www.jefco.com

JHP Enterprises LLC
534 West Road
New Canaan, CT 06840
Phone: 203-652-0548
Fax: 917-591-7580
contact@jhpenter.com
www.jhpenter.com

Johnsen Securities, Inc.
1931 Black Rock Turnpike
Fairfield, CT 06432
Phone: 203-332-4106
Fax: 203-332-1547

Johnson Butler & Co.
2600 Mission Street, Suite 206
San Marino, CA 91108
Phone: 626-799-5200
Fax: 626-799-5274
www.johnsonbutler.com

Jopling, Inc.
2100 Georgetowne Drive, Suite 203
Sewickley, PA 15143
Phone: 724-933-8180
info@joplinginc.com
www.joplinginc.com

Josephberg Grosz & Co.
633 Third Avenue, 13th Floor
New York, NY 10017
Phone: 212-974-9926
Fax: 212-397-5832

Kaufman & Co.
45 Milk Street
Boston, MA 02109
Phone: 617-426-0444
Fax: 617-542-6506
www.kaufmanandco.com

Kelso & Co.
320 Park Avenue, 24th Floor
New York, NY 10022
Phone: 212-751-3939
Fax: 212-223-2379
www.kelso.com

KTL Industries
3150 Lenox Park Boulevard, Suite 220

Memphis, TN 38115
Phone: 901-273-2250
Fax: 901-273-2255
www.ktlindustries.com

L. R. Nathan Associates
167 Dwight Road
Longmeadow, MA 01106
Phone: 413-567-1766
Fax: 413-567-1697

Ladenburg Thalmann & Co.
590 Madison Avenue, 35th Floor
New York, NY 10022
Phone: 212-409-2000
Fax: 212-409-2169
www.ladenburg.com

Laux & Co.
672 W. Liberty Street
Medina, OH 44256
Phone: 330-721-0100
Fax: 330-721-0111
www.lauxco.com

LeCorgne Loewenbaum & Co., LLC
1110 Poydras Street, Suite 1750
New Orleans, LA 70163
Phone: 504-582-2121
Fax: 504-539-7124
www.lecorgne.com

Legacy Partners—New York
520 Madison Avenue 27th Floor
New York, NY 10022
Contact: Robert McMullen
Phone: 212-649-0000
Fax: 212-649-0001
http://legacypartnersgroup.com

Legacy Partners—Washington, D.C.
1919 Pennsylvania Avenue NW
Washington, DC 20006
Phone: 202-736-5252
Fax: 202-736-5253

Legacy Securities
4684 Roswell Road, N.E.
Atlanta, GA 30342
Contact: Chris Battel
Phone: 404-965-2420
www.legacysecurities.com

Legg Mason Wood Walker, Inc.
100 Light Street
Baltimore, MD 21202
Phone: 410-539-0000
Fax: 410-454-4508
www.leggmason.com

Lehman Brothers, Inc.
745 Seventh Avenue, 30th Floor

New York, NY 10019
Phone: 212-526-7000
www.lehman.com

Lepercq De Neuflize & Co.
1675 Broadway
New York, NY 10019
Phone: 212-698-0762
Fax: 212-262-0155

Lightyear Capital LLC
375 Park Avenue, 11th Floor
New York, NY 10152
Phone: 212-328-0555
Fax: 212-328-0516
lycapinfo@lycap.com
www.lycap.com

Lincoln Partners
500 W. Madison, Suite 3900
Chicago, IL 60661
Phone: 312-580-8339
Fax: 312-580-8317
tgillick@lincolnpartners.com
www.lincolnpartners.com

LM Capital Corporation
1200 N. Federal Highway, Suite 312
Boca Raton, FL 33432
Phone: 561-981-8410
Fax: 561-981-8418
www.lmcapitalsecurities.com

Loeb Partners Corporation
61 Broadway
New York, NY 10006
Phone: 212-483-7000
Fax: 212-425-7090

Loehr & Associates
4309 Courtland Drive
Metairie, LA 70002
Phone: 504-455-5613
Fax: 504-455-5613

M. H. Meyerson & Co.
525 Washington Boulevard, 34th Floor
Jersey City, NJ 07310
Phone: 201-459-9500
Fax: 201-459-9534
www.mhmeyerson.com

M. R. Beal & Co.
67 Wall Street, Suite 1701
New York, NY 10005
Phone: 212-983-3930
Fax: 212-983-4539

Macadam Capital Partners
4800 SW Macadam Avenue, Suite 311
Portland, OR 97201
Phone: 503-225-0889

Fax: 503-225-0009
www.macadamcapital.com

Mallory Capital Group LLC
19 Old King's Highway South, Suite 14
Darien, CT 06820
Phone: 203-655-1571
Fax: 203-662-3682
info@mallorycapital.com
www.mallorycapital.com

March Group LLLP
William D. Roebuck Park
Building One, Suite 100
Kingshill 850 U.S. Virgin Islands
Phone: 340-773-7300
Fax: 340-773-7915
mmay@marchgroup.com
www.marchgroup.com

MASI Ltd.
1419 Lake Cook Road, Suite 220
Deerfield, IL 60015
Phone: 847-948-7300
Fax: 847-948-7379
www.masiltd.com

Mayfair Capital Partners, Inc.
P.O. Box 30
New York, NY 10021
Phone: 212-288-0500
Fax: 212-737-0039
www.mayfaircapital.com

McCormick & Pryor Ltd.
26 Broadway, Suite 1640
New York, NY 10004
Phone: 212-968-9090
Fax: 212-363-9433

McDonald Investments, Inc.
127 Public Square
Cleveland, OH 44114
Phone: 216-443-2300
www.mcdinvest.com

McFarland Grossman & Co.
9821 Katy Freeway, Suite 500
Houston, TX 77024
Phone: 713-464-7770
Fax: 713-464-1827
www.mcfarlandgrossman.com

McLean Group LLC
1660 International Drive, Suite 450
McLean, VA 22102
Phone: 703-827-0020
Fax: 703-827-0175
www.mcleanllc.com

MelCap Partners LLC
3995 Medina Road, Suite 230

Medina, OH 44256
Phone: 330-721-1990
Fax: 330-721-1991

Memhard Investment Bankers, Inc.
P.O. Box 617
Old Greenwich, CT 06870
Phone: 203-637-5494
Fax: 203-637-9414
www.memhard.com

Meridian Group
The Benedum-Trees Building
223 Fourth Avenue, Suite 1700
Pittsburgh, PA 15222
Phone: 412-232-0113
Fax: 412-232-0502
www.themeridiangrp.com

Merrill Lynch & Co.
4 World Financial Center
250 Vesey Street
New York, NY 10080
Phone: 212-449-1000
www.merrilllynch.com

Mesirow Financial, Inc.
350 N. Clark Street
Chicago, IL 60610
Phone: 312-595-6000
Fax: 312-595-6988
www.mesirowfinancial.com

MidMark Investments, Inc.
380 N. Old Woodward Avenue, Suite 255
Birmingham, MI 48009
Phone: 248-594-4010
Fax: 248-594-4013
www.midmarketcapital.com

Milestone Merchant Partners LLC
1775 Eye Street NW, Suite 800
Washington, DC 20006
Phone: 202-367-3000
Fax: 202-367-3001
www.milestonecap.com

Mille Capital
590 Madison Avenue, 21st Floor
New York, NY 10022
Phone: 212-758-0607
Fax: 212-758-0608
www.millecap.com

Miller Johnson Steichen Kinnard, Inc.
60 S. Sixth Street, Suite 200
Minneapolis, MN 55402
Phone: 612-455-5555
Fax: 612-455-5600
www.mjsk.com

Montauk Financial Group
Parkway 109 Office Center

328 Newman Springs Road
Red Bank, NJ 07701
Phone: 732-747-2332
Fax: 732-224-1468
www.montaukfinancial.com

Montgomery & Co.
100 Wilshire Boulevard, Suite 400
Santa Monica, CA 90401
Phone: 310-260-6006
Fax: 310-260-6095
www.monty.com

Morgan Joseph & Co.
600 Fifth Avenue
New York, NY 10022
Phone: 212-218-3708
Fax: 212-218-3719
wcrooks@mlga.com
www.morganjoseph.com

Morgan Keegan & Co.
Morgan Keegan Tower
50 N. Front Street
Memphis, TN 38103
Phone: 800-366-7426
Fax: 901-579-4355
www.morgankeegan.com

Morgan Stanley
1585 Broadway, 33rd Floor
New York, NY 38103
Phone: 212-761-4000
www.morganstanley.com

MSI Capital Corporation
6500 Greenville Avenue, Suite 350
Dallas, TX 75206
Phone: 214-265-1801
Fax: 214-265-1804

Nassau Group, Inc.
245 Park Avenue
New York, NY 10167
Phone: 212-497-4107
www.thenassaugroup.com

NatCity Investments, Inc.
1900 E. Ninth Street
Cleveland, OH 44114
Phone: 888-462-8289
Fax: 216-222-0158
www.natcity.com

Needham & Co.
445 Park Avenue, 3rd Floor
New York, NY 10022
Phone: 212-371-8300
Fax: 212-371-8415
www.needhamco.com

Neidiger Tucker Bruner, Inc.
1675 Larimer Street, Suite 300

Denver, CO 80202
Phone: 303-825-1825

New England Business Exchange
60 Walnut Street
Wellesley, MA 02481
Phone: 781-431-0909
Fax: 781-431-7221
www.nebex.com

Newbury Piret & Co.
1 Boston Place, 28th Floor
Boston, MA 02108
Phone: 617-367-7300
Fax: 617-367-7301
www.newburypiret.com

NewCap Partners, Inc.
5777 W. Century Boulevard, Suite 1135
Los Angeles, CA 90045
Phone: 310-645-7900
Fax: 310-215-1025

Newfield Capital, Inc.
555 Fifth Avenue, 14th Floor
New York, NY 10017
Phone: 212-599-5000
Fax: 212-986-5316

Newman & Associates, Inc.
1801 California Street, Suite 3700
Denver, CO 80202
Phone: 303-293-8500
Fax: 303-296-6804
www.newmanfs.com

Noble Financial Group
6501 Congress Avenue, Suite 100
Boca Raton, FL 33487
Phone: 561-994-1191
Fax: 561-994-4809
www.noblefinancialgroup.com

Nomura Securities International, Inc.
2 World Financial Center, Building B
New York, NY 10281
Phone: 212-667-9433
Fax: 212-667-1054
www.nomurany.com

North American Capital Corporation
510 Broad Hollow Road
Melville, NY 11747
Phone: 631-752-9600
Fax: 631-752-9618
www.northamericancapital.com

Northbridge Equity Partners, Inc.
1010 Sherbrooke Street West, Suite 2210
Montreal, Quebec H3A 2R7
Canada
Phone: 514-845-9884

Noveltek Capital Group
521 Fifth Avenue, Suite 1700
New York, NY 10175
Phone: 212-286-1963
Fax: 212-661-7606
www.noveltek.com

Nuveen Investments
333 W. Wacker Drive
Chicago, IL 60606
Phone: 312-917-7700
Fax: 312-917-8367
www.nuveen.com

OEM Capital Corporation
230 Park Avenue, Suite 456
New York, NY 10169
Phone: 212-983-9500
Fax: 212-983-9018
www.oemcapitalcorp.com

Orion International Group
360 Central Avenue, Suite 1505
St. Petersburg, FL 33710
Phone: 727-823-4000
Fax: 727-823-6518

Pacific Crest Securities
111 SW Fifth Avenue, 42nd Floor
Portland, OR 97204
Phone: 503-248-0721
Fax: 503-227-3608
www.pacific-crest.com

Pacific Growth Equities, Inc.
1 Bush Street, Suite 1700
San Francisco, CA 94104
Phone: 415-274-6800
Fax: 415-274-6866
www.pacificgrowth.com

Pangaea Partners Ltd.
402 Laurel Lane
Madison, WI 53704
Phone: 608-242-1801
Fax: 608-242-1606
www.pangaeapartners.com

Paramax CFG Corporation
333 International Drive, Suite A
Williamsville, NY 14221
Phone: 716-626-1200
Fax: 716-626-4800
www.paramaxcorp.com

Parker/Hunter Inc.
600 Grant Street, 31st Floor
Pittsburgh, PA 15219
Phone: 412-562-8050
Fax: 412-562-7843

Paulson Investment Co.
811 Naito Parkway, Suite 200

Portland, OR 97204
Phone: 503-243-6000
Fax: 503-243-6018
www.paulsoninvestment.com

Peacock Hislop Staley & Given, Inc.
2999 N. 44th Street
Phoenix, AZ 85018
Phone: 602-952-6800
Fax: 602-952-0220

Philpott Ball & Werner
227 W. Trade Street, Suite 2170
Charlotte, NC 28202
Phone: 704-358-8094
Fax: 704-358-0021
www.pbandw.com

Pierce Financial Corporation
8300 Greensboro Drive, Suite 800
Vienna, VA 22102
Phone: 571-641-3032
Fax: 571-641-3036
info@piercefinancial.net
www.piercefinancial.net

Pine South Capital
13400 U.S. Highway 42, Suite 300
Prospect, KY 40059
Phone: 502-292-2920
Fax: 502-292-2921

PNC Capital Markets, Inc.
249 Fifth Avenue, 26th Floor
Pittsburgh, PA 15222
Phone: 412-762-9940
Fax: 412-762-7568

Porter White & Co.
15 Richard Assington Jr. Boulevard
North Birmingham, AL 35230
Phone: 205-252-3681
Fax: 205-252-8803

Prime Charter Ltd.
810 Seventh Avenue
New York, NY 10019
Phone: 212-699-7701
Fax: 212-977-0639

Prospect Capital Advisors LLC
30 Prospect Avenue
Darien, CT 06820
Phone: 203-655-6155
Fax: 203-656-3055

Prudential Financial
1 New York Plaza
New York, NY 10292
Phone: 212-214-1000
www.prusec.com

Pundmann & Co.
P.O. Box 446

St. Charles, MO 63302
Phone: 636-940-0400
Fax: 636-925-0000

R. F. Lafferty & Co.
The Colonnades, 82 Bishops Bridge Road
London W2 6BB
United Kingdom
Phone: 44-20-7563-5700
Fax: 44-20-7563-5701
www.lafferty.com

Raymond James Capital, Inc.
880 Carillon Parkway
St. Petersburg, FL 33716
Phone: 727-573-3800
Fax: 727-573-8733
www.raymondjames.com

RBC Dain Rauscher
Dain Rauscher Plaza
60 S. Sixth Street
Minneapolis, MN 55502
Phone: 612-371-2711
Fax: 612-371-7619
www.rbcdain.com

Regions Financial Corp.
P.O. Box 10247
Birmingham, AL 35202
Contact: Doyle Rippee
Phone: 205-244-2830
www.regions.com

Resilience Capital Partners
25201 Chagrin Boulevard, Suite 360
Cleveland, OH 44122
Phone: 216-292-0200
Fax: 212-292-4750
www.rcpmb.com

Resource Financial Corporation
550 W. Van Buren Street, Suite 1410
Chicago, IL 60607
Phone: 312-525-2600
Fax: 312-525-2610
www.resource-financial.com

Rittenhouse Financial Services
5 + B362 Radnor Corporate Center
100 Matsonford Road, Suite 300
Radnor, PA 19087
Phone: 800-847-6369
Fax: 610-225-3824
www.rittenhousefinancial.com

Robert W. Baird & Co.
777 E. Wisconsin Avenue
Milwaukee, WI 53202
Phone: 414-765-3500
Fax 414-765-3912
www.rwbaird.com

Robinson Capital, Inc.
5460 Yonge Street
P.O. Box 1000
Toronto, Ontario M2N 5T5
Canada
Phone: 905-882-8405
Fax: 905-882-8516

Rothschild, Inc.
1251 Avenue of the Americas
New York, NY 10020
Phone: 212-403-3500
Fax: 212-403-3501
www.rothschild.com

RoyNat, Inc.
Scotia Plaza
40 King Street West, 26th Floor
Toronto, Ontario M5H 1H1
Canada
Phone: 416-933-2730
Fax: 416-933-2783
info@roynat.com
www.roynat.com

RSM EquiCo
575 Anton Boulevard, 11th Floor
Costa Mesa, CA 92626
Phone: 714-327-8800
Fax: 714-327-8850
info@rsmequico.com
www.rsmequico.com

Ryan Beck & Co.
18 Columbia Turnpike
Florham Park, NJ 07932
Phone: 973-597-6000
Fax: 973-597-1258
www.ryanbeck.com

S. K. Platt & Co.
P.O. Box 158
Hinsdale, IL 60522
Phone: 630-920-1844
Fax: 630-920-1843

Sanders Morris Harris, Inc.
3100 JPMorgan Chase Tower
600 Travis, Suite 3100
Houston, TX 77002
Phone: 713-224-3100
Fax: 713-993-4677
www.smhhou.com

Sandton Financial Group
21550 Oxnard Street, Suite 300
Woodland Hills, CA 91367
Phone: 818-702-9283

Schnitzius & Vaughan
700 Louisiana Street, Suite 2450
Houston, TX 77002

Phone: 713-222-2170
Fax: 713-227-4412
www.sch-vau.com

SCO Financial Group LLC
1285 Avenue of the Americas, 35th Floor
New York, NY 10019
Phone: 212-554-4158
Fax: 212-554-4058
www.scogroup.com

Scott-Macon Ltd.
800 Third Avenue, 16th Floor
New York, NY 10022
Phone: 212-755-8200
Fax: 212-755-8255
www.scottmaconltd.com

SEG Cos.
6 Hutton Centre Drive, Suite 860
South Coast Metro, CA 92707
Phone: 714-444-3833
Fax: 714-435-9410
info@segco.com
www.segco.com

Seidler Cos.
515 S. Figueroa Street
Los Angeles, CA 90071
Phone: 213-683-4500
Fax: 213-683-1247
www.seidlercos.com

Selkirk Investments
222 N. Wall Street, Suite 310
Spokane, WA 99201
Phone: 509-623-1300
Fax: 509-623-1709

Sentra Securities Corporation
2800 N. Central Avenue, Suite 2100
Phoenix, AZ 85004
Phone: 619-471-3700
Fax: 619-640-9091
www.sentraspelman.com

SG Cowen
1221 Avenue of the Americas, 10th Floor
New York, NY 10020
Phone: 212-278-6000
Fax: 212-278-6789
www.sgcowen.com

Shipley Raidy Capital Partners LLC
P.O. Box 32
Conshohocken, PA 19428
Phone: 610-941-9090
Fax: 610-828-4131
www.srcapital.com

Sierra Trading Co.
2045 Palisades Drive

Fullerton, CA 92831
Phone: 714-992-2150
Fax: 714-992-4395
www.mnawizards.com

Silicon Valley Bank
3003 Tasman Drive
Santa Clara, CA 95054
Phone: 408-654-7400
www.svb.com

Simmons & Co. International
700 Louisiana, Suite 5000
Houston, TX 77002
Phone: 713-236-9999
Fax: 713-223-7800
www.simmonsco-intl.com

Sorrento Associates, Inc.
4370 LaJolla Village Drive, Suite 1040
San Diego, CA 92122
Phone: 858-452-3100
Fax: 858-452-7607
www.sorrentoventures.com

Southeastern Capital Advisors LLC
3390 Peachtree Road NE, Suite 1000
Atlanta, GA 30326
Phone: 404-969-3333
Fax: 404-969-3601
www.southeastern-capital.com

Southwest Securities, Inc.
1201 Elm Street, Suite 3500
Dallas, TX 75270
Phone: 214-859-1800
Fax: 214-658-9441
www.southwestsecurities.com

Stamford Financial
Stamford Financial Boulevard
Stamford, NY 12167
Phone: 607-652-3311
Fax: 607-652-6301

State Street Corporation
1 Lincoln Street
Boston, MA 02111
Phone: 617-654-4000
Fax: 617-350-4020
www.statestreet.com

Stenton Leigh Group, Inc.
1900 Corporate Boulevard, Suite 305W
Boca Raton, FL 33431
Phone: 561-241-9921
Fax: 561-241-7011
www.stentonleighgroup.com

Stephens Inc.
111 Center Street
Little Rock, AR 72201

Phone: 501-374-4361
Fax: 501-377-8011
www.stephens.com

Stern Brothers Valuation Advisors
1044 Main Street, Suite 900
Kansas City, MO 64105
Phone: 816-471-0005
Fax: 816-842-2789
www.sternbv.com

Stevenson & Co.
1603 Orrington Avenue, Suite 1100
Evanston, IL 60201
Phone: 847-866-1188
Fax: 847-866-1199
www.StevensonCo.com

Stifel Nicolaus & Co.
501 N. Broadway
St. Louis, MO 63102
Phone: 314-342-2000
Fax: 314-342-2151
www.stifel.com

Stonehenge Partners
191 W. Nationwide Boulevard, Suite 600
Columbus, OH 43215
Phone: 614-246-2500
Fax: 614-246-2441
www.stonehengepartners.com

Stout Risius Ross, Inc.
Bank One Center, 7th Floor
600 Superior Avenue East
Cleveland, OH 44114
Phone: 216-685-5000
Fax: 216-685-5001
www.gosrr.com

Strategic Advisors, Inc.
400 Southpointe Boulevard, Plaza I, Suite 120
Canonsburg, PA 15317
Phone: 724-743-5800
Fax: 724-742-5870
www.strategicad.com

Strategica Group
701 Brickell Avenue, Suite 2500
Miami, FL 33149
Phone: 305-536-1414
Fax: 305-536-1486
www.strategica.net

Sucsy Fischer & Co.
799 Central Avenue, Suite 350
Highland Park, IL 60035
Phone: 312-554-7575
Fax: 312-554-7501
www.sfco.com

SunTrust Robinson Humphrey
3333 Peachtree Road NE, 11th Floor
Atlanta, GA 30326
Phone: 404-926-5250
Fax: 404-926-5872
www.suntrustrh.com

Symphony Capital LLC
875 Third Avenue, 18th Floor
New York, NY 10022
Phone: 212-632-5400
Fax: 212-632-5401
www.symphonycapital.com

TD Securities
66 Wellington Street West
P.O. Box 1, TD Bank Tower
Toronto, Ontario M5K 1A2
Canada
Phone: 416-982-6160
Fax: 416-307-0338
www.tdsecurities.com

Texada Capital Corporation
62 Greenwood Shoals, Suite A
Grasonville, MD 21638
Phone: 410-827-4888
Fax: 410-827-3109
www.texada.com

Thompson Capital Corporation
31 Ridge Road
Ridgewood, NJ 07450
Phone: 201-447-4121
Fax: 201-447-6723

TM Capital Corporation
1 Battery Park Plaza, 35th Floor
New York, NY 10004
Phone: 212-890-1360
Fax: 212-890-1450
www.tmcapital.com

TransAction Group, Inc.
Hanna Building, Suite 500
1422 Euclid Avenue
Cleveland, OH 44115
Phone: 216-348-1666
Fax: 216-348-1416
www.transactiongroup.com

Trenwith Securities LLC
3200 Bristol Street, 4th Floor
Costa Mesa, CA 92626
Phone: 714-668-7333
Fax: 714-668-7377
www.trenwith.com

Triangle Capital Partners LLC
3600 Glenwood Avenue, Suite 104
Raleigh, NC 27612

Phone: 919-719-4770
www.trianglecapitalpartners.com

TriCapital Corporation
11140 Rockville Pike, Suite 600
North Bethesda, MD 20852
Phone: 301-230-8900
Fax: 301-231-7227
www.tricapital.com

Tully & Holland, Inc.
36 Washington Street, Suite 190
Wellesley Hills, MA 02481
Phone: 781-239-2900
Fax: 781-239-2901
www.tullyandholland.com

UBS Investment Bank
677 Washington Boulevard
Stamford, CT 06901
Phone: 203-719-3000
Fax: 203-719-6898
www.ubs.com

Union Bank of California N.A.
445 S. Figueroa Street
Los Angeles, CA 90017
Phone: 213-236-7700
Fax: 213-236-7734
www.uboc.com

USBX
2425 Olympic Boulevard, Suite 500E
Santa Monica, CA 90404
Phone: 310-315-6750
Fax: 310-315-6751
www.usbx.com

Veber Partners LLC
605 NW 11th Avenue
Portland, OR 97209
Phone: 503-229-4400
Fax: 503-227-5067
advisors@veber.com
www.veber.com

Vector Fund Management
1751 Lake Cook Road, Suite 350
Deerfield, IL 60015
Phone: 847-374-3947
Fax: 847-374-3899
www.vectorfund.com

Venture Associates Ltd.
4950 E. Evans, Suite 105
Denver, CO 80222-5209
Phone: 303-758-8710
Fax: 303-758-8747
www.venturea.com

Venture Business Group, Inc.
601 Carlson Center, Suite 1050

Minneapolis, MN 55305
Phone: 952-449-5247
merger@vbgi.net
www.vbgi.net

Veronis Suhler Stevenson
350 Park Avenue
New York, NY 10022
Phone: 212-935-4990
Fax: 212-381-8168
www.vss.com

vFinance Investments, Inc.
880 Third Avenue
New York, NY 10022
Phone: 212-508-4745
www.vfinance.com

Via Inc.
545 Middlefield Road, Suite 175
Menlo Park, CA 94025
Phone: 650-853-6464
Fax: 650-853-6474
www.viaincorporated.com

W.P. Carey & Co. LLC
50 Rockefeller Plaza
New York, NY 10020
Phone: 212-492-1100
Fax: 212-492-8922
www.wpcarey.com

W. Y. Campbell & Co.
1 Woodward Avenue, 26th Floor
Detroit, MI 48226
Phone: 313-496-9000
Fax: 313-496-9001
www.wycampbell.com

Wachovia IJL Corporation
191 Peachtree Street NE
Atlanta, GA 30301
Phone: 404-332-4116
Fax: 404-332-1026
www.wachovia.com

Walden Group
560 White Plains Road
Tarrytown, NY 10591
Phone: 914-332-9700
Fax: 914-332-0020
www.waldenmed.com

Wall Street Access
17 Battery Place, 11th Floor
New York, NY 10004
Phone: 800-925-5781
Fax: 212-709-9522
www.wsaccess.com

Wedbush Morgan Securities
1000 Wilshire Boulevard

Los Angeles, CA 90017
Phone: 213-688-8000
Fax: 213-688-6642
www.wedbush.com

Wellington Associates, Inc.
6500 N. Belt Line Road, Suite 160
Irving, TX 75063
Phone: 972-999-4570
Fax: 972-999-4572
rwellington@wellington-associates.com
www.wellington-associates.com

Western America Capital Group
10025-102A Avenue Edmonton, Suite 1500
Edmonton, Alberta T5J 2Z2
Canada
Phone: 780-496-9171
Fax: 780-496-9172
www.wacapital.com

William Blair & Co. LLC
222 W. Adams Street
Chicago, IL 60606
Phone: 312-236-1600
Fax: 312-236-8654
www.wmblair.com

Wilson-Davis & Co.
39 W. Market Street, 3rd Floor
Salt Lake City, UT 84101
Phone: 801-532-1313
Fax: 801-578-2823
www.wdco.com/wd/wdco.html

Windsor Group Securities LLC
12010 Sunset Hills Road, Suite 700
Reston, VA 20190

Phone: 703-471-8500
Fax: 703-471-3888
www.windsorgroupllc.com

Winmill & Co.
11 Hanover Square
New York, NY 10005
Phone: 212-785-0900
Fax: 212-785-1102
www.winmillco.com

Wm Sword & Co.
34 Chambers Street
Princeton, NJ 08542
Phone: 609-924-6710
contact@wmswordco.com

Woodward Capital Advisors
355 S. Old Woodward Avenue
Birmingham, MI 48009
Phone: 248-430-2632
Fax: 248-430-2635
www.woodwardcapital.com

Wye River Capital, Inc.
7 King Charles Place
Annapolis, MD 21401
Phone: 410-267-8811
Fax: 410-267-8235
www.wyeriver.net

Zachary Scott & Co.
500 Union Street, Suite 1000
Seattle, WA 98101
Phone: 206-224-7380
Fax: 206-224-7384
info@zacharyscott.com
www.zacharyscott.com

APPENDIX B-4. ACCOUNTANTS

Altschuler Melvoin & Glasser
1 S. Wacker Drive, Suite 800
Chicago, IL 60606
Phone: 312-384-6000
Fax: 312-634-3410
www.amgnet.com

Anchin Block & Anchin
1375 Broadway
New York, NY 10018
Phone: 212-840-3456
Fax: 212-840-7066
www.anchin.com

BDO Seidman LLP
330 Madison Avenue

New York, NY 10017
Phone: 212-885-8000
Fax: 212-697-1299
www.bdo.com

Beers & Cutler
1700 K Street, NW, Suite 410
Washington, DC 20006
Contact: Scott Barnard
Phone: 202-331-0300
Fax: 202-778-0259
www.beersandcutler.com

BISYS Private Equity Services
245 Fifth Avenue
New York, NY 10016

Phone: 212-224-0909
Fax: 212-447-7020
www.bisysprivateequity.com

CAS
2775 Algonquin Road, Suite 250
Rolling Meadows, IL 60008
Phone: 847-255-3500
Fax: 847-255-3566

Crowe Chizek & Co. LLC
1 Mid America Plaza, Suite 700
Oak Brook, IL 60522-3697
Phone: 630-574-7878
Fax: 630-574-1608
www.crowechizek.com

Deloitte & Touche LLP
2 World Financial Center
New York, NY 10281-1414
Phone: 800-776-4449
www.deloitte.com//m&a

Eisner LLP
750 Third Avenue
New York, NY 10017
Phone: 212-949-8700
Fax: 212-891-4100
thall@eisnerllp.com
www.eisnerllp.com

Ellin & Tucker Chartered
100 S. Charles Street, Suite 1300
Baltimore, MD 21201
Phone: 410-727-5735
www.etnet.com

Ernst & Young LLP
5 Times Square
New York, NY 10036
Phone: 212-773-3000
Fax: 212-773-6350
www.ey.com

Geller & Co.
800 Third Avenue
New York, NY 10022
Phone: 212-583-6000
Fax: 212-583-6243
hshore@gellerco.com
www.gellerco.com

Goldstein Golub Kessler LLP
1185 Avenue of the Americas
New York, NY 10036-2602
Phone: 212-372-1800
Fax: 212-372-1801
www.ggkllp.com

Grant Thornton LLP
226 Causeway Street

Boston, MA 02114
Phone: 617-848-4890

Harb Levy & Weiland LLP
The Landmark @ 1 Market Street, Suite 620
San Francisco, CA 94105
Phone: 415-974-6000
Fax: 415-974-5488
www.hlwcpa.com

Invient
1388 Terra Bella Avenue
Mountain View, CA 94043
Phone: 650-316-5990
Fax: 650-316-5901
info@invient.com
www.invient.com

KPMG LLP—Private Equity Group
345 Park Avenue
New York, NY 10154
Phone: 212-758-9700
Fax: 212-758-9819
www.kpmg.com

Marcum & Kliegman LLP
130 Crossways Park Drive
Woodbury, NY 11797
Phone: 516-390-1000
Fax: 516-390-1001

McGladrey & Pullen LLP
3600 American Boulevard West
Bloomington, MN 55341
Phone: 952-835-9930
Fax: 952-921-7702
www.mcgladrey.com

Mohler Nixon & Williams
635 Campbell Technology Parkway,
    Suite 100
Campbell, CA 95008-5059
Phone: 408-369-2400
Fax: 408-879-9485
www.mohlernixon.com

Moss Adams LLP
1001 Fourth Avenue, Suite 2900
Seattle, WA 98154
Phone: 206-223-1820
Fax: 206-622-9975
www.mossadams.com

Mourant
22 Grenville Street
St. Helier, Jersey JE4 8PX
United Kingdom
Phone: 44-1534-609-000
Fax: 44-1534-609-333
mifa@mourant.com
www.mourant.com

Northport LLC
100 Walnut Avenue, Suite 103
Clark, NJ 07066
Phone: 732-943-3400
info@northportpm.com
www.northportpm.com

Palmeri Fund Administrators, Inc.
16-00 Route 208 South
Fair Lawn, NJ 07410
Phone: 201-475-8072
Fax: 201-475-8076
www.pfadmin.com

PricewaterhouseCoopers LLP
300 Madison Avenue
New York, NY 10017
Phone: 646-471-3000
Fax: 646-471-3188
www.pwcglobal.com

Ravix Group, Inc.
2109 Landings Drive
Mountain View, CA 94011
Phone: 650-691-1500
Fax: 650-691-9909

Rotenberg Meril Solomon Bertiger & Guttilla
Park 80 West, Plaza One
Saddle Brook, NJ 07663
Phone: 201-487-8383
Fax: 201-490-2068
cpas@rmsbg.com
www.rmsbg.com

Rothstein Kass & Co.
1350 Avenue of the Americas, 15th Floor
New York, NY 10019
Phone: 212-997-0500
Fax: 212-730-6892
admin@rkco.com
www.rkco.com

APPENDIX B-5. LAW FIRMS

Akin Gump Strauss Hauer & Feld LLP
590 Madison Avenue
New York, NY 10022
Phone: 212-872-1000
Fax: 212-872-1002
newyorkinfo@akingump.com
www.akingump.com

Arnold & Porter
555 12th Street NW
Washington, DC 20004-1206
Phone: 202-942-5000
Fax: 202-942-5999
www.arnoldporter.com

Baker & McKenzie
1 Prudential Building
130 E. Randolph Drive
Chicago, IL 60601
Phone: 312-861-8000
Fax: 312-861-2899
www.bakernet.com

Bingham McCutchen LLP
150 Federal Street
Boston, MA 02110
Phone: 617-951-8000
Fax: 617-951-8736
www.bingham.com

Buchanan Ingersoll PC
One Oxford Centre
301 Grant Street, 20th Floor
Pittsburgh, PA 15219-1410
Phone: 412-562-8800

Fax: 412-562-1041
E-mail: info@bipc.com
www.buchananingersoll.com

Buchanan Ingersoll PC (Washington, D.C.)
1776 K Street, N.W.
Suite 800
Washington, DC 20006-2365
Phone: 202-452-7900
Fax: 202-452-7989

Cadwalader, Wickersham & Taft LLP
1 World Financial Center
New York, NY 10281
Phone: 212-504-6000
Fax: 212-504-6666
cwtinfo@cwt.com
www.cadwalader.com

Chadbourne & Parke LLP
30 Rockefeller Plaza
New York, NY 10112
Phone: 212-408-5100
Fax: 212-541-5369
www.chadbourne.com

Christensen, Miller, Fink, Jacobs,
Glaser, Weil & Shapiro LLP
10250 Constellation Boulevard, 19th Floor
Los Angeles, CA 90067
Phone: 310-553-3000
Fax: 310-556-2920
jsoza@chrismill.com
www.chrismill.com

Cleary Gottlieb Steen & Hamilton
1 Liberty Plaza
New York, NY 10006
Phone: 212-225-2000
Fax: 212-225-3999
www.clearygottlieb.com

Clifford Chance
10 Upper Bank Street
London E14 5JJ United Kingdom
Phone: 44-20-7006-1000
Fax: 44-20-7006-5555
www.cliffordchance.com

Cohen & Grigsby PC
11 Stanwix Street, 15th Floor
Pittsburgh, PA 15222-1319
Phone: 412-297-4900
Fax: 412-209-0672
www.cohenlaw.com

Cooley Godward LLP
4401 Eastgate Mall
San Diego, CA 92121-1909
Phone: 858-550-6000
Fax: 858-550-6420
sandiego@cooley.com
www.cooley.com

Covington & Burling
1330 Sixth Avenue
New York, NY 10019
Phone: 212-841-1000
Fax: 212-841-1010
www.cov.com

Cravath, Swaine & Moore LLP
Worldwide Plaza
825 Eighth Avenue
New York, NY 10019-7475
Phone: 212-474-1000
Fax: 212-474-3700
cravath@cravath.com
www.cravath.com

Davis Polk & Wardwell
450 Lexington Avenue
New York, NY 10017
Phone: 212-450-4000
Fax: 212-450-3800
www.dpw.com

Debevoise & Plimpton LLP
919 Third Avenue
New York, NY 10022
Phone: 212-909-6000
Fax: 212-909-6836
mailbox@debevoise.com
www.debevoise.com

Dechert LLP
30 Rockefeller Plaza

New York, NY 10112-2200
Phone: 212-698-3500
Fax: 212-698-3599
www.dechert.com

Dewey Ballantine LLP
1301 Avenue of the Americas
New York, NY 10019
Phone: 212-259-8000
Fax: 212-259-6421
marketingdepartment@deweyballantine.com
www.deweyballantine.com

Dickinson Wright PLLC
500 Woodward Avenue, Suite 4000
Detroit, MI 48226-3425
Phone: 313-223-3500
Fax: 313-223-3598
www.dickinsonwright.com

DLA Piper Rudnick Gray Cary
2000 University Avenue
East Palo Alto, CA 94303
Phone: 650-833-2000
info@dlapiper.com
www.dlapiper.com

Duval & Stachenfeld LLP
300 E. 42nd Street, 3rd Floor
New York, NY 10017
Phone: 212-883-1700
Fax: 212-883-8883
info@dsllp.com
www.dsllp.com

Dykema Gossett PLLC
400 Renaissance Center
Detroit, MI 48243
Phone: 313-568-6800
Fax: 313-568-6893
www.dykema.com

Edwards & Angell LLP
101 Federal Street
Boston, MA 02110
Phone: 617-439-4444
Fax: 617-439-4170
www.edwardsangell.com

Elias, Matz, Tiernan & Herrick LLP
734 15th Street NW, 12th Floor
Washington, DC 20005
Phone: 202-347-0300
Fax: 202-347-2172
www.emth.com

Fenwick & West LLP
Silicon Valley Center
801 California Street
Mountain View, CA 94041
Phone: 650-335-7616

info@fenwick.com
www.fenwick.com

Fried, Frank, Harris, Shriver & Jacobson LLP
1 New York Plaza
New York, NY 10004
Phone: 212-859-8000
Fax: 212-859-4000
www.friedfrank.com

Fulbright & Jaworski LLP
Fulbright Tower
1301 McKinney, Suite 5100
Houston, TX 77010
Phone: 713-651-5151
Fax: 713-651-5246
info@fulbright.com
www.fulbright.com

Gibson Dunn & Crutcher LLP
200 Park Avenue, 47th Floor
New York, NY 10166-0193
Phone: 212-351-4000
Fax: 212-351-4035
www.gdclaw.com

Goodwin Procter LLP
Exchange Place
53 State Street
Boston, MA 02109
Phone: 617-570-1000
Fax: 617-523-1231
www.goodwinprocter.com

Greenberg Traurig LLP
1221 Brickell Avenue
Miami, FL 33131
Phone: 305-579-0500
Fax: 305-579-0717
info@gtlaw.com
www.gtlaw.com

Gunderson Dettmer Stough Villeneuve
Franklin & Hachigian LLP
155 Constitution Drive
Menlo Park, CA 94025
Phone: 650-321-2400
Fax: 650-321-2800
www.gunder.com

Harris Beach
99 Garnsey Road
Pittsford, NY 14534
Phone: 585-419-8800
Fax: 585-419-8801
www.harrisbeach.com

Haynes and Boone LLP
901 Main Street, Suite 3100
Dallas, TX 75202
Phone: 214-651-5000

Fax: 214-651-5940
www.haynesboone.com

Heller Ehrman LLP
333 Bush Street
San Francisco, CA 94104
Phone: 415-772-6000
Fax: 415-772-6268
info@hellerehrman.com
www.hellerehrman.com

Hogan & Hartson LLP
555 13th Street NW
Washington, DC 20004
Phone: 202-637-5600
Fax: 202-637-5910
www.hhlaw.com

Hutchison & Mason PLLC
3110 Edwards Mill Road, Suite 100
Raleigh, NC 27612
Phone: 919-829-9600
Fax: 919-829-9696
rtyler@hutchlaw.com
www.hutchlaw.com

Jones Day
901 Lakeside Avenue
Cleveland, OH 44114-1190
Phone: 216-586-3939
Fax: 216-579-0212
info@jonesday.com
www.jonesday.com

Katten Muchin Rosenman
525 W. Monroe Street, Suite 1600
Chicago, IL 60661-3693
Phone: 312-902-5200
Fax: 312-902-1061
www.kmzr.com

Kaye Scholer
425 Park Avenue
New York, NY 10022-3598
Phone: 212-836-8000
Fax: 212-836-8689
www.kayescholer.com

Kennedy Covington Lobdell & Hickman LLP
Hearst Tower, 47th Floor
214 N. Tryon Street
Charlotte, NC 28202
Phone: 704-331-7400
Fax: 704-331-7598
jstensrud@kennedycovington.com
www.kennedycovington.com

Kilpatrick Stockton LLP
1100 Peachtree Street, Suite 2800
Atlanta, GA 30309-4530
Phone: 404-815-6500
Fax: 404-815-6555

aguthrie@kilpatrickstockton.com
www.kilstock.com

King & Spalding LLP
191 Peachtree Street
Atlanta, GA 30303-1763
Phone: 404-572-4600
Fax: 404-572-5100
kingspalding@kslaw.com
www.kslaw.com

Kirkland & Ellis LLP
Citigroup Center
153 E. 53rd Street
New York, NY 10022-4675
Phone: 212-446-4800
Fax: 212-446-4900
www.kirkland.com

Kirkpatrick & Lockhart
Nicholson Graham LLP
599 Lexington Avenue
New York, NY 10022-6030
Phone: 212-536-3900
Fax: 212-536-3901
www.klng.com

Klehr Harrison Harvey
Branzburg & Ellers
260 S. Broad Street
Philadelphia, PA 19102-5003
Phone: 215-568-6060
Fax: 215-568-6603
www.klehr.com

Latham & Watkins
633 W. Fifth Street, Suite 4000
Los Angeles, CA 90071-2007
Phone: 213-485-1234
Fax: 213-891-8763
www.lw.com

Loeb & Loeb LLP
345 Park Avenue
New York, NY 10154
Phone: 212-407-4000
Fax: 212-407-4990
www.loeb.com

Manatt, Phelps & Phillips LLP
11355 W. Olympic Boulevard
Los Angeles, CA 90064
Phone: 310-312-4000
Fax: 310-312-4224
bkelly@manatt.com
www.manatt.com

Maples & Calder
P.O. Box 309GT
Ugland House, S. Church Street
George Town, Grand Cayman
Cayman Islands

Phone: 345-949-8066
Fax: 345-949-8080
info@maplesandcalder.com
www.maplesandcalder.com

Mayer, Brown, Rowe & Maw LLP
190 S. LaSalle Street
Chicago, IL 60603-3441
Phone: 312-782-0600
Fax: 312-701-7711
www.mayerbrownrowe.com

McCarter & English LLP
4 Gateway Center
100 Mulberry Street
Newark, NJ 07102-4056
Phone: 973-622-4444
Fax: 973-624-7070
www.mccarter.com

McDermott Will & Emery LLP
227 W. Monroe Street
Chicago, IL 60606-5096
Phone: 312-372-2000
blynch@mwe.com
www.mwe.com

Milbank, Tweed, Hadley & McCloy LLP
1 Chase Manhattan Plaza
New York, NY 10005
Phone: 212-530-5000
Fax: 212-530-5219
www.milbank.com

Mintz Levin Cohn Ferris
Glovsky and Popeo PC
1 Financial Center
Boston, MA 02111
Phone: 617-542-6000
Fax: 617-542-2241
comments.@mintz.com
www.mintz.com

Morgan, Lewis & Bockius LLP
101 Park Avenue
New York, NY 10178-0060
Phone: 212-309-6000
Fax: 212-309-6001
www.morganlewis.com

Morrison & Foerster LLP
425 Market Street
San Francisco, CA 94105-2482
Phone: 415-268-7000
Fax: 415-268-7522
kmuller@mofo.com
www.mofo.com

Morrison Cohen Singer & Weinstein LLP
909 Third Avenue
New York, NY 10022-4731
Phone: 212-735-8600

Fax: 212-735-8708
info@morrisoncohen.com
www.mcsw.com

Morrison Mahoney LLP
250 Summer Street
Boston, MA 02210
Phone: 617-737-8804
Fax 617-342-4958
boston@morrisonmahoney.com
www.morrisonmahoney.com

Nixon Peabody LLP
437 Madison Avenue
New York, NY 10022
Phone: 212-940-3000
Fax: 212-940-3111
www.nixonpeabody.com

Norris McLaughlin & Marcus, PA
721 Route 202-206
Bridgewater, NJ 08807
Phone: 908-722-0700
Fax: 908-722-0755
www.nmmlaw.com

O'Melveny & Myers LLP
7 Times Square Tower
New York, NY 10036
Phone: 212-326-2000
Fax: 212-326-2061
www.omm.com

Orrick, Herrington & Sutcliffe LLP
666 Fifth Avenue
New York, NY 10103
Phone: 212-506-5000
Fax: 212-506-5151
info@orrick.com
www.orrick.com

Patton Boggs LLP
2550 M Street
Washington, DC 20037
Phone: 202-457-6000
Fax: 202-457-6315
www.pattonboggs.com

Paul, Hastings, Janofsky & Walker
515 S. Flower Street, 25th Floor
Los Angeles, CA 90071-2228
Phone: 213-683-6000
Fax: 213-683-0705
www.paulhastings.com

Paul, Weiss, Rifkind, Wharton & Garrison
   LLP
1285 Avenue of the Americas
New York, NY 10019-6064
Phone: 212-373-3000
Fax: 212-757-3990
www.mailbox.com

Pillsbury Winthrop Shaw Pittman LLP
2300 N Street NW
Washington, DC 20037-1128
Phone: 202-663-8000
Fax: 202-663-8007
www.pillsburylaw.com

Preston Gates
925 Fourth Avenue, Suite 2900
Seattle, WA 98104-1158
Phone: 206-623-7580
Fax: 206-623-7022
www.prestongates.com

Proskauer Rose LLP
1585 Broadway
New York, NY 10036
Phone: 212-969-3000
Fax: 212-969-2900
www.proskauer.com

Reed Smith LLP
1999 Harrison Street, Suite 2400
Oakland, CA 94612-3572
Phone: 510-763-2000
Fax: 510-273-8832
www.reedsmith.com

Ropes & Gray LLP
1 International Place
Boston, MA 02110-2624
Phone: 617-951-7000
Fax: 617-951-7050
contactus@ropesgray.com
www.ropesgray.com

Sadis & Goldberg LLC
551 Fifth Avenue, 21st Floor
New York, NY 10176
Phone: 212-947-3793
Fax: 212-573-8147
www.sglawyers.com

Schulte Roth & Zabel LLP
919 Third Avenue
New York, NY 10022
Phone: 212-756-2000
Fax: 212-593-5955
www.mail@srz.com
www.srz.com

Shearman & Sterling LLP
599 Lexington Avenue
New York, NY 10022
Phone: 212-848-4000
www.shearman.com

Sidley Austin Brown & Wood
Bank One Plaza
10 S. Dearborn Street
Chicago, IL 60603
Phone: 312-853-7000

Fax: 312-853-7036
www.sidley.com

Simpson Thacher & Bartlett LLP
425 Lexington Avenue
New York, NY 10017
Phone: 212-455-2000
Fax: 212-455-2502
www.simpsonthacher.com

Skadden, Arps, Slate, Meagher
& Flom LLP and Affiliates
4 Times Square
New York, NY 10036
Phone: 212-735-3000
Fax: 212-735-2000
www.skadden.com

Sonnenschein Nath & Rosenthal LLP
101 JFK Parkway
Short Hills, NJ 07078
Phone: 973-912-7100
Fax: 973-912-7199
svtg@sonnenschein.com
www.sonnenschein.com

Stradley Ronon Stevens & Young LLP
2600 1 Commerce Square
Philadelphia, PA 19103
Phone: 215-564-8000
Fax: 215-564-8120
www.stradley.com

Stroock & Stroock & Lavan LLP
180 Maiden Lane
New York, NY 10038
Phone: 212-806-5400
www.stroock.com

Sullivan & Worcester LLP
1 Post Office Square
Boston, MA 02109
Phone: 617-338-2800
Fax: 617-338-2880
info@sandw.com
www.sandw.com

Torys LLP
237 Park Avenue
New York, NY 10017
Phone: 212-880-6000
Fax: 212-682-0200
info@torys.com
www.torys.com

Vinson & Elkins LLP
First City Tower
1001 Fannin Street, Suite 2300
Houston, TX 77002-6760
Phone: 713-758-2222
Fax: 713-758-2346
www.vinson-elkins.com

Weil, Gotshal & Manges LLP
767 Fifth Avenue
New York, NY 10153
Phone: 212-310-8000
Fax: 212-310-8007
www.weil.com

Willkie Farr & Gallagher LLP
787 Seventh Avenue
New York, NY 10019-6099
Phone: 212-728-8000
Fax: 212-728-8111
www.willkie.com

Wilmer Cutler Pickering Hale and Dorr LLP
60 State Street
Boston, MA 02109
Phone: 617-526-6000
Fax: 617-526-5000
law@wilmerhale.com
www.wilmerhale.com

Wilson Sonsini Goodrich & Rosati
650 Page Mill Road
Palo Alto, CA 94304-1050
Phone: 650-493-9300
wsgr@wsgr.com
www.wsgr.com

Winston & Strawn LLP
35 W. Wacker Drive
Chicago, IL 60601
Phone: 312-558-5600
Fax: 312-558-5700
info@winston.com
www.winston.com

Yigal Arnon & Co.
1 Azrieli Center
Tel Aviv 67021 Israel
Phone: 972 3608 7777
Fax: 972 3608 7724
info@arnon.co.il
www.arnon.co.il

APPENDIX B-6. PRIVATE EQUITY INVESTMENT FIRMS

It's important to identify a private equity investment firm whose interests match your transaction. Some firms only work on very large deals, and many venture capital firms only invest in technology companies and do not back management buyouts. Fortunately, the Internet has made searching for firms much easier, and with this list I've tried to provide you with the Web addresses of the various firms. Review those Web sites carefully before you send out any material. For many of the firms listed, I have included the amount of capital and made some annotations about its focus, which can help you initially identify a firm that may best match your needs.

This list of firms is not by any means a complete list. There are hundreds of firms, and if I tried to list them all, the list would comprise the whole book. While a majority of the firms listed have multiple office locations, for the most part I have included only their primary office location, so check their website to see if they have an office close to you. You'll be able to get detailed personal contact information from most sites as well.

Please note that there are also a very large group of firms backed by the Small Business Administration (called SBICs, or "Small Business Investment Companies"). You can find that list of firms at www.sba.gov. These farms target investments in smaller companies.

If you are an investor and I left your firm off this list, or an investor who would have preferred to have been left off the list, I apologize. This list, and additional updates and links, can also be found online at the website for the book.

ABS Capital Partners
1 South Street
Baltimore, MD 21202
Contacts: Don Hebb, Tim Weglicki
Phone: 410-895-4400
Fax: 410-895-4380
www.abscapital.com
Capital: More than $900 million

Acacia Venture Partners
101 California Street, Suite 3160
San Francisco, CA 94111
Contacts: Harold Friedman, Sage Givens
Phone: 415-433-4200
Fax: 415-433-4250

www.acaciavp.com
Capital: More than $200 million

Accel Partners
428 University Avenue
Palo Alto, CA 94301
Contact: Jim Breyer
Phone: 650-614-4800
Fax: 650-614-4880
www.accel.com
Capital: More than $2 billion

Advanced Technology Ventures
281 Winter Street, Suite 350
Waltham, MA 02451

Phone: 781-290-0707
Fax: 781-684-0045
www.atvcapital.com
Capital: More than $300 million

Advent International
75 State Street
Boston, MA 02109
Phone: 617-951-9400
Fax: 617-951-0566
www.adventinternational.com
Capital: More than $3.5 billion
Leading global investment firm with large
   domestic and European capabilities.

Agio Capital Partners I, LP
US Bank Place, Suite 4600
601 Second Avenue South
Minneapolis, MN 55402
Phone: 612-339-8408
Fax: 612-349-4232
www.agiocap@aol.com
Capital: Approximately $42 million

Allen & Co. LLC
711 Fifth Avenue
New York, NY 10022
Phone: 212-832-8000
Fax: 212-832-7057

Allied Capital Corporation
1919 Pennsylvania Avenue, 3rd Floor
Washington, DC 20006-3434
Contact: John Fruehwirth
Phone: 202-331-1112
Fax: 202-659-2053
www.alliedcapital.com

Alta Communications
One Post Office Square, Suite 3800
Boston, MA 02109
Phone: 617-482-8020
Fax: 617-482-1944

ARCH Venture Partners
8725 W. Higgins Road, Suite 290
Chicago, IL 60631
Phone: 773-380-6600
Fax: 773-380-6606
www.archventure.com

Arlington Partners
600 New Hampshire Avenue, 6th Floor
Washington, DC 20037
Contact: Jeffrey Freed
Phone: 202-337-7500
Fax: 202-337-7525
Capital: More than $800 million

Austin Ventures
114 W. 7th Street, Suite 1300
Austin, TX 78701

Phone: 512-485-1900
Fax: 512-476-3952
www.austinventures.com
Capital: More than $1 billion
Large Internet and telecom investment firm.

Bain Capital, Inc.
Two Copley Plaza
Boston, MA 02116
Phone: 617-572-3000
Fax: 617-572-3274
www.baincap.com

Baker Capital Corp.
540 Madison Avenue, 29th Floor
New York, NY 10022
Phone: 212-848-2000
Fax: 212-486-0660
www.bakercapital.com

BancBoston Capital/BancBoston Ventures
175 Federal Street, 10th Floor
Boston, MA 02110
Phone: 617-434-2509
Fax: 617-434-1153
www.BKB.com
Capital: More than $2 billion
Large equity investor affiliated with the
   commercial bank in Boston. Many of the
   large banks such as Chase Manhattan, First
   Union, and BankAmerica have equity
   groups.

Banc of America Capital Corporation
100 N. Tryon Street, 10th Floor
Charlotte, NC 28255
Phone: 704-386-8063
Fax: 704-386-6432

BankAmerica Ventures
950 Tower Lane, Suite 700
Foster City, CA 94404
Phone: 650-378-6000
Fax: 650-378-6040
www.bankamerica.com

Battery Ventures
20 William Street, Suite 200
Wellesley, MA 02481
Phone: 781-577-1000
Fax: 781-577-1001
www.battery.com

Behrman Capital, Inc.
126 E. 56th Street
New York, NY 10022
Contact: Bill Matthes
Phone: 212-980-6500
Fax: 212-980-7024
Capital: More than $2.0 billion

Benchmark Capital
2480 Sandhill Road, Suite 200
Menlo Park, CA 94025
Phone: 650-854-8180
Fax: 650-854-8183
www.benchmark.com

Berkshire Partners LLC
One Boston Place
Boston, MA 02108
Phone: 617-227-0050
Fax: 617-227-6105
www.berkshirepartners.com

Bessemer Venture Partners
83 Walnut Street
Wellesley Hills, MA 02481
Phone: 781-237-6050
Fax: 781-235-7068
www.bessemervp.com

Blue Chip Venture Company
1100 Chiquita Center
250 E. Fifth Street
Cincinnati, OH 45202
Phone: 513-723-2300
Fax: 513-723-2306
www.bcvc.com
Capital: More than $150 million

Blue Water Capital, LLC
8300 Greensboro Drive, Suite 440
McLean, VA 22101
Phone: 703-448-8821
Fax: 703-448-1849
www.bluewatercapital.com

Boston Capital Ventures
Old City Hall
45 School Street
Boston, MA 02108
Phone: 617-227-6550
Fax: 617-227-3847
www.bcv.com
Capital: More than $100 million

Boston Ventures Management, Inc.
One Federal Street, 10th Floor
Boston, MA 02110
Phone: 617-350-1500
Fax: 617-350-1572

Bradford Ventures Ltd.
1 Rockefeller Plaza, Suite 1722
New York, NY 10020
Phone: 212-218-6900
Fax: 212-218-6901

Brantley Partners
20600 Chagrin Boulevard, Suite 1150
Cleveland, OH 44122
Phone: 216-283-4800

Fax: 216-283-5324
Capital: More than $150 million

Brentwood Associates
11150 Santa Monica Boulevard, Suite 1200
Los Angeles, CA 90025
Contacts: Bill Barnum, David Wong
Phone: 310-477-6611
www.brentwoodvc.com
Capital: More than $800 million
Long-standing Los Angeles–based buyout
and growth equity investor.

Brinson Partners, Inc.
209 S. LaSalle Street
Chicago, IL 60604-1295
Phone: 312-220-7100
Fax: 312-220-7110
www.brinsonpartners.com
Capital: Approximately $7.6 billion
Large fund advisor and equity investment
firm.

Brockway Moran & Partners
225 NE Mizer Boulevard
Boca Raton, FL 33432
Contact: Mike Moran
Phone: 561-750-2000
Fax: 561-750-2001
Capital: More than $700 million

The Cambria Group
1600 El Camino Real, Suite 155
Menlo Park, CA 94025
Contact: Lew Davies
Phone: 650-329-8600
Fax: 650-329-8601
www.cambriagroup.com

Canaan Partners
105 Rowayton Avenue
Rowayton, CT 06853
Phone: 203-855-0400
Fax: 203-854-9117
www.canaan.com

Capital Resource Partners
85 Merrimac Street, Suite 200
Boston, MA 02114
Phone: 617-723-9000
Fax: 617-723-9819
www.crp.com
Capital: More than $800 million

Capital Southwest Corporation
12900 Preston Road, Suite 700
Dallas, TX 75230
Phone: 972-233-8242
Fax: 972-233-7362
www.capitalsouthwest.com
Capital: More than $20 million

Cardinal Health Partners, L.P.
221 Nassau Street
Princeton, NJ 08542
Phone: 609-924-6452
Fax: 609-683-0174
www.cardinalhealthpartners.com

The Carlyle Group
1001 Pennsylvania Avenue, N.W.
Washington, DC
Contact: David Rubenstein, Ed Mathias
Capital: More than $20 billion
www.thecarlylegroup.com

The Centennial Funds
1428 15th Street
Denver, CO 80202-1318
Phone: 303-405-7500
Fax: 303-405-7575
www.centennial.com
Capital: More than $700 million

CenterPoint Venture Partners
Two Galleria Tower
13455 Noel Road, Suite 1670
Dallas, TX 75240
Phone: 972-702-1101
Fax: 972-702-1103
www.cpventures.com
Capital: More than $150 million

Charles River Ventures
1000 Winter Street, Suite 3300
Waltham, MA 02451
Phone: 781-487-7060
Fax: 781-487-7065
www.crv.com
Capital: More than $500 million

Chase Capital Partners
380 Madison Avenue, 12th Floor
New York, NY 10017-2070
Phone: 212-622-3100
Fax: 212-622-3101
www.chasecapital.com

Chisholm Private Capital Partners, L.P.
10830 E. 45th Street, Suite 307
Tulsa, OK 74146
Phone: 918-663-3500
Fax: 918-663-1140
www.chisholmvc.com
Capital: More than $10 million

Code Hennessy & Simmons LLC
10 S. Wacker Drive, Suite 3175
Chicago, IL 60606
Phone: 312-876-1840
Fax: 312-876-3854
www.chsonline.com

Columbia Capital
201 N. Union Street, #300
Alexandria, VA 22314
Contacts: Jim Fleming, Harry Hopper
Phone: 703-519-2000
Fax: 703-519-3904
www.colcap.com
Capital: More than $1 billion

Commerce Capital, L.P.
611 Commerce Street, Suite 2602
Nashville, TN 37203
Phone: 615-244-1432
Fax: 615-242-1407
www.commercecap.com
Capital: More than $10 million

Core Capital Partners
901 15th Street, N.W.
Suite 950
Washington, D.C. 20005
Phone: 202-589-0090
Contact: Jonathan Silver
Fax: 202-589-0091
Email: info@core-capital.com
www.core-capital.com
Capital: Approximately $500 million

Cornerstone Equity Investors, LLC
717 Fifth Avenue, 11th Floor
New York, NY 10022
Phone: 212-753-0901
Fax: 212-826-6798
www.cornerstone-equity.com

Cravey, Green & Wahlen Inc.
12 Piedmont Center, Suite 210
Atlanta, GA 30305
Phone: 404-816-3255
Fax: 404-816-3258
Capital: More than $250 million

Crescendo Venture Management, LLC
800 LaSalle Avenue, Suite 2250
Minneapolis, MN 55402
Phone: 612-607-2800
Fax: 612-607-2801
www.crescendoventures.com
Capital: More than $400 million

Crosspoint Venture Partners
2925 Woodside Road
Woodside, CA 94062
Phone: 650-851-7600
Fax: 650-851-7661
www.cpvp.com
Capital: More than $500 million

The Crossroads Group
1717 Main Street, Suite 2500
Dallas, TX 75201

Phone: 214-698-2777
Fax: 214-698-2778
www.crossroadsgroup.com
Capital: More than $1.5 billion

Delphi Ventures
3000 Sand Hill Road
Building 1, Suite 135
Menlo Park, CA 94025
Phone: 650-854-9650
Fax: 650-854-2961
www.delphiventures.com
Capital: More than $300 million

Desai Capital Management, Inc.
540 Madison Avenue, 36th Floor
New York, NY 10022
Phone: 212-838-9191
Fax: 212-838-9807
www.desaicapital.com

Draper International
50 California Street, Suite 2925
San Francisco, CA 94111
Phone: 415-616-4050
Fax: 415-616-4060
www.draperintl.com
Capital: More than $50 million

E. M. Warburg, Pincus & Co., LLC
466 Lexington Avenue
New York, NY 10017-3146
Phone: 212-878-9358
Fax: 212-878-6167
www.warburgpincus.com
Capital: More than $20 billion
One of the largest and most long-standing
  equity firms.

Edison Venture Fund
1009 Lenox Drive #4
Lawrenceville, NJ 08648
Phone: 609-896-1900
Fax: 609-896-0066
www.edisonventure.com
Capital: More than $200 million

Emigrant Capital
6 E. 43rd Street, 8th floor
New York, NY 10017
Contact: Joe Hart
Phone: 212-850-4460
www.emigrant.com

Enterprise Partners
7979 Ivanhoe Avenue, Suite 550
La Jolla, CA 92037
Phone: 858-454-8833
Fax: 858-454-2489
www.ent.com
Capital: More than $400 million

Equus Capital Corporation
2929 Allen Parkway, 25th Floor
Houston, TX 77019
Phone: 713-529-0900
Fax: 713-529-9545
Capital: More than $100 million

Evercore Partners, Inc.
65 E. 55th Street
New York, NY 10022
Phone: 212-857-3100
Fax: 212-857-3101
Capital: More than $1 billion

Fenway Partners, Inc.
152 W. 57th Street, 59th Floor
New York, NY 10019
Phone: 212-698-4000
Fax: 212-581-1205

First Analysis Corporation
233 S. Wacker Drive, Suite 9500
Chicago, IL 60606
Phone: 312-258-1400
Fax: 312-258-0334
www.firstanalysisvc.com
Capital: More than $300 million

Flatiron Partners
257 Park Avenue, 12th Floor
New York, NY 10010
Phone: 212-228-3800
Fax: 212-228-0552
www.flatironpartners.com

Fleet Equity Partners
50 Kennedy Plaza
Providence, RI 02903
Phone: 401-278-6770
Fax: 401-278-6387
www.fleetequitypartners.com
Capital: More than $1 billion

Florida Capital Ventures, Ltd.
880 Riverside Plaza
100 W. Kennedy Boulevard
Tampa, FL 33602
Phone: 813-229-2294
Fax: 813-229-2028
Capital: More than $300 million

Francisco Partners
One Maritime Plaza, Suite 2500
San Francisco, CA 94111
Contacts: Dave Stanton, Neil Garfinkel
Phone: 415-277-2900
Fax: 415-986-1320
www.franciscopartners.com
Capital: Approximately $3 billion

Friedman, Fleischer & Lowe, LLC
One Maritime Plaza, Suite 1000

San Francisco, CA 94111
Contact: Spencer Fleischer
Phone: 415-445-9850
Fax: 415-445-9851
www.fflpventures.com
Capital: Approx. $1 billion

Frontenac Company
135 S. LaSalle Street, Suite 3800
Chicago, IL 60603
Phone: 312-368-0044
Fax: 312-368-9520
www.frontenac.com

GE Capital Equity Group
120 Long Ridge Road
Stamford, CT 06927
Phone: 203-357-3100; 800-976-0675
Fax: 203-357-3945
Capital: More than $250 million

Greenwich Street Capital Partners, Inc.
388 Greenwich Street, 36th Floor
New York, NY 10013
Phone: 212-816-8600
Fax: 212-816-0166
Capital: More than $1 billion

Greylock Management Corporation
One Federal Street, 26th Floor
Boston, MA 02110-2065
Phone: 617-423-5525
Fax: 617-482-0059
www.greylock.com
Capital: More than $500 million
One of the most successful and enduring
  venture firms.

GTCR Golder Rauner, LLC
6100 Sears Tower
Chicago, IL 60606-6402
Phone: 312-382-2200
Fax: 312-382-2201
www.gtcr.com
Capital: More than $2.5 billion
Long-standing Chicago-based buildup equity
  firm.

Halifax Group, LLC
1133 Connecticut Avenue, N.W., Suite 700
Washington, D.C. 20036
Contact: David Dupree
Phone: 202-530-8300
Fax: 202-296-7133
www.thehalifaxgroup.com

Hancock Park Associates
1925 Century Park East, #810
Los Angeles, CA 90067
Contact: Mike Fourticq
Phone: 310-553-5550
Capital: More than $200 million

Harbourvest Partners, LLC
One Financial Center, 44th Floor
Boston, MA 02111
Phone: 617-348-3707
Fax: 617-350-0305
www.hvpllc.com
Capital: Approximately $5.3 billion

Harvest Partners, Inc.
230 Park Avenue, 33rd Floor
New York, NY 10017-1216
Phone: 212-838-7776
Fax: 212-593-0734
Capital: More than $600 million

HealthCare Ventures, LLC
44 Nassau Street
Princeton, NJ 08542
Phone: 609-430-3900
Fax: 609-430-9525
www.hcven.com
Capital: Approximately $475 million

Hellman and Friedman
One Maritime Plaza, 12th Floor
San Francisco, CA 94111
Phone: 415-788-5111
Fax: 415-788-0176
www.HF.com
Capital: More than $12 billion

Hicks, Muse, Tate & Furst, Inc.
200 Crescent Court, Suite 1600
Dallas, TX 75201
Phone: 214-740-7300
Fax: 214-720-7888
www.hmtf.com
Capital: More than $5 billion

Highland Capital Partners
Two International Place
Boston, MA 02110
Phone: 617-531-1500
Fax: 617-531-1550
www.hcp.com
Capital: Approximately $500 million

Houston Partners
P.O. Box 2023
401 Louisiana, 8th Floor
Houston, TX 77252-2023
Phone: 713-222-8600
Fax: 713-222-8932
Capital: More than $20 million

Intersouth Partners
P.O. Box 13546
Research Triangle Park, NC 27709
Phone: 919-481-6889
Fax: 919-481-0225
www.intersouth.com
Capital: More than $60 million

InterWest Partners
3000 Sand Hill Road
Building 3, Suite 225
Menlo Park, CA 94025-7112
Phone: 650-854-8585
Fax: 650-854-4706
www.interwest.com
Capital: More than $800 million

IVP—Institutional Venture Partners
3000 Sand Hill Road
Building 2, Suite 290
Menlo Park, CA 94025
Phone: 650-854-0132
Fax: 650-854-5762
www.ivp.com
Capital: More than $1 billion

J. H. Whitney & Company
177 Broad Street, 15th Floor
Stamford, CT 06901
Contacts: Peter Castleman, Bill Laverack
Phone: 203-973-1400
Fax: 203-973-1422
www.jhwhitney.com
Capital: More than $2 billion

Kansas City Equity Partners
233 W. 47th Street
Kansas City, MO 64112
Phone: 816-960-1771
Fax: 816-960-1777
www.kcep.com
Capital: More than $75 million

Kelso & Company
320 Park Avenue, 24th Floor
New York, NY 10022
Phone: 212-751-3939
Fax: 212-223-2379
Capital: More than $2 million

Key Equity Capital Corporation
127 Public Square, 6th Floor
Cleveland, OH 44114
Phone: 216-689-5776
Fax: 216-689-3204
Capital: Approximately $125 million

Kinetic Ventures, LLC
Two Wisconsin Circle, Suite 620
Chevy Chase, MD 20815
Contact: Jake Tarr
Phone: 301-652-8066
Fax: 301-652-8310
Capital: More than $300 million

Kleiner Perkins Caufield & Byers
2750 Sand Hill Road
Menlo Park, CA 94025
Phone: 650-233-2750

Fax: 650-233-3300
www.kpcb.com
Capital: More than $1.2 billion
The biggest name in the venture capital world.

Kohlberg Kravis Roberts & Company
9 W. 57th Street, Suite 4200
New York, NY 10019
Phone: 212-750-8300
Fax: 212-750-0003
www.kkr.com
Capital: More than $20 billion
The granddaddy of the big leveraged buyout.

Landmark Partners, Inc.
760 Hopmeadow Street
Simsbury, CT 06070
Phone: 860-651-9760
Fax: 860-651-8890
www.landmarkpartners.com

Leonard Green & Partners, LP
11111 Santa Monica Boulevard, Suite 2000
Los Angeles, CA 90025
Phone: 310-954-0444
Fax: 310-954-0404
Capital: Approximately $5 billion

Littlejohn & Levy, Inc.
450 Lexington Avenue, Suite 3350
New York, NY 10017
Phone: 212-286-8600
Fax: 212-286-8626
Capital: More than $1 billion

Madison Dearborn Partners
Three First National Place, Suite 3800
Chicago, IL 60602
Phone: 312-895-1000
Fax: 312-895-1001
www. mdcp.com

Marquette Venture Partners
520 Lake Cook Road, Suite 450
Deerfield, IL 60015
Phone: 847-940-1700
Fax: 847-940-1724
Capital: More than $150 million

Maveron, LLC
800 Fifth Avenue, Suite 4100
Seattle, WA 98104
Phone: 206-447-1300
Fax: 206-470-1150
www.maveron.com
Capital: More than $100 million

Mayfield Fund
2800 Sand Hill Road, Suite 250
Menlo Park, CA 94025
Phone: 650-854-5560
Fax: 650-854-5712

www.mayfield.com
Capital: More than $1 billion

Menlo Ventures
3000 Sand Hill Road
Building 4, Suite 100
Menlo Park, CA 94025
Phone: 650-854-8540
Fax: 650-854-7059
www.menloventures.com
Capital: More than $1 billion

Morganthaler Ventures
Terminal Tower
50 Public Square, Suite 2700
Cleveland, OH 44113
Contact: Peter Taft
Phone: 216-416-7500
Fax: 216-416-7501
www.morganthaler.com
Capital: Approximately $1 billion

Nassau Capital, LLC
22 Chambers Street, 2nd Floor
Princeton, NJ 08542
Phone: 609-924-3555
Fax: 609-924-8887
www.nassau.com
Firm affiliated with Princeton University.
   Several of the larger universities, such as
   Princeton, Harvard and Yale, have
   investment firms associated with their
   endowments.

New Enterprise Associates
1119 St. Paul Street
Baltimore, MD 21202
Phone: 410-244-0115
Fax: 410-752-7721
www.nea.com
Capital: More than $7 billion

Noro-Moseley Partners
9 N. Parkway Square
4200 Northside Parkway NW
Atlanta, GA 30327
Phone: 404-233-1966
Fax: 404-239-9280
Capital: Approximately $100 million

The North Carolina Enterprise Fund, L.P.
3600 Glenwood Avenue, Suite 107
Raleigh, NC 27612
Phone: 919-781-2691
Fax: 919-783-9195
www.ncef.com
Capital: More than $20 million

Norwest Venture Partners
245 Lytton Avenue, Suite 250
Palo Alto, CA 94301

Phone: 650-321-8000
Fax: 650-321-8010
www.norwestvp.com
Capital: More than $800 million

Oak Investment Partners
One Gorham Island
Westport, CT 06880
Phone: 203-226-8346
Fax: 203-227-0372
www.oakinv.com
Capital: More than $1.6 billion

Oaktree Capital Management, LLC
550 S. Hope Street, 22nd Floor
Los Angeles, CA 90071
Phone: 213-694-1501
Fax: 213-694-1594
Capital: Approximately $8.5 billion

Patricof & Co. Ventures, Inc.
445 Park Avenue
New York, NY 10022
Contact: George Jenkins
Phone: 212-753-6300
Fax: 212-319-6155
www.patricof.com
Capital: More than $1 billion

Pine Creek Partners
1055 Thomas Jefferson Street, NW
Suite 218
Washington, DC 20007
Contacts:
George McCabe
george@pinecreekpartners.com
Rick Rickertsen
rick@pinecreekpartners.com
Phone: 202.333.7780
Fax: 202.333.7786
Capital: More than $50 million

Polaris Venture Partners
Bay Colony Corporate Center
1000 Winter Street, Suite 3350
Waltham, MA 02451
Contact: Alan Spoon
Phone: 781-290-0770
Fax: 781-290-0880
www.polarisventures.com
Capital: More than $1 billion

Providence Equity Partners, Inc.
50 Kennedy Plaza, 9th Floor
Providence, RI 02903
Contact: Paul Salem
Phone: 401-751-1700
Fax: 401-751-1790

Questor
9 W. 57th Street, 34th Floor

New York, NY 10019
Phone: 212-297-1599
Fax: 212-297-1588
Capital: More than $1 billion
Firm targets turnaround situations.

Redpoint Ventures
3000 Sand Hill Road, Suite 290
Menlo Park, CA 94025
Contact: John Walecka
Phone: 650-926-5600
Fax: 650-854-5762
www.redpointventures.com
Capital: More than $800 million

Riordan, Lewis and Haden
300 S. Grand Avenue, 29th Floor
Los Angeles, CA 90071
Phone: 213-229-8500
Fax: 213-229-8597

RRE Investors
126 E. 56th Street
New York, NY 10022
Phone: 212-418-5110
www.rre.com

Saugatuck Capital Company
One Canterbury Green
Stamford, CT 06901
Phone: 203-348-6669
Fax: 203-324-6995
www.saugatuckcapital.com
Capital: More than $90 million

Saunders Karp & Meguire
667 Madison Avenue
New York, NY 10021
Phone: 212-303-6600
Fax: 212-755-1624
www.skmequity.com

Schroder Ventures
787 Seventh Avenue
New York, NY 10019
Phone: 212-735-0700
Fax: 212-735-0711
Capital: Approximately $1.7 billion

Sevin Rosen Funds
Two Galleria Tower
13455 Noel Road, Suite 1670, LB 24
Dallas, TX 75240
Phone: 972-702-1100
Fax: 972-702-1103
www.srfunds.com
Capital: More than $500 million

Sierra Ventures
3000 Sand Hill Road
Building 4, #210
Menlo Park, CA 94025

Phone: 650-854-1000
Fax: 650-854-5593
www.sierraven.com

South Atlantic Venture Funds
614 W. Bay Street
Tampa, FL 33606-2704
Phone: 813-253-2500
Fax: 813-253-2360
www.southatlantic.com
Capital: More than $70 million

Sterling Venture Partners
111 S. Calvert Street, Suite 2810
Baltimore, MD 21202
Phone: 410-347-2905
Fax: 410-347-3140
www.sterlingcap.com
Capital: More than $50 million

St. Paul Venture Capital
10400 Viking Drive, Suite 550
Eden Prairie, MN 55344
Phone: 612-995-7474
Fax: 612-995-7475
www.stpaulvc.com
Capital: More than $800 million

Summit Partners
600 Atlantic Avenue, 28th Floor
Boston, MA 02210
Contact: Marty Mannion
Phone: 617-824-1000
Fax: 617-824-1100
www.summitpartners.com
Capital: More than $4 billion

Sutter Hill Ventures
755 Page Mill Road, Suite A-200
Palo Alto, CA 94304
Phone: 650-493-5600
Fax: 650-858-1854
www.shv.com
Capital: More than $400 million

TA Associates, Inc.
High Street Tower, Suite 2500
125 High Street
Boston, MA 02110
Phone: 617-574-6700
Fax: 617-574-6728
www.ta.com
Capital: More than $5 billion

TCW/Crescent Mezzanine, LLC
11100 Santa Monica Boulevard, Suite 2000
Los Angeles, CA 90025
Phone: 310-235-5900
Fax: 310-235-5967

Texas-Pacific Group
201 Main Street, Suite 2420

Forth Worth, TX 76102
Contact: Kelvin Davis
Phone: 817-871-4000
Fax: 817-871-4010
www.texpac.com
Capital: More than $17 billion

Thayer Capital Partners
1455 Pennsylvania Avenue NW, Suite 350
Washington, DC 20004
Phone: 202-371-0150
Fax: 202-371-0391
www.thayercapital.com
Capital: More than $1.2 billion

Thoma Cressey Equity Partners
233 S. Wacker Drive, Suite 4460
Chicago, IL 60606
Phone: 312-777-4444
Fax: 312-777-4445
www.tc.nu
Capital: More than $450 million

Three Cities Research, Inc.
650 Madison Avenue, 24th Floor
New York, NY 10022
Phone: 212-838-9660
Fax: 212-980-1142
www.tcr-ny.com
Capital: More than $440 million

Trident Capital
2480 Sand Hill Road, Suite 100
Menlo Park, CA 94025
Contact: Don Dixon
Phone: 650-233-4300
Fax: 650-233-4333
www.tridentcap.com
Capital: More than $1 billion

U.S. Venture Partners
2180 Sand Hill Road, Suite 300
Menlo Park, CA 94025
Phone: 650-854-9080
Fax: 650-854-3018
www.usvp.com
Capital: More than $700 million

Venrock Associates
30 Rockefeller Plaza, Room 5508
New York, NY 10112
Phone: 212-649-5600
Fax: 212-649-5788
www.venrock.com
Capital: More than $500 million

Vestar Capital Partners
245 Park Avenue, 41st Floor
New York, NY 10067-4098
Phone: 212-351-1600
Fax: 212-808-4922

www.vestarcap.com
Capital: More than $1 billion

Wakefield Group
1110 E. Morehead Street
P.O. Box 36329
Charlotte, NC 28236
Phone: 704-372-0355
Fax: 704-372-8216
www.wakefieldgroup.com

Weiss, Peck & Greer Venture Partners
555 California Street, Suite 3130
San Francisco, CA 94104
Phone: 415-622-6864
Fax: 415-989-5108
www.wpgvp.com
Capital: More than $700 million

Welsh, Carson, Anderson & Stowe
320 Park Avenue, 25th Floor
New York, NY 10022
Contact: Russ Carson
Phone: 212-893-9500
Fax: 212-893-9575
www.welshcarson.com
Capital: More than $7 billion
Long-standing information technology and
    health care investor.

Wellspring Associates, LLC
620 Fifth Avenue, Suite 216
New York, NY 10020-1579
Phone: 212-332-7555
Fax: 212-332-7575

Weston Presidio Capital
One Federal Street, 21st Floor
Boston, MA 02110
Phone: 617-988-2500
Fax: 617-988-2515
www.westonpresidio.com
Capital: More than $900 million

Willis Stein & Partners, LLC
227 W. Monroe Street, Suite 4300
Chicago, IL 60606
Phone: 312-422-2400
Fax: 312-422-2418
Capital: More than $1 billion

Private Equity Funds: Europe

Abingworth Management Limited
Princess House
38 Jermyn Street
London SW1Y 6DN
United Kingdom
Phone: 44-020-7534-1500
Fax: 44-020-7287-0480
www.abingworth.com
Capital: Approximately £100 million

Abtrust Fund Managers Limited
One Albyn Place
Aberdeen AB10 1YG
United Kingdom
Phone: 44-1224-631999
Fax: 44-1224-647010
Capital: Approximately £60 million

A.C.T. Venture Capital Limited
The Merrion Business Centre
58 Howard Street
Belfast BT1 6PJ
United Kingdom
Phone: 44-1232-247266
Fax: 44-1232-247372
Capital: Approximately £75 million

Advent Venture Partners
25 Buckingham Gate
London SW1E 6LD
United Kingdom
Phone: 44-171-630-9811
Fax: 44-171-828-1474
E-mail: info@advent.ventures.com
Capital: Approximately $250 million

Allianz Capital Partners GmbH
Theresienstrasse 1-5
80333 Munich
Germany
Phone: 49-89-3800-7582
Fax: 49-89-3800-7586
E-mail: margit.kaserer@allianz.de
Capital: More than $1 billion

Alpha Group
89 rue Taitbout
75009 Paris
France
Phone: 33-1-5321-8888
Fax: 33-1-4016-4323
More than Euro 550 million

Alpinvest Holding NV
3 Postbus 5073
1410 AB Naarden
Netherlands
Phone: 31-35-695-2600
Fax: 31-35-694-7525
www.alpinvest.com
Capital: More than Euro 750 million

Apax Partners and Co. Ventures Ltd.
15 Portland Place
London W1N 3AA
United Kingdom
Phone: 44-171-872-6300
Fax: 44-171-636-6475
www.apax.com
Capital: More than $300 million

Apax Partners et Cie.
45 Avenue Kléber
75784 Paris Cedex 16
France
Phone: 33-1-6365-0100
Fax: 33-1-5365-0101/06
www.apax.com

AXA Asset Management Gestion
58 Avenue de La Gramdearmee
75017 Paris
France
Phone: 33-1-5537-5000
Fax: 33-1-5537-5501
Capital: More than Ffr500 million

Banexi Ventures Partners
12 rue Chauchat
75009 Paris
France
Phone: 33-1-4014-2663
Fax: 33-1-4014-3896
www.banexiventurej.com
Capital: More than Ffr400 million

Barclays Acquisition Finance
Barclays Bank plc
54 Lombard Street
London EC3P 3AH
United Kingdom
Phone: 44-171-699-3186
Fax: 44-171-699-2770

Baring Venture Partners Ltd.
33 Cavendish Square
London W1M 0BQ
United Kingdom
Phone: 44-171-290-5000
Fax: 44-171-290-5020
www.bpep.com
Capital: More than £285 million

BC Partners
185 Piccadilly
London W1V 9FN
United Kingdom
Phone: 44-171-408-1282
Fax: 44-171-493-1368
www.bcpartners.com
Capital: More than $1 billion

BNP Private Equity
12 rue Chauchat
75009 Paris
France
Phone: 33-1-6016-8600
Fax: 33-1-6016-6960
E-mail: bnppeinfo@bnpgroup.com
Capital: More than Ffr4 billion

Candover
20 Old Bailey

London EC4M 7LN
United Kingdom
Phone: 44-20-7489-9848
Fax: 44-20-7248-5483
www.candover.com
Capital: Approximately £850 million

Capital for Companies
Quayside House
Canal Wharf
Leeds LS11 5PU
United Kingdom
Phone: 44-113-243-8043
Fax: 44-113-245-1777
www.cfc.vct.co.uk
Capital: Approximately £22 million

Cinven Limited
Pinners Hall
105-108 Old Broad Street
London EC2N 1EH
United Kingdom
Phone: 44-171-661-3333
Fax: 44-171-256-2225
www.cinven.com
Capital: More than $2.5 billion

Commerz Beteiligungsgesellschaft mbH
Kaiserstrasse 16
D-60311 Frankfurt am Main
Germany
Phone: 49-69-136-2 96 82
Fax: 49-69-136-2 98 76
www.obg.commerzbank.de

Copernicus Capital Management
u. Krak. Przedmiescie 79, 2nd Floor
00079 Warsaw
Poland
Phone: 48-22-268580
Fax: 48-22-254462
E-mail: 100710.1515@compuserve
Capital: Approximately $25 million

Credit Agricole Indosuez
122 Leadenhall Street
London EC3V 4QH
United Kingdom
Phone: 44-171-971-4454/4405
Fax: 44-171-628-4362
E-mail: mary.clippingdale@indosuez.co.uk
Capital: Approximately £30 million

CVC Capital Partners Ltd.
Huson House
8-10 Tavistock Street
London WC2E 7PP
United Kingdom
Phone: 44-020-7420-4200
Fax: 44-020-7420-4231

www.cvceurope.com
Capital: Approximately $2.5 billion

DLJ Phoenix Private Equity Limited
99 Bishopsgate
London EC2M 34F
United Kingdom
Phone: 44-207-655-7600
Fax: 44-207-655-7683
E-mail: dljppe@dlj.com
Capital: Approximately £350 million

Elderstreet Investments Ltd.
32 Bedford Row
London EC1N 4HE
United Kingdom
Phone: 44-171-831-5088
Fax: 44-171-831-5099
www.elderstreet.com
Capital: £40 million

Englefield Capital LLP
Michelin House
81 Fulham Road
London SW3 6RD
Contact: Dominic Shorthouse
Phone: 44-20-7591- 4200
Fax: 44-20-7591-4222
www.englefieldcapital.com

Euroventures France
27 rue de la Ville l'Eveque
75008 Paris
France
Phone: 33-1-4007-0518
Fax: 33-1-4924-9972
Capital: Approximately Ffr240 million

Excel Partners
Claudio Coelle 78
28001 Madrid
Spain
Phone: 34-1-578-3676
Fax: 34-1-431-9303
www.excelpartners.com
Capital: Approximately $100 million

Four Seasons Venture Capital AB
Sveavagen 17
P.O. Box 1415
11184 Stockholm
Sweden
Phone: 46-8-15420
Fax: 46-8-216995
www.fourseasons.se
Capital: Approximately Sek 475 million

Gemini Capital Fund Management Ltd.
Maskit Street
P.O. Box 12548
Industrial Zone

Herzliya 46733
Israel
Phone: 972-9-958-3596
Fax: 972-9-958-4842
Capital: Approximately $25 million

Glaxo Wellcome plc.
Glaxo Wellcome House
Berkeley Avenue
Greenford
Middlesex WB6 0NN
United Kingdom
Phone: 44-0207-493-4060
Fax: 44-0208-966-8330
www.glaxowellcome.co.uk
Capital: Approximately $1.4 billion

Goldman Sachs International
Peterborough Court
133 Fleet Street
London EC4A 2BB
United Kingdom
Phone: 44-171-774-1000
Fax: 44-171-774-4123
www.gs.com
Capital: Approximately £1 billion

H.S.B.C. Ventures UK Limited
H.S.B.C. Bank plc, 2nd Floor
27-32 Poultry
London EC2P 2BX
United Kingdom
Phone: 44-171-260-7935
Fax: 44-171-260-6767
Capital: Approximately £25 million

Hannover Finanz GmbH
Gunther Wagner Allee 13
30177 Hanover
Germany
Phone: 49-511-280-070
Fax: 49-511-280-0737
www.hannoverfinanz.de
Capital: Approximately DM 730 million

HSBC Private Equity
Vintner's Place
68 Upper Thames Street
London EC4V 3BJ
United Kingdom
Phone: 44-171-336-9955
Fax: 44-171-336-9961
Capital: Approximately £1.1 billion

Innoventure Equity Partners AG
Gerbergasse 5
8023 Zurich
Switzerland
Phone: 41-1-211-4171
Fax: 41-1-211-4230
www.innoventure.ch

Kleinwort Benson Development Capital
Limited
P.O. Box 18075
Riverbank House
2 Swan Lane
London EC4R 3UX
United Kingdom
Phone: 44-020-7623-8000
Fax: 44-020-7626-8616
www.drkbpe.com
Capital: Approximately Euro 180 million

Kreditanstalt Für Wiederaufbau (KFW)
Palmengartenstrasse 5-9
60325 Frankfurt am Main
Germany
Phone: 49-69-74310
Fax: 49-69-7431-2944
Capital: Approximately DM 1.13 billion

LBO France
1 rue François 1 er
75008 Paris
France
Phone: 33-1-4235-0021
Fax: 33-1-4561-0064

Mercury Private Equity
33 King William Street
London EC4R 9AS
United Kingdom
Phone: 44-171-280-2800
Fax: 44-171-203-5833
Capital: Approximately £600 million

Murray Johnstone Private Equity Limited
7 W. Nile Street
Glasgow G1 2PX
United Kingdom
Phone: 44-141-226-3131
Fax: 44-141-248-5636
www.murrayj.com
Capital: Approximately £300 million

Nash, Sells and Partners Limited
25 Buckingham Gate
London SW1E 6LD
United Kingdom
Phone: 44-171-828-6944
Fax: 44-171-828-9958
www.nashsells.co.uk
Capital: Approximately £100 million

Natwest Acquisition Finance
38 Bishopsgate
London EC2N 4DP
United Kingdom
Phone: 44-020-7665-6000
Fax: 44-020-7665-6101
www.nwacqfin.com
Capital: Approximately £2 billion

Nordic Capital
Stureplan 4 A
SE-11435 Stockholm
Sweden
Phone: 46-8-440-5050
Fax: 46-8-611-7998
www.nordiccapital.se
Capital: Approximately Skr 3.2 billion

Northern Venture Managers Limited
Northumberland House
Princess Square
Newcastle Upon Tyne NE1 8ER
United Kingdom
Phone: 44-191-232-7068
Fax: 44-191-232-4070
Capital: Approximately £35 million

NSM Finances SA
3 avenue Hoche
75008 Paris
France
Phone: 33-1-4766-6609
Fax: 33-1-4888-5348
Capital: Approximately Ffr550 million

Pantheon Ventures Limited
43-44 Albermarle Street
London W1X 3FE
United Kingdom
Phone: 44-171-493-5685
Fax: 44-171-629-0844
Capital: Approximately £500 million

Proven Private Equity
42 Craven Street
London WC2N 5NG
United Kingdom
Phone: 44-171-451-6500
Fax: 44-171-839-8349
E-mail: info@proven.co.uk
Capital: Approximately £70 million

Royal Bank of Scotland Leveraged Finance
138-142 Holburn
London EC1N 2TH
United Kingdom

Phone: 44-171-427-8304
Fax: 44-171-427-8473

Siparex Group
139 rue Vendôme
69477 Lyon Cedex 06
France
Phone: 33-04-7283-2323
Fax: 33-04-7283-2300
www.siparex.com
Capital: Approximately Euro 453 million

Skandia Investment
Box 5295
10246 Stockholm
Sweden
Phone: 46-8-788-1030
Fax: 46-8-203566
www.skandia.se/ski
Capital: Approximately Skr 1.600 million

Sofinnova Partners SA
17 rue de Surène
75008 Paris
France
Phone: 33-1-53-054100
Fax: 33-1-53-064129
www.sofinnova.fr
Capital: Approximately $250 million

Swedfund International A
P.O. Box 3286
SE-10365 Stockholm
Sweden
Phone: 46-8-725-9400
Fax: 46-8-203093
www.swedfund.se
Capital: Approximately Skr 600 million

3i Group plc
91 Waterloo Road
London SE18XP
United Kingdom
Phone: 44-171-928-3131
Fax: 44-171-928-0058
Capital: More than $3 billion

APPENDIX B-7. MEZZANINE LENDERS

The mezzanine market is a huge and highly efficient market. There are large and small mezzanine investors. The group below is only a small sample. Also, there are many Small Business Investment Company (SBIC) mezzanine funds, so be sure to look them up at www .sba.gov.

Allied Capital Corporation
1919 Pennsylvania Avenue, 3rd Floor
Washington, DC 20006-3434
Contact: John Fruehwirth
Phone: 202-331-1112
Fax: 202-659-2053
www.alliedcapital.com

American Capital Strategies, Ltd.
Three Bethesda Metro Center, Suite 860
Bethesda, MD 20814
Contact: Jon Isaacson
Phone: 301-951-6122
Fax: 301-654-6714
www.american-capital.com

CapitalSource
4445 Willard Avenue
12th Floor
Chevy Chase, MD 20815
Contact: Joseph Kenary
Phone: 866-876-8723
info@capitalsource.com
www.capitalsource.com

Chevy Chase Bank
7926 Jones Branch Drive
Suite 230
McLean, VA 22102
Contact: Richard Amador
Phone: 703-287-7233
www.chevychasebank.com

DLJ Merchant Banking Partners
277 Park Avenue, 19th Floor
New York, NY 10172
Phone: 212-892-3000
Fax: 212-892-7552
www.dlj.com

Emigrant Bank
6 E. 43rd Street
8th Floor
New York, NY 10017
Contact: John Hart
Phone: 212-850-4460
www.emigrant.com

Gladstone Capital
1521 Westbranch Drive, Suite 200
McLean, VA 22102

Contact: George "Chipp" Stelljes
Phone: 703-287-5800
Fax: 703-287-5801
Info@GladstoneCapital.com
www.gladstonecapital.com

Key Community Development Corporation
127 Public Square, 13th Floor
Mailcode: OH-01-27-1319
Cleveland, OH 44114-1306
Contact: Amy Dosen
Phone: 800-523-7247 (Ohio only)
Phone: 800-523-7248 (Outside of Ohio)
www.keybank.com

MCG Capital Corporation
1100 Wilson Boulevard
Suite 3000
Arlington, VA 22209
Contact: Bill Ford
Phone: 703-247-7500
Fax: 703-247-7505
www.mcgcapital.com

Mercantile Bank
2 Hopkins Plaza
Baltimore, MD 21201
Contact: Greg Barger
Phone: 800-896-9758
www.mercantile.com

Sankaty Advisors, LLC (Bain)
111 Huntington Avenue
Boston, MA 02199
Phone: 617-516-2700
Fax: 617-516-2710
http://www.sankatyadvisors.com

TCW/Crescent Mezzanine, LLC
11100 Santa Monica Boulevard, Suite 2000
Los Angeles, CA 90025
Phone: 310-235-5900
Fax: 310-235-5967

Triangle Capital Partners
3600 Glenwood Avenue
Suite 104
Raleigh, NC 27612
Contact: Brent P.W. Burgess
Phone: 919-719-4770
www.trianglecapitalpartners.com

APPENDIX B-8. DEBT-FINANCING SOURCES

Commercial Banks and Senior Lenders

The banks below are only a small fraction of the lenders out there. Contact your largest local banks first if a bank loan could help your situation.

ABN AMRO Bank N.V.
135 S. LaSalle Street, Suite 725
Chicago, IL 60674-9135
Phone: 312-904-2051
Fax: 312-904-4456

Allied Capital Corporation
1919 Pennsylvania Avenue, 3rd Floor
Washington, DC 20006-3434
Contact: John Fruehwirth
Phone: 202-331-1112
Fax: 202-659-2053
www.alliedcapital.com

American Capital Strategies, Ltd.
Three Bethesda Metro Center, Suite 860
Bethesda, MD 20814
Contact: Jon Isaacson
Phone: 301-951-6122
Fax: 301-654-6714
www.american-capital.com

Antares Capital Corporation
311 S. Wacker Drive, Suite 275
Chicago, IL 60606
Phone: 312-697-3999
Fax: 312-697-3998
E-mail: antareslev@msc.com

BancBoston Securities, Inc.
Corporate Finance Department
Mail Stop 01-09-03
100 Federal Street
Boston, MA 02110
Phone: 617-434-2200

Banc One Capital Markets
120 S. LaSalle Street
Chicago, IL 60603
Phone: 312-661-5211
Fax: 312-661-7352

Bankamerica Business Credit, Inc.
231 S. LaSalle Street, 16th Floor
Chicago, IL 60697
Phone: 312-974-2400
Fax: 312-974-8744

Bank of America
555 S. Flower Street
Department 3283, 11th Floor
Los Angeles, CA 90071
Phone: 213-228-2694
Fax: 213-228-2641

Banque Paribas Merchant Banking Group
787 Seventh Avenue
New York, NY 10019-6016
Phone: 212-841-2115
Fax: 212-841-2363

Business Capital Group, Inc.
3503 NW 63rd Street, Suite 600
Oklahoma City, OK 73116

Phone: 405-842-1010
Fax: 405-842-9981

CapitalSource
4445 Willard Avenue
12th Floor
Chevy Chase, MD 20815
Contact: Joseph Kenary
Phone: 866-876-8723
info@capitalsource.com
www.capitalsource.com

Chevy Chase Bank
7926 Jones Branch Drive
Suite 230
McLean, VA 22102
Contact: Richard Amador
Phone: 703-287-7233
www.chevychasebank.com

CIGNA Investments, Inc.
Leveraged Investments
S-307
900 Cottage Grove Road
Hartford, CT 06152-2307
Phone: 860-726-4077
Fax: 860-726-7203

CITICORP Securities, Inc.
399 Park Avenue, 6th Floor, Zone 4
New York, NY 10022
Phone: 212-559-3540
Phone: 212-793-1290

Citizens Business Credit Corporation
Citizens Bank Building
28 State Street
Boston, MA 02109
Phone: 617-725-5830
Fax: 617-725-5827

Congress Financial Corporation
1133 Avenue of the Americas
New York, NY 10036
Phone: 212-840-2000
Fax: 212-545-4555

Credit Lyonnais Leveraged and Financial
    Sponsor Group
1301 Avenue of the Americas
New York, NY 10019
Phone: 212-261-7871
Fax: 212-459-3176

Emigrant Bank
6 E. 43rd Street
8th Floor
New York, NY 10017
Contact: John Hart
Phone: 212-850-4460
www.emigrant.com

Fleet Capital Corporation
200 Glastonbury Boulevard

Glastonbury, CT 06033
Phone: 860-659-3200
Fax: 860-657-7768
www.fleetcapital.com

Foothill Capital Corporation
11111 Santa Monica Boulevard, Suite 1500
Los Angeles, CA 90025-3333
Phone: 310-996-7000
Fax: 310-478-4860

Fremont Financial Corporation
2020 Santa Monica Boulevard, Suite 600
Santa Monica, CA 90404-2023
Phone: 310-315-5550
Fax: 310-315-5561

GE Capital Commercial Finance
201 High Ridge Road
Stamford, CT 06927-5100
Phone: 203-316-7500
Fax: 203-316-7815
www.gecommercialfinance.com

HSBC Bank
452 Fifth Avenue
New York, NY 10018
Contact: James Marley
Phone: 212-525-5000
www.us.hsbc.com

HSBC Securities, Inc.
140 Broadway, 5th Floor
New York, NY 10005-1185
Phone: 212-658-2751
Fax: 212-658-2587
www.hsbc.com

Indosuez Capital
1211 Avenue of the Americas, 7th Floor
New York, NY 10036
Phone: 212-278-2222
Fax: 212-278-2203

Key Community Development Corporation
127 Public Square, 13th Floor
Mailcode: OH-01-27-1319
Cleveland, OH 44114-1306
Contact: Amy Dosen
Phone: 800-523-7247 (Ohio only)
Phone: 800-523-7248 (Outside of Ohio)
www.keybank.com

LaSalle Business Credit, Inc.
135 S. LaSalle Street, Suite 400
Chicago, IL 60603
Phone: 312-904-7410
Fax: 312-904-7425

Mellon Business Credit
Mellon Bank Center
1735 Market Street, 6th Floor

Philadelphia, PA 19103
Phone: 215-553-2162
Fax: 215-553-0201

Mercantile Bank
2 Hopkins Plaza
Baltimore, MD 21201
Contact: Greg Barger
Phone: 800-896-9758
www.mercantile.com

New York Life Insurance Company
51 Madison Avenue, Room 203
New York, NY 10010
Phone: 212-576-6525

PNC Business Credit
70 E. 52nd Street, 25th Floor
New York, NY 10022
Phone: 212-223-3626
Fax: 212-223-6780

Presidential Bank
4600 East-West Highway
Suite 400
Bethesda, MD 20814
Contact: A. Bruce Cleveland
Phone: 800-808-1424
www.presidential.com

Regions Financial Corp.
P.O. Box 10247
Birmingham, AL 35202
Contact: Doyle Rippee
Phone: 205-244-2830
www.regions.com

Sanwa Business Credit Corporation
500 Glenpointe Centre West, 4th Floor
Teaneck, NJ 07666-6802
Phone: 201-836-4006
Fax: 201-836-4744

Société Générale
1221 Avenue of the Americas, 8th Floor
New York, NY 10020
Phone: 212-278-6000
Fax: 212-278-6178

State Street Bank & Trust Company
3414 Peachtree Road NE, Suite 1010
Atlanta, GA 30326
Phone: 404-364-9500
Fax: 404-261-4469

SunAmerica Corporate Finance
One SunAmerica Center, 38th Floor
Los Angeles, CA 90067
Phone: 310-772-6300
Fax: 310-772-6078

APPENDIX B-9. WEALTH MANAGEMENT RESOURCES

The wealth management advisory world is huge, comprising thousands of large and small firms. This list is but a tiny group. Always be careful and work with advisers with deep experience and a long track record.

Allen & Co. LLC
711 Fifth Avenue
New York, NY 10022
Contact: Kim Wieland
Phone: 212-832-8000
Fax: 212-832-7057

Bessemer Trust
New York City
630 Fifth Avenue
New York, New York 10111-0333
Contact: Donovan Moore
Phone: 212-708-9364

Bessemer Trust
Washington, D.C.
1050 Connecticut Avenue N.W.
Suite 1060
Washington, D.C. 20036-5303
Contact: Lawrence P. Fisher II
Phone: 202-659-3330
www.bessemer.com

Chevy Chase Bank
7926 Jones Branch Drive
Suite 230
McLean, VA 22102
Contact: Richard Amador
Phone: 703-287-7233
www.chevychasebank.com

Deutsche Bank Private Wealth Management
280 Park Avenue
New York, NY 10017
Phone: 212-454-3600
www.pwm.db.com

Emigrant Bank
6 E. 43rd Street
8th Floor
New York, NY 10017
Contact: John Hart
Phone: 212-850-4460
www.emigrant.com

Friedman Billings Ramsey & Co.
1001 19th Street North
Arlington, VA 22209
Contact: J. Rock Tonkel, Jr.
Phone: 703-312-9500

Fax: 703-312-9501
www.fbr.com

Goldman, Sachs & Co.
Private Wealth Management
Goldman Sachs & Co.
85 Broad Street
New York, NY 10004
Contact: Scott Belveal
Phone: 1-800-874-1815
scott.belveal@gs.com
www.gs.com/client_services/
    private_wealth_management/

Hogan & Hartson LLP
555 13th Street, NW
Washington, DC 20004
Contact: Molly James
Phone: 202-637-5600
Fax: 202-637-5910
www.hhlaw.com

HSBC
452 Fifth Avenue
New York, NY 10018
Contact: James Marley
Phone: 212-525-5000
www.us.hsbc.com

Mercantile Bank
2 Hopkins Plaza
Baltimore, MD 21201
Contact: Greg Barger
Phone: 800-896-9758
www.mercantile.com

Mellon Private Wealth Management
One Mellon Center
Pittsburgh, PA 15258
Phone: 412-234-5000
www.mellon.com/
    privatewealthmanagement/

Merrill Lynch & Co., Inc.
4 World Financial Center
250 Vesey Street
New York, NY 10080
Phone: 212-449-1000
individual.ml.com

Presidential Bank
4600 East-West Highway